D1495737

How-To With Wood

by Pete Prlain

Reston Publishing Company, Inc.
A Prentice-Hall Company
Reston, Virginia

Contents

Acknowledgments

We wish to express our appreciation to the following companies and associations for their cooperation and contributions to this book: American Hardboard Association, American Plywood Association, California Redwood Association, Fine Hardwoods/American Walnut Association, Fir and Hemlock Door Association, Georgia-Pacific, Hardwood Plywood Manufacturers Association, Koppers Company, Inc., Louisiana-Pacific, Masonite Corporation, Red Cedar Shingles and Handsplit Shake Bureau, Western Wood Products Association, Western Wood Moulding and Millwork Producers Association.

Popular Science contributed the following projects: a Weight Lifting Bench, designed by Greg Sollie of Huntsville, Alabama; a Slip-Together Bed/Desk, designed by Donald A. Maxwell, Jr. of Richmond, Virginia; and a Swing-Wing Liquor Cabinet, designed by Norbert Marklin of St. Louis, Missouri.

ISBN 0—8359—2982—5
ISBN 0—8359—2983—3

©1983 by
Reston Publishing Company, Inc.
A Prentice-Hall Company
Reston, Virginia, 22090

10   9   8   7   6   5   4   3   2   1

Printed in the United States of America.

Be sure that you understand all steps of construction and verify all dimensions before cutting any material. While every effort has been made to insure accuracy in the design and reproduction of all project plans, the possibility of error always exists, and Louisiana-Pacific Corporation and the distributor of this book shall not be responsible for injury, damage, or loss resulting from information contained herein.

CHAPTER
— 1 —

INTRODUCTION TO WOOD AND WOOD PRODUCTS

Wood is one of man's oldest, yet most modern materials. Even in this age of synthetic and metallurgical miracles, wood still enhances and serves innumerable needs of modern living as no other material can. However, you may have heard some people say, "They don't make houses today like they used to," or "Somehow, the wood we get today isn't what it used to be." Both statements are very true, but usually not in the sense that the speaker had in mind at the time. What the person said was right, but what he/she meant was wrong.

Today, better lumber and better houses have been produced. Better materials for building, better design, greater efficiency, and better workmanship are utilized. Standardization both in the lumber industry and in the building trades has brought about a better selection and use of materials. You no longer build with whatever is available at the corner lumberyard or the local sawmill.

More efficient mill practices have improved the preparation of lumber and have found uses for nearly all the by-products. The chips and sawdust are now made into several types of hardboard and particleboard. These materials are sometimes harder and stronger than the wood from which they are made.

Plywoods are made from several types of wood and given finish surfaces of almost every variety. The sheets are thinner, stronger, made in larger sizes, not subject to shrinkage, warpage, checking, or splitting; therefore, they are far more useful than the lumber from which they are made. In the forest, trees are grown to maturity before cutting. Selective methods eliminate the culls and harvest the better trees at the right time. Wood is prepared better at the mill, better seasoned and machined, and is marketed with better standards in quality and size than it formerly was.

STRUCTURE AND CHARACTERISTICS OF WOOD

For strictly botanical reasons, wood from the needle-leaved coniferous trees is called *softwood* (Fig. 1-1A). That from the broad-leaved deciduous trees which shed their leaves each year is called *hardwood* (Fig. 1-1B). These terms do not refer to the working hardness or softness of the wood because some of the softwoods, such as southern pine and fir, are harder than many of the hardwoods. Poplar and basswood are in the hardwood groups yet are among the softest

A

B

Fig. 1-1: The terms softwood and hardwood refer to broad categories of trees: (A) evergreens and (B) deciduous.

woods in working qualities. By far, the greatest bulk of wood for all commercial purposes comes from the softwood group. The hardwoods are more generally used for furniture, trim, flooring, and cabinetwork.

The way in which wood is formed in nature has a lot to do with its uses and working qualities. When you harvest a tree and slice the log into sections of lumber, you can see that wood grows both vertically and in width, or girth, of the tree (Fig. 1-2). In the cross section of the log, you can see a number of circles forming a more or less uniform pattern around a center core. Near the center, these rings are somewhat closer together and are usually darker in color. If you test the wood in this central area, you will find that it is harder than the lighter wood in the outer part of the log.

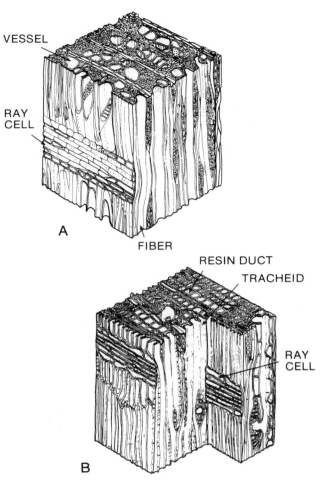

A = CAMBIUM LAYER
B = INNER BARK
C = OUTER BARK

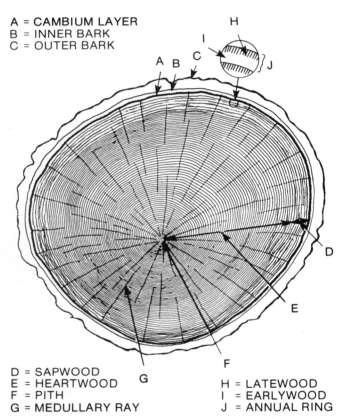

D = SAPWOOD
E = HEARTWOOD
F = PITH
G = MEDULLARY RAY
H = LATEWOOD
I = EARLYWOOD
J = ANNUAL RING

Fig. 1-2: A cross section of a log reveals the tree's growth pattern in the annual rings as well as other growth characteristics.

The split section of the tree, too, shows that the wood grows in slivers or fibers that run lengthwise of the trunk. If you examine these fibers with a magnifying glass (Fig. 1-3), you will see that they are composed of minute cells of varying size and thickness. It is the thickness of the walls of these cells that determines the weight and strength of the wood, and the uses to which it can be put.

Fig. 1-3: A magnified section of (A) hardwood and (B) softwood fibers. Note that the hardwood cells are smaller and arranged more densely than the softwood cells—a fact which explains the greater weight, strength, and hardness of most hardwoods.

Looking at the cross section of the tree trunk again, you will find an outside shell which is called the outer bark. Just inside of that is a thinner layer of soft and moist material called the inner bark. This section carries the food material made in the leaves to all live parts of the tree. Beneath the inner bark is a thin and darker layer, the cambium, in which the wood cells as well as the bark cells are formed for growth. Next comes a thicker section of light-colored wood which is known as the sapwood. This part of the tree trunk is the living part of the wood that carries the sap from the roots to the leafy sections.

The largest section of darker wood is the heartwood of the tree. This is the inactive part of the wood which has been pressed more solidly by the annual growth of the trunk and has become the harder and more durable part of the wood. The annual layers of growth are shown by the thin, concentric rings which begin at the very center and continue outward to the bark.

Through these growth rings, extending from the pith and out through the heartwood, are thin lines called medullary rays or wood rays, which function in transferring food throughout the tree trunk. Splits that sometimes occur in radiating lines from the center of the tree are called *heartshakes.* These are defects associated with decay at the center of the trunk.

If a tree is harvested too early in its life, it doesn't have much heartwood. While both sapwood and heartwood are about equal in strength, the heartwood has better working qualities, is better in appearance, and is more durable. The sapwood will absorb preservatives to a greater extent and is much better for outdoor use with such treating processes. A mature tree ready to be cut for lumber will have a large area of heartwood that can be cut into lumber for various purposes.

If you look closely at the individual bands of wood in each section marked by the annual growth rings, you will find that there is a difference from light to dark in the color of the fibers. The light-colored portion is the part that has grown in the spring. The darker section is the summer or autumn wood. The ratios of the portions of springwood and summerwood are very important to the strength and other characteristics of the wood. Generally, the varieties which grow rapidly and form wide growth rings having a large percentage of springwood are coarse-grained and not as strong as the slower-growing trees having narrow growth bands and denser summerwood.

Upon examining different types of wood, you will also find that some have fibers that grow straight and parallel to the bark. In others, the fibers seem to run in many directions or at an angle with the sides of the lumber. The two types are designated as straight-grained and cross-grained. You can readily see that it makes a difference how the logs are cut into lumber if you expect to get the best grain and strength qualities from the wood.

Sawing a Tree into Lumber

Boards are cut from logs in two *major* ways. The most common and economical way is called *flat-grained* (when it is a softwood tree) or *plain-sawn* (when it is a hardwood tree). Figure 1-4A shows typical boards that have been sawn from a log using the flat-grain or plain-sawn technique. Several distinctive features clearly identify this type of grain. First, by looking at the grain (annual rings) on the board's end, you can observe the slight arc of the rings. In some cases, as Fig. 1-4B shows, the arcs are incomplete. This type of display indicates that the board,

although flat cut, is cut very near the center of the tree, or cut from heartwood. Second, looking at the top surface, you'll probably see both a fairly wide section with no annual rings and toward the edges, smaller spaces between rings. Third, turning the board over, you should see a reverse pattern of the top and also closer annual rings.

Vertical- or *edge-grain sawing* for softwood (or *quarter-sawing* for hardwood) is a more expensive method of cutting (Fig. 1-5). It shows a better grain pattern especially in oak and other hardwoods. Quarter-sawn or edge-grain cutting provides a general uniform spacing of annual rings both on the surface and the edges.

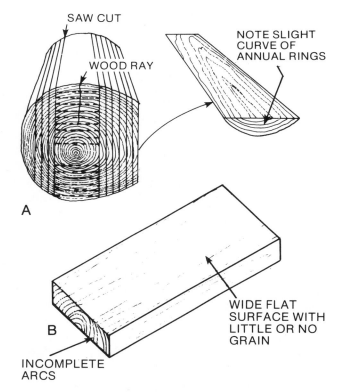

Fig. 1-4: Grain characteristics of flat-grained or plain-sawn lumber: (A) slight arc of end grain; (B) incomplete arcs indicate that the piece was cut very near the tree's center.

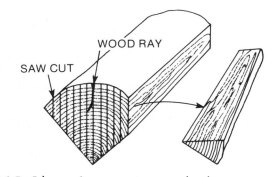

Fig. 1-5: Edge-grain or quarter-sawn lumber.

A third but less common method of cutting hardwood is *rift-sawing* (Fig. 1-6). This method is similar to quarter-sawing, except that the boards are sawn from the quarter log at an off-perpendicular angle. That is, the boards are sawn at not less than 35° nor more than 65° to the annual rings.

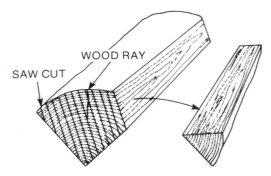

Fig. 1-6: Rift-sawn lumber.

Moisture Content of Lumber

When a tree is first harvested, it contains from 30 to 300% more moisture than it will after the wood is properly seasoned. The moisture in the green wood exists as free water in the cell cavities and as water absorbed in the cell walls. When the wood is dried, any free water is removed. Wood is at the fiber saturation point (approximately 23 to 30% moisture content) when it contains just enough water to saturate the cell fibers.

The wood's size does not change when the free water is removed. During additional drying after the fiber saturation point, the wood's size is reduced in proportion to the amount of free water removed. This exact proportion is dependent upon the wood type and the method in which it was cut from the log.

Because of the composition of wood cells, wood shrinks very little in length when drying. With the grain, the length of a piece of wood will not be altered due to moisture content. Across the grain shrinkage, however, is much more likely and may depend on the method in which the wood has been cut. Flat-grained or plain-sawn lumber will be altered almost twice as much in width as quarter-sawn or vertical-grain stock. Shrinkage affecting lumber cut from different sections of a log is shown in Fig. 1-7.

Remember, don't use freshly cut or green lumber for any of the projects described in this book. Although it costs less than lumber that has been dried, it's usually more expensive in the end because of difficulties resulting from shrinkage—nail-popping, warping, checking, and so on.

Lumber should be dried to about the same moisture

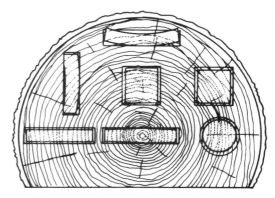

Fig. 1-7: The way a piece of lumber shrinks depends on the area from which the piece was cut.

content it will have when it is put into use. Problems can be expected if the moisture content exceeds 20%. Softwood lumber now is classified by the American Softwood Lumber Standard as either "dry" or "green"; dry lumber has been seasoned to a maximum moisture content of 19% or less. Electric moisture meters can be used to check moisture content if the dryness of the lumber is questionable.

The two common methods of seasoning or drying lumber are air-drying and kiln-drying.

Air-drying. Wood is stacked and allowed to season out-of-doors (Fig. 1-8). This method is impracticable in cold, damp weather; in hot, dry weather, the green lumber may warp or check since shrinkage is difficult to control.

Kiln-drying. Lumber is placed in a large "oven" where the rate of seasoning is controlled by adjusting humidity, air temperature, and air circulation (Fig. 1-9). Kiln-drying is more expensive than air-drying but the lumber can be dried faster and to a lower moisture content by the former method. Kiln-dried lumber usually is stamped with a "KD" to indicate that it's dried by this process.

Fig. 1-8: Lumber that is stacked to air-dry.

Fig. 1-9: Kiln-drying seasons to a lower moisture content in a shorter period of time and with fewer adverse effects than does air-drying.

Lumber dried to the same moisture content by either method will give equal satisfaction if it does not warp or check in drying.

Regardless of how it is dried, lumber will pick up or lose moisture until it reaches a balance with the moisture content of the air. Paint does not prevent wood from absorbing moisture as the finishes do not completely seal the wood. Paint does slow the rate of moisture absorption and the subsequent drying of wood as atmospheric conditions change.

Storing Lumber. To avoid warping, staining, and other possible ill effects, lumber delivered to a job should be stored in a dry place and stacked as it is in lumberyards. If the lumber must be stored out-of-doors, put it on a level foundation off the ground. Protect it from rain and ground moisture with tarpaulins or moisture resistant coverings. It's also very important that air be allowed to circulate along all surfaces of the stock. Stacking is the most universal method. Notice that the spacer sticks are evenly positioned vertically and horizontally. If done in this manner, no bending or warping of the stock should occur while it's being stored.

BUYING LUMBER

Before buying lumber from your local home center or lumber dealer, you should know something about the general grading and finishing of yard and specialty lumber. Availability of any particular wood in sufficient quantity and grade, or quality, is perhaps of first importance. The character of the wood, its color, strength, durability, and finishing qualities in relation to the project on which it is to be used also have to be

considered. Cost is always another important factor in the selection of lumber. The cost will be determined not only by the type of lumber and the sizes needed, but the grade of a particular wood that can be used.

Lower grades of lumber are always cheaper in price than the higher grades. It is often possible to save money in buying lumber by using a lower grade of wood or a higher grade of a cheaper wood. A particular piece of lumber can often be upgraded by careful selection and cutting out the imperfections of a low-grade board. When the sizes of lumber are considered, it is often possible to use a better grade of cheaper wood to better advantage than a lower grade of costly wood. Therefore, when selecting wood you should be aware of the various defects found in lumber.

Knots. Knots are created where a limb grows out from the trunk of the tree. As the tree continues to grow in diameter, the limb becomes partially recessed into the tree. When the limb dies, the recessed portions will be entrapped and incorporated into the trunk. Although the knot itself is as strong as the rest of the wood, the irregular grain which develops around the knot weakens the lumber. Furthermore, when the lumber is being dried, checks and cracks often develop in this irregular grain.

If the knot represents a live limb, the knot will be tight and will not affect the strength of the lumber a great deal (Fig. 1-10A); if the knot was formed when the trunk grew around a dead limb, the knot will be surrounded with bark and is apt to fall out. Such knots are called either encased or loose knots (Fig. 1-10B) and may impair the lumber's strength. If the knot passes across the wide face of the piece, it renders the lumber almost useless for structural purposes. This is called a spike knot (Fig. 1-10C) and occurs when

A   B   C

Fig. 1-10: Several types of knots: (A) Tight knots are intergrown into the log or piece of lumber. (B) Encased knots are surrounded with bark and may fall out. (C) Spike knots greatly reduce the strength of a piece of lumber.

the board is split by radial or quarter sawing. On plain-sawn boards, the knots will appear round or oval and are called round knots. The grade of a piece of lumber will be in part determined by the size and number of knots it has.

Checks, Splits, and Shakes. Checks and splits are separations of the wood along the grain (Figs. 1-11A and B). A split extends through lumber; a check does not. Checks and splits usually develop as a result of unequal shrinkage in a piece of lumber. How much they weaken lumber depends on their size and where they are located in the piece. Small checks from drying have little effect on strength.

Shakes (Fig. 1-11C) differ from splits in that a shake is a separation between two growth rings; a split usually runs across growth rings. The size and location of checks, splits, and shakes determine the board's suitability for your needs. In some cases, you can cut them off the board or fill them with patching compound.

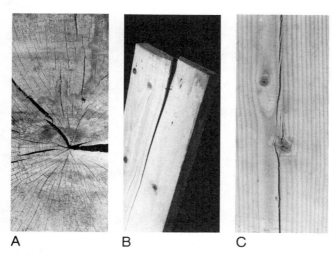

Fig. 1-11: Separations of wood fibers known as (A) checks, (B) splits, and (C) shakes.

Warpage. During the seasoning of boards, warpage in the form of bowing, cupping, kinking, diamonding, twisting, and crooking can take place (Fig. 1-12). This is especially true when the boards are flat- or plain-cut. The reason for this is that because of the different spacing of annual rings caused by flat- or plain-cutting, the surfaces tend to dry at different rates. The closer grains on the bottom of the board tend to dry faster than the wide grains on the top. Their shrinkage causes compression and warping. On the other hand, quarter-sawn or vertical-grain lumber has a tendency to shrink and swell less. It cups and twists less, and does not surface-check or split as badly in seasoning and use. It also wears more evenly, and raised grain caused by the annual rings is not as pronounced.

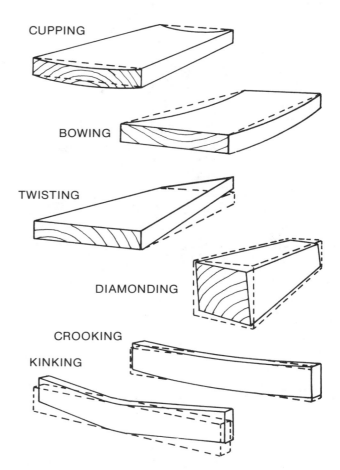

Fig. 1-12: Warpage may occur in several different planes.

Pitch Pockets and Wanes. Pitch pockets are openings which contain solid or liquid pitch (Fig. 1-13). They are found in pine, spruce, Douglas fir, tamarack, and western larch. Filling pitch pockets is difficult because the pitch usually bleeds through. If you decide to use a board with pitch pockets, clean away the pitch with turpentine. Then shellac the surface before finishing.

When a board is cut, it may be cut to include a portion of the bark. The bark, an area where the bark has fallen off, or any lack of wood for any reason on the edge or corner of a piece of lumber is called *wane* (Fig. 1-14). Wane will not affect the strength of a piece, but it doesn't help from an appearance standpoint.

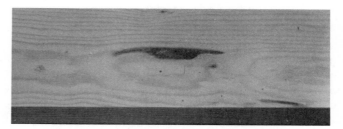

Fig. 1-13: Pitch pockets often occur in softwoods.

Fig. 1-14: Wane is the presence of bark or lack of wood on the edge or corner of a piece of lumber.

Decay and Stain. When the moisture in wood is excessive, the wood is susceptible to decay, stain, or mold. Decay is caused by fungi, small plant organisms which feed on wood until it becomes soft and punky. Even though this wood may appear to be sound, it loses some of its strength.

Fungi require favorable temperature, air, and water to remain active. There is no such thing as "dry rot" since the so-called dry-rot fungi can carry moisture several feet into dry wood.

As Chapter 3 describes, certain woods, such as cedar, cypress, and redwood, are more resistant to decay and insect attack than others because the heartwood contains chemicals which are poisonous to fungi. Sapwood is generally not as resistant to decay as heartwood but absorbs wood preservatives better.

Chemical preservatives, which poison the food supply of the fungi and give the wood resistance to insect attack, are frequently used to treat the more susceptible woods. Methods of applying wood preservatives are fully described in Chapter 3.

Some fungi do not rot the wood but cause only stain or mold which affects the wood's appearance. For example, blue stain in pine is a result of a non-destructive fungus in the sapwood of drought- and beetle-plagued trees in the western United States. Once an affected tree is harvested, sawn, and dried, the fungus ceases to grow and leaves a permanent coloration in the resulting lumber. It's not just a surface coloration but penetrates deeply through the affected sapwood. Blue stain doesn't, however, adversely affect workability, paint-holding quality, the ability to be glued or nailed, or finishing properties. In fact, blue stain is now much sought after for its unique, appealing appearance. Patterned boards finish into a beautiful, distinctive interior paneling with blue-tinged streaks of grain. In heavier dimensions it is used in chairs, tables, and furniture.

The way the various defects affect the grading of the two types of lumber—softwood and hardwood—is fully covered in Chapters 2 and 3.

TIPS ON WORKING WITH WOOD

Specific tips on working with wood and wood products are given in later chapters. When wood types and products are discussed in detail, there are certain general procedures that hold true for all woods. These general procedures are discussed in the following sections.

Fasteners to Use

Fasteners used in the projects shown in this book include nails and screws. As a rule, these fasteners are the weakest link in all forms of construction and in all materials; therefore, the resistance offered by the wood to the withdrawal of nails and screws is important. Usually, the denser and harder the wood, the greater is the inherent nail-holding ability, assuming the wood does not split.

Nails. The nail industry still clings to the penny system to indicate the length of the most commonly used nails, ranging in length from 1" to 6". The symbol for penny is d. The length, diameter, head size, and approximate number to a pound of the various penny sizes of common nails and finishing nails are shown in Table 1-1. Actually, the size, quantity, and placement of nails have a marked effect on the strength of a joint. Thus, more nails are required in woods of medium holding power than in woods of high holding power.

The resistance of a nail to withdrawal increases almost directly with its diameter; if the diameter of the nail is doubled, the holding strength is doubled,

TABLE 1-1: COMMON NAILS AND FINISHING NAILS

		Common Nails		
Size	Length (inches)	Diameter Gauge Number	Diameter of Head (inches)	Approximate Number per Pound
2d	1	15	11/64	830
3d	1-1/4	14	13/64	528
4d	1-1/2	12-1/2	1/4	316
5d	1-3/4	12-1/2	1/4	271
6d	2	11-1/2	17/64	168
7d	2-1/4	11-1/2	17/64	150
8d	2-1/2	10-1/4	9/32	106
9d	2-3/4	10-1/4	9/32	96
10d	3	9	5/16	69
12d	3-1/4	9	5/16	63
16d	3-1/2	8	11/32	49
20d	4	6	13/32	31
30d	4-1/2	5	7/16	24
40d	5	4	15/32	18
50d	5-1/2	3	1/2	14
60d	6	2	17/32	11

TABLE 1-1:   COMMON NAILS AND FINISHING NAILS
(Continued)

Finishing Nails

Size	Length (inches)	Diameter Gauge Number	Diameter of Head Gauge Number	Approximate Number per Pound
2d	1	16-1/2	13-1/2	1,351
3d	1-1/4	15-1/2	12-1/2	807
4d	1-1/2	15	12	584
5d	1-3/4	15	12	500
6d	2	13	10	309
8d	2-1/2	12-1/2	9-1/2	189
10d	3	11-1/2	8-1/2	121
16d	3-1/2	11	8	90
20d	4	10	7	62

providing the nail doesn't split the wood when it's driven. The lateral resistance of nails increases as the diameter increases.

Nails that are commonly used in construction work are shown in Fig. 1-15. The nail generally used in wood-frame construction is the common nail. However, galvanized and aluminum nails are used extensively in applying siding and exterior trim because these nails resist rusting. The galvanized nail is slightly better than the common bright nail in retaining its withdrawal resistance.

Superior withdrawal resistance has been shown by the deformed-shank nail, which is produced in two general forms, the ring- or annular-groove and the spiral-groove shanks. The annular-groove nail is outstanding in its resistance to withdrawal loads and is

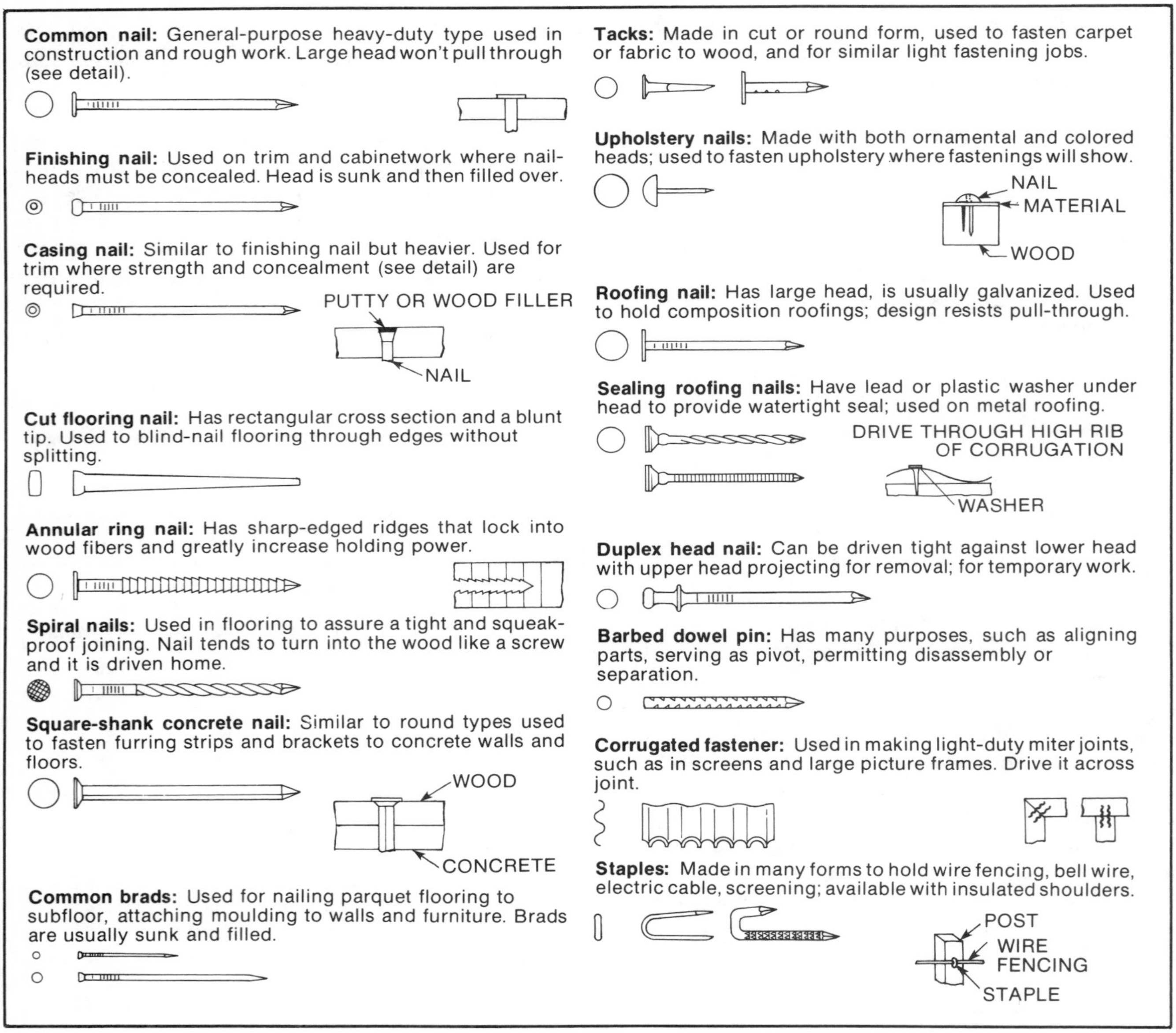

Common nail: General-purpose heavy-duty type used in construction and rough work. Large head won't pull through (see detail).

Finishing nail: Used on trim and cabinetwork where nailheads must be concealed. Head is sunk and then filled over.

Casing nail: Similar to finishing nail but heavier. Used for trim where strength and concealment (see detail) are required.

PUTTY OR WOOD FILLER

NAIL

Cut flooring nail: Has rectangular cross section and a blunt tip. Used to blind-nail flooring through edges without splitting.

Annular ring nail: Has sharp-edged ridges that lock into wood fibers and greatly increase holding power.

Spiral nails: Used in flooring to assure a tight and squeak-proof joining. Nail tends to turn into the wood like a screw and it is driven home.

Square-shank concrete nail: Similar to round types used to fasten furring strips and brackets to concrete walls and floors.

WOOD

CONCRETE

Common brads: Used for nailing parquet flooring to subfloor, attaching moulding to walls and furniture. Brads are usually sunk and filled.

Tacks: Made in cut or round form, used to fasten carpet or fabric to wood, and for similar light fastening jobs.

Upholstery nails: Made with both ornamental and colored heads; used to fasten upholstery where fastenings will show.

NAIL
MATERIAL
WOOD

Roofing nail: Has large head, is usually galvanized. Used to hold composition roofings; design resists pull-through.

Sealing roofing nails: Have lead or plastic washer under head to provide watertight seal; used on metal roofing.

DRIVE THROUGH HIGH RIB OF CORRUGATION

WASHER

Duplex head nail: Can be driven tight against lower head with upper head projecting for removal; for temporary work.

Barbed dowel pin: Has many purposes, such as aligning parts, serving as pivot, permitting disassembly or separation.

Corrugated fastener: Used in making light-duty miter joints, such as in screens and large picture frames. Drive it across joint.

Staples: Made in many forms to hold wire fencing, bell wire, electric cable, screening; available with insulated shoulders.

POST
WIRE
FENCING
STAPLE

Fig. 1-15: General purpose and woodworking nails.

commonly used in construction of pole-type buildings.

Interior carpentry uses the small-headed finish nail, which can be set and puttied over. That is, where the nail head must not show or must be inconspicuous, it is driven well below the surface with a nail set. The hole in the wood over the nail head can then be filled flush with the surface, with putty, plastic wood, or sawdust mixed with glue. Nail sets are made in several sizes, usually 1/32″, 2/32″, and 4/32″; the size is indicated by the diameter of the small end of the tapered shank. The end of a nail set is often "cupped" or hollowed, which prevents it from "walking" or slipping on the nail. Use a nail set of a size which will not enlarge the hole made by the head of the nail.

The moisture content of the wood at the time of nailing is extremely important for good nail holding. If plain-shank nails are driven into wet wood, they will lose about three-fourths of their full holding ability when the wood becomes dry. This loss of holding power is so great that siding, barn boards, or fence pickets are likely to become loose when plain-shank nails are driven into green wood that subsequently dries. Thus the most important rule in obtaining good joints and high nail-holding ability is to use well-seasoned wood.

The splitting of wood by nails greatly reduces their holding ability. Even if the wood is split only slightly around the nail, considerable holding strength is lost. Because of hardness and texture characteristics, some woods split more in nailing than do others. The heavy, dense woods, such as maple, oak, and hickory, split more in nailing than do the lightweight woods, such as basswood, spruce, balsam, and white fir. Location of nails as shown in Fig. 1-16 is good practice.

Predrilling is a good practice when working with dense woods; especially when large-diameter nails are used. The drilled hole should be about 75% of the nail diameter. Woods without a uniform texture, like southern yellow pine and Douglas fir, split more than do uniform-textured woods such as northern and Idaho white pine, sugar pine, or ponderosa pine. In addition to predrilling, the most common means taken to reduce splitting is the use of small-diameter nails. The number of small nails must be increased to maintain the same gross holding strength as with larger nails. Slightly blunt-pointed nails have less tendency to split wood than do sharp-pointed nails. Too much blunting, however, results in a loss of holding ability.

There is a simple rule to follow when selecting nail lengths for both rough (framing) and finish (trim, cabinets) carpentry. The rule applies to hardwoods and softwoods. Figure 1-17 shows the rule graphically. Suppose that pieces A and B are to be nailed together. In the case of hardwoods, the nail penetration, X, into

the bottom piece should be one-half the length of the nail. For softwoods, the penetration, Y, into the bottom piece should be two-thirds the length of the nail. Thus, the thickness of the top piece determines the required nail length.

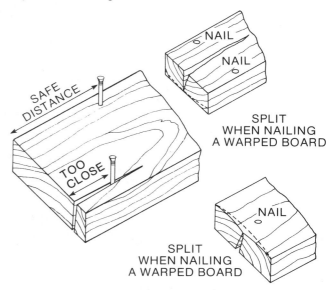

Fig. 1-16: Positioning nails to prevent splitting.

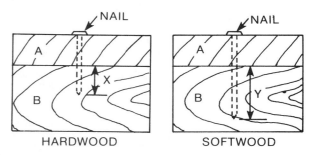

Fig. 1-17: Proper nail penetration in hardwood and softwood.

Screws. Screws have much greater holding power than nails. An added advantage to using screws is that work held together by them is easily taken apart and put together again without damaging the pieces. But screws take longer to install and are generally used only in finish carpentry work. The most commonly used screws are shown in Fig. 1-18.

Wood screws are sized according to diameter and length. The length is indicated in inches or fractions thereof; the diameter is indicated by a number. The smallest diameter is #0, and the largest common size is #24. The most generally used sizes are #3 to #16.

The method of measuring screws is shown in Fig. 1-19. The length of a flathead wood screw is the overall length, but the length of roundhead and fillister-head screws is measured from the point to the underside of the head. The length of an ovalhead screw is measured from the point to the edge of the head.

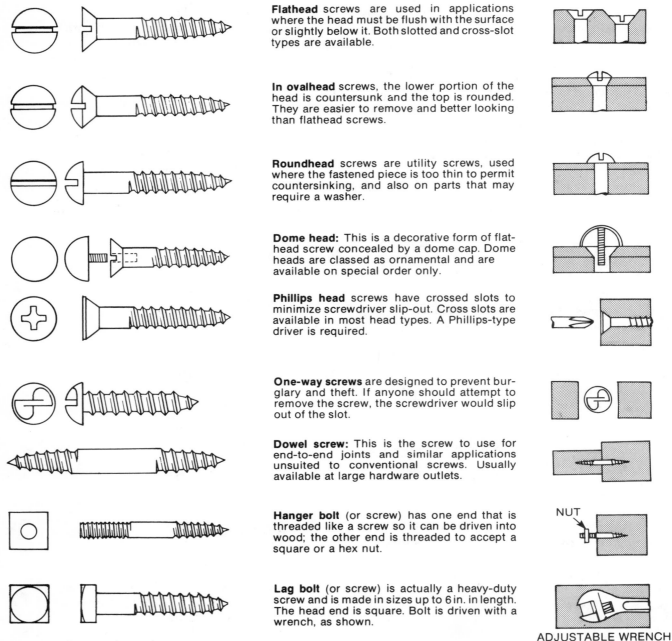

Flathead screws are used in applications where the head must be flush with the surface or slightly below it. Both slotted and cross-slot types are available.

In ovalhead screws, the lower portion of the head is countersunk and the top is rounded. They are easier to remove and better looking than flathead screws.

Roundhead screws are utility screws, used where the fastened piece is too thin to permit countersinking, and also on parts that may require a washer.

Dome head: This is a decorative form of flat-head screw concealed by a dome cap. Dome heads are classed as ornamental and are available on special order only.

Phillips head screws have crossed slots to minimize screwdriver slip-out. Cross slots are available in most head types. A Phillips-type driver is required.

One-way screws are designed to prevent burglary and theft. If anyone should attempt to remove the screw, the screwdriver would slip out of the slot.

Dowel screw: This is the screw to use for end-to-end joints and similar applications unsuited to conventional screws. Usually available at large hardware outlets.

Hanger bolt (or screw) has one end that is threaded like a screw so it can be driven into wood; the other end is threaded to accept a square or a hex nut.

NUT

Lag bolt (or screw) is actually a heavy-duty screw and is made in sizes up to 6 in. in length. The head end is square. Bolt is driven with a wrench, as shown.

ADJUSTABLE WRENCH

Fig. 1-18: Commonly used screws.

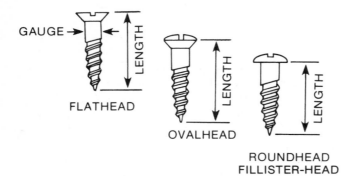

GAUGE

FLATHEAD

OVALHEAD

ROUNDHEAD
FILLISTER-HEAD

LENGTH

Fig. 1-19: Method of measuring common screws.

Standards for screws have been established by cooperation between the manufacturers and the United States Bureau of Standards so that standard screws of all screw manufacturers are alike. The standard diameters are given in Table 1-2.

If a screw is driven in without first boring a pilot hole for the threaded part, the wood may split and in some instances the screw head may be twisted off. (As shown in Fig. 1-20, a little bar soap rubbed into the threads of a wood screw makes it easier to drive.) Bore holes for small screws with a small brad awl; for large screws use bits or twist drills. If the wood is soft (pine, spruce, basswood, tulip), bore the hole only about half as deep as the threaded part of the screw. If the wood is hard (oak, maple, birch), the hole must be almost as deep as the screw.

If the screw is large or made of brass, bore a screw body hole slightly smaller in diameter than the threaded part of the screw. Enlarge the top of this body hole into a lead hole, using a second drill the same diameter as the unthreaded portion of the screw. Table 1-3 lists the body and lead hole drill sizes for standard screw gauges.

Screws are sometimes set below the surface of the wood and concealed by a wooden plug. Plugs can be cut with a tool called a plug cutter, which fits into an ordinary brace. Plugs should be cut from the same kind of wood as that in which they are to be inserted, and the grain should match as closely as possible. They should be cut so that the grain runs across the plug, not lengthwise.

TABLE 1-2: STANDARD WOOD SCREW DIAMETERS

| Number | Diameter | | |
	Basic	Maximum	Minimum
0	.060	.064	.053
1	.073	.077	.066
2	.086	.090	.079
3	.099	.103	.092
4	.112	.116	.105
5	.125	.129	.118
6	.138	.142	.131
7	.151	.155	.144
8	.164	.168	.157
9	.177	.181	.170
10	.190	.194	.183
11	.203	.207	.196
12	.216	.220	.209
14	.242	.246	.235
16	.268	.272	.261
18	.294	.298	.287
20	.320	.324	.313
24	.372	.376	.365

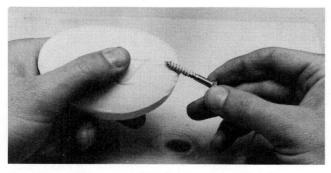

Fig. 1-20: A little soap rubbed on a screw will make it easier to turn.

TABLE 1-3: BODY AND LEAD HOLES FOR WOOD SCREWS

Screw Gauge	Diameter (in decimals)	Body Hole Drill Number	Lead Hole Drill Number	Counter-sink Drill Number
0	.060	53	unnecessary	32
1	.073	49	unnecessary	20
2	.086	44	56	16
3	.099	40	56	4
4	.112	33	52	B
5	.125	1/8	52	F
6	.138	28	47	L
7	.151	24	47	O
8	.164	19	42	S
9	.177	15	42	T
10	.190	10	42	X
11	.203	5	38	7/16
12	.216	7/32	38	29/64
14	.242	D	31	33/64
16	.268	1/4	28	37/64
18	.294	19/64	23	41/64

First bore a hole at least 3/8″ deep with a spade or auger bit the same size as the wood plug (Fig. 1-21). Then bore the proper pilot and clearance holes. Drive the screw in as far as it will go with a screwdriver. Select a suitable plug, put some glue on its sides, and insert it in the hole, with the grain on the end of the plug running in the same direction as the grain on the surface of the work. Drive the plug in as far as it will go. When the glue has dried, use a chisel or a plane to pare the plug off level with the surface.

Fig. 1-21: Screws may be hidden by countersinking and filling the hole with a wood plug.

Gluing. Gluing is another popular method of fastening wood together. Any good wood gluing job depends on several factors, the most important of which are:

1. Selection and preparation of the adhesive.
2. Preparation of the wood surfaces to be joined.
3. Design of the joints.
4. Application of the adhesive.

5. Assembly of the parts and proper use of clamps and other clamping devices.

(Factors 2 and 3 will be discussed in later chapters.)

For most wood projects described in this book, one of the ready-to-use adhesives, such as liquid hide, aliphatic, and polyvinyl acetate (white glue), can be used. But where a waterproof joint is a must, use a resorcinol type. This is a two-part adhesive and must be mixed as directed by the manufacturer. Just mix enough glue for the bonding job at hand so that the batch is fresh.

Make a trial assembly to be certain that the joints are well fitted. Do this by clamping all the pieces together. While checking the parts, carefully inspect each one to make sure that all sandpapering has been completed. This will open the pores of the wood, giving the adhesive more holding power. Also, the joints should be square; the more the surfaces touch, the better the grip will be. After all the parts line up square and true, mark all companion pieces with a soft pencil or carpenter's chalk as 1 and 1, 2 and 2, etc. (Fig. 1-22); then indicate front right, front left, etc. (In edge gluing several pieces together, it is a good idea to draw a large X across the face of the pieces.) Once this is done, the different pieces will fit together as they should for the actual gluing without further adjustment; this is important since the assembly time should go as quickly and smoothly as possible. The clamps should also be set to the correct opening beforehand to facilitate the gluing operation. Also, have the wood pieces and the glue at room temperature, since cold glue and cold wood will not bond properly. No type of wood glue will function properly if it or the piece to be glued is too cold. For best results, gluing and drying of glue should be done in room temperatures of 70 to 75°F.

The common methods of applying wood adhesives are with a squeeze bottle, wood stick or paddle, paintbrush, glue roller, or spray gun. The glue may be ap-

plied either to one surface (single spreading) or to both surfaces (double spreading). When applying glue to porous surfaces such as end grain, it is wise to spread a thin coat of glue on both surfaces to be joined; let it stand until tacky. This first coat will dry partly by evaporation, partly by being drawn into the pores of the material. Then spread on a second coat.

Glue from a squeeze bottle should be applied in a zigzag line (Fig. 1-23). Then, the two parts should be pressed together and moved back and forth to produce an even spread. As a rule, the proper amount of applied adhesive will cause tiny beads of glue to appear along the glue line at regular intervals of 2" to 4" when clamped. A starved glue joint will generally result from using too little adhesive or too great a clamping pressure. Too much adhesive will cause squeeze-out and running of the glue down the wood surface. This can be a messy problem, especially when the project is to be finished with stain or varnish.

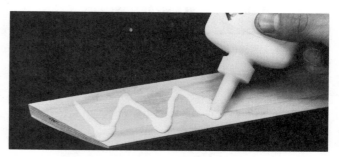

Fig. 1-23: Applying glue in a zigzag pattern.

Most good wood gluing requires the use of some type of clamps. The purpose of the clamps is to bring the members being glued in close enough contact to produce a thin uniform glue line and to hold them in this position until the glue has developed enough strength to hold the assembly together. If the members of a glued construction were to fit together perfectly so that a thin, even glue line could be produced, no clamp pressure would be required. But, from a practical standpoint, since machining of stock is never perfect, a certain amount of clamping pressure must be used.

To ensure close contact in edge gluing and lumber laminating operations, 100 to 150 pounds per square inch (psi) is usually required. This pressure can usually be obtained by tightening the clamp with your fingers only. Sometimes, it's a good idea to give the clamp a turn or two after a few minutes. But, do not distort the piece; it can be extremely frustrating to break a delicate piece which took a great deal of time to make. In some instances, nails can be used as temporary clamps.

Keep in mind that heavy pressures will crush the softer woods. To prevent injuries of this sort, as men-

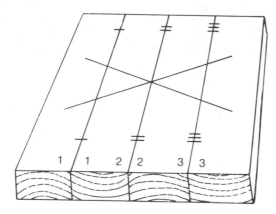

Fig. 1-22: Method of marking pieces before gluing.

tioned earlier, place small pieces of hardwood, leather, or hardboard between the metal clamping feet and the material being clamped. For very delicate work, you can make blocks of wood with felt or foam rubber strips cemented to one face, and use these between the work and the clamps. Also, it is a good idea to put waxed paper between the glue joints and the clamps or clamping blocks so they do not become glued to the stock (Fig. 1-24). If possible, use clamps in pairs on both ends of the work to prevent one end from separating while the other is being joined. For large surfaces, additional clamps are needed. Apply even pressure on all clamps, but avoid pressing in the sides of the work. If you have a job that requires pressure and the workpiece is too wide for any of the clamps you have available, just open one clamp to approximately its full length and hook its jaw over the jaw of a second clamp. Then, tighten the second clamp to the tension desired, and your problem is solved. Regardless of which clamps are used, there is usually a tendency for long-glued joints to spring apart at the ends. Greater clamping pressure should therefore be applied to the ends than to the center, and the center clamps should be tightened before the end clamps.

Fig. 1-24: Waxed paper between work and glue blocks prevents clamp or blocks from adhering to the work.

After the clamps have been applied, test the job for squareness. Use a damp cloth to wipe excess glue off clamps and stock surfaces. Do this as soon as the material is clamped securely together, so that later sanding and smoothing will be easier and clamps won't get clogged with glue. If you throw sawdust over the squeeze-out as it oozes out of the joint, the sawdust will absorb the moisture of the glue, making it easier to peel or scratch off the excess. The latter can be done by using a sharp chisel along the squeeze-out line. Hold the chisel with the bevel side up. Cutting across the grain (where possible), remove all glue that still remains. Follow this with a thorough sandpapering of all such parts. Give a final sanding to all parts of the furniture with fine and then very fine abrasive paper. Never *wash off* excess glue with water.

This would only coat the wood with a thin layer of glue that might show when it dries; it might also make the wood swell, which is very undesirable.

Minor gaps between joints can usually be filled with wood filler after the adhesive hardens. However, if the defect is detected before the adhesive has set, it's a good idea to fill it with a glue-coated wood sliver.

Sawing Wood

Sawing wood to the size necessary for the project is one of the first steps you must undertake. When a board is cut with a saw, it is either ripped with the grain or crosscut across the grain. Each type of cut requires a special type of saw tooth and configuration. Figure 1-25 shows that a hand ripsaw has 5-1/2 teeth per inch and that a crosscut handsaw may have as few as 8 teeth per inch to 12 and more.

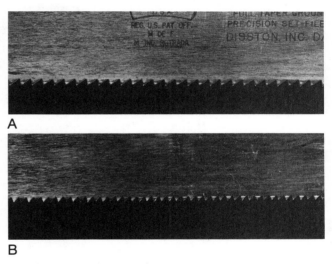

A

B

Fig. 1-25: (A) Ripsaw and (B) crosscut saw.

The reason for so few teeth per inch on the ripsaw is that the cutting action is in line with the cell wall structure of the wood fibers. The fibers offer minimal opposition to cutting, thereby allowing for larger teeth and wider spacing. This ripping action results in a very rough saw-cut surface (Fig. 1-26A). Planing is absolutely essential after cutting.

In contrast, the crosscutting of a board requires a saw with many small teeth. As the term implies, crosscutting saws across the cell walls instead of along the cell walls. The saw teeth slice rather than rip through the wood and produce a much smoother cut than when ripsawing (Fig. 1-26B). The more teeth per inch, the smoother the cut. Therefore, when building cabinets and furniture, all crosscutting should be done with a sharp, 11- or 12-point crosscut saw.

Fig. 1-26: The results of (A) ripping with a 5-point ripsaw and (B) crosscutting with a 10-point crosscut saw.

But what if you have an electric saw? The same principles apply. If ripping, use a ripsaw blade; if crosscutting, use a crosscut blade. In ripping operations your ripsaw blade should be properly set. Since most of the lumber is very dry, a standard set of teeth minimizes the gouging and tearing effects on the wood fibers. Thus the planing and sanding requirements that follow are also reduced.

Crosscutting saw blades are made in many configurations. The combination blade has the largest teeth since this blade may be used for ripping as well as crosscutting. Its set is usually standard or minimal. Its cut is fairly smooth with only a little tearing. The crosscut saw blade is also made *hollow ground*. This means that the blade's teeth area thickness is thicker than the blade's steel body. There is a general taper toward the center hole. This type of blade has little if any set and results in a cut approaching a sanded wood surface. Obviously this is the best type of blade to use for the final fitting and cutting of mouldings, trims, and open shelf ends.

Saber saw blades also are made for rough and smooth cutting action. If ripping, use a rough (large tooth) blade to ease cutting. Change to a smooth (small tooth) blade for crosscuts and circles or arcs.

Hand Sawing. To saw across the grain of the stock, use a crosscut saw; to saw with the grain, use a ripsaw. Study the teeth in both kinds of saws so you can readily identify the saw that you need.

Place the board on a sawhorse or some other suitable object, or in a vise. Hold the saw firmly, and extend the first finger along the handle as shown in Figs. 1-27A and B. When crosscutting, grasp the board as shown in Fig. 1-27C and take a position so that an imaginary line passing lengthwise along the forearm

will be at an angle of approximately 45° with the face of the board (Fig. 1-28A). Be sure the side of the saw is plumb, or at right angles, with the face of the board. Place the heel of the saw on the mark. Keep the saw in line with the forearm, and pull it toward you to start the cut. When ripping, the best saw angle is about 60° (Fig. 1-28B).

A

B

C

D

Fig. 1-27: Hints regarding the use of handsaws: (A) ripping a board on a sawhorse, (B) ripping a board held in a vise, (C) board held in a vise for crosscutting, and (D) testing a saw cut with a try square.

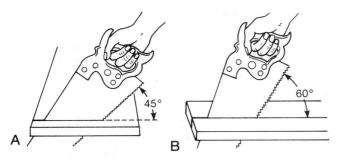

Fig. 1-28: Proper angle for (A) crosscutting and (B) ripping.

Well-made saws are designed to make starting cuts easily. Ripsaws are usually one point finer at the tip than at the butt, so start the cut with the tip end of the blade. In crosscutting, start with a draw stroke at the butt end of the blade. Repeat once or twice until a groove is started; then use full strokes. That is, to begin with, take short, light strokes, gradually increasing the strokes to the full length of the saw. Don't force or jerk the saw; such a procedure will only make sawing more difficult. The arm that does the sawing should swing clear of your body so that the handle of the saw operates at your side rather than in front of you.

Use only one hand to operate the saw. You may be tempted to use both hands at times, but one hand will serve you better if your saw is sharp. The weight of the saw is sufficient to make it cut. If the saw sticks or binds, it may be because the saw is dull and is poorly "set." The wood may have too much moisture in it, or you may have forced the saw and thus caused it to leave the straight line.

Keep your eye on the line, rather than on the saw, while sawing. Watching the marked line enables you to see instantly any tendency to leave the line. If the saw veers away from the marked line, a slight twist or flex of the handle and taking a few short strokes while sawing will bring the saw back. But don't flex it much or it may "oversteer" and veer across to the other side. (Also, too much flex could cause the saw to jam or buckle, causing permanent damage.) Blow away the sawdust frequently, so you can see the marked layout line. The final strokes of the cut should be taken slowly. Hold the waste piece in your other hand so the wood won't split when you take the last stroke.

When it is important that your cut be perfectly square, use a small try square as a guide (Fig. 1-27D). Another way to keep the cut true and square is to clamp a piece of scrap stock to your work and use it as a guide (Fig. 1-29).

When sawing across the grain, if the nature of the work permits, place the board as shown in Fig. 1-30B. This avoids splintering at the last resin ring, as sometimes happens when the board is placed as shown in Fig. 1-30A. Also when ripping or crosscutting, keep

the saw on the waste side of the marked line—don't try to saw on the line, or "saw out the line." This ensures that the board will be of the right width or length after it is cut (Fig. 1-30C). When cutting on the line, you cut into the board as well as the waste, as shown in Fig. 1-30D.

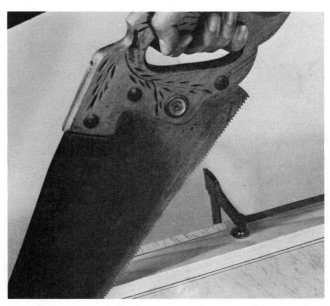

Fig. 1-29: Scrap stock clamped to the work along the kerf line will help keep the kerf straight.

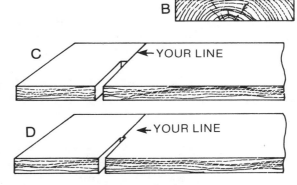

Fig. 1-30: How to make a saw kerf.

Power Sawing. The portable electric circular saw is a right-handed tool and is used very much like the handsaw. The difference is that the cut is made in the opposite direction: the blade cuts from the bottom to the top of the work. For this reason, when using a portable circular saw, always place the work with its "good" side—the one on which appearance is more important—down. Set the depth of cut 1/4" to 1/2" greater than the thickness of the stock to be cut. A good rule of thumb is that the blade should protrude through the work by one tooth depth (Fig. 1-31). More protrusion will only increase the cutting friction and,

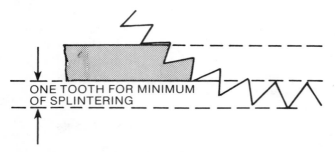

Fig. 1-31: Depth of power saw blade should be one tooth greater than thickness of the work.

in some cases, make for a rougher surface. The exception is carbide-tipped blades, for which only half a tooth tip should project below the material. Be sure to tighten the wing nut well, after making the depth adjustment.

Always maintain a firm grip on the handle and operate the switch with a decisive action. Place the saw base on the stock, with the blade clear, before turning on the switch. That is, the saw should be running at full speed before the blade contacts the work. Advance the saw into the wood. The telescoping lower guard will swing back by itself. Feed the tool at the speed at which the blade cuts willingly. Never force the saw. Always use a light and continuous pressure. Remember that hardness and roughness can vary even in the same piece. A knotty or damp section can put a heavy load on the saw; when this happens, feed more slowly. Your ear and your muscles will tell you when the saw is overloaded; feed hard enough to keep it working without much decrease in speed. Forcing it beyond this makes for rough cuts, inaccuracy, and overheating of the motor.

Should your cut begin to go off the line, don't try to force it back on. It is best, of course, to make errors on the waste side of the line. Then you can withdraw the saw, sight again, and start a new cut a trifle inside the wrong one. In any event, withdraw the saw if you must shift the cut. Forcing a correction inside the cut can stall the saw, cause kickbacks, and perhaps spoil the work. Also never attempt to remove a portable circular saw from the work while the blade is in motion, or kickback may occur. When making an incomplete cut or when the cut is interrupted, release the switch and hold the saw motionless in the material until the blade comes to a complete stop.

The workpiece should also be placed face down when cutting with a saber saw (Fig. 1-32). The saber saw blade moves up and down, cutting as it moves up through the wood. Keeping the good side down will assure that feathered and splintered edges will appear on the rough side of the workpiece.

The up-and-down action of the blade also produces a lot of vibration. Keep a firm and steady downward

pressure on the saw when cutting. Start the cut by placing the shoe plate firmly on the workpiece with the blade not touching the workpiece. Start the saw. When it is running at the proper speed, move the saw into the wood. Don't force the saw; let the saw do the cutting, just as with the circular saw.

The operation of a stationary table saw and radial-arm saw is basically the same as the portable circular saw except that the "good" side should be up. Before operating *any* power saw be sure to read the owner's manual carefully and follow the safety rules most *carefully.*

Fig. 1-32: Cutting with a saber saw.

Using Wood Chisels

Another wood cutting tool used in some of the projects in this book is a chisel. For light cuts in softwood, the chisel can usually be operated with hand pressure only. For most hardwood, however, a soft-face hammer or mallet is employed to force the chisel into the wood. The chisel is held in one hand, beveled edge down against the wood, and the end of the handle is struck lightly with the mallet, which is held in the other hand. For finish work, the chisel is used with the beveled edge of the blade turned away from the finished surface. Whether striking or hand pressure is employed, be sure to secure the work.

When using hand pressure, the chisel should be held and guided by your left hand and powered with your right. Don't start to cut directly on the marked line, but a little away from it, so that any accidental splitting will occur in the waste portion rather than in the finished work. Cut with the grain as much as possible, since then the chisel's cutting edge tends to sever the wood fibers cleanly, leaving the wood fairly smooth. Cutting against the grain splits the fibers of the wood, leaving it rough. That is, the chisel acts as a wedge, forcing the fibers apart in advance of the cutting edge. The cut thus can't easily be controlled.

In cutting with a chisel, be very careful (especially when finishing) to make the shavings thin and to cut with the grain of the wood so the surface will be left smooth and bright. Hold the chisel, when possible, at a slight angle to the cut, instead of square across the direction of motion. This gives a paring or sliding cut that is easier to make, and one that leaves the work smoother both on the end grain and with the grain.

The two principal chisel cuts are horizontal and vertical paring. To chisel horizontally with the grain, always hold the tool turned toward one side, and push it with your hand, removing moderate or small portions of the wood. To chisel horizontally against the grain, press your forefinger and thumb together on the chisel to act as a brake while you push the chisel with your other hand (Fig. 1-33A). To avoid splintering the corners, cut halfway from each edge toward the center and remove the center stock last. While a chisel is frequently used for roughing, it is usually better to remove as much waste as possible with a saw.

A   B

Fig. 1-33: Chiseling against the grain (A) horizontally and (B) vertically.

To cut vertically against the grain, the chisel can either be tilted to one side, or held straight and moved to a side as the chisel cuts down into the wood. If the surface to be cut is wider than the chisel, part of the chisel should be pressed against the portion just cut out (Fig. 1-33B). This helps to guide and keep in line the part of the chisel cutting out a new portion of the work.

To chisel vertically with the grain (Fig. 1-34), keep the chisel slanted as you would when cutting across the grain. If you're working along an edge of a board, work from the guideline toward the end so that the wood will split away from the line. If you work from the end toward the guideline, you could ruin your work if the wood splits too far.

Fig. 1-34: Chiseling vertically with the grain.

Planing Boards

The primary rule that must never be violated when planing a board is "Plane in the direction of grain." What does this mean? Using Fig. 1-35, observe that the grain indicated at the point of the arrow has a slight angle toward the top edge of the board. This fact indicates that the direction of grain for planing purposes is from left to right. Planing in this manner results in a smooth cut because the wood cells are being cut toward their top surfaces. Figure 1-36 shows the proper position of the plane when planing a board's edge. The ribbon of wood leaving the plane's cutting edge provides a good example.

The sharp edge of the plane's blade continually slides along the board without cutting because the

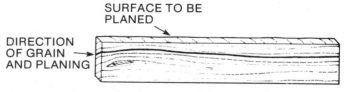

Fig. 1-35: Plane in the direction of the rise and run of the grain.

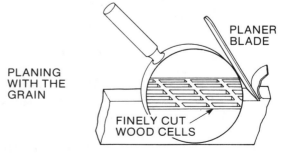

Fig. 1-36: Planing in the direction of grain.

direction of grain encourages it. However, when a downward pressure is applied to the plane, its blade cuts into a layer or several layers of cells and they peel away.

A serious problem can occur if the plane is used in the *against-the-grain manner*. Figure 1-37 shows that the blade, rather than sliding along the surface, tends to dig deeply into the wood by following the grain. This action results in tearing the wood fibers, uneven cutting, and severe damage. Because the blade is fixed at a specific depth in the plane, it can't continue along the direction of the grain. Therefore, it must rip the fibers as it travels along the board's surface.

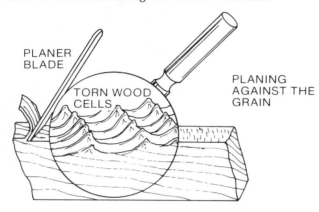

Fig. 1-37: *Planing against the grain tears the wood fibers instead of cutting them.*

The torn portions of wood present two problems: The surface area is lower than surrounding areas, and many of the cell walls are torn. Both conditions make it virtually impossible to obtain an even finish during finishing operations. Stain takes faster and darker in torn fibers, causing an uneven coloring. If filling is used, so much of it accumulates in the depressions that the grain pattern is lost, stain takes lighter or darker, and a blotch effect is obtained.

To avoid these problems your procedure in planing a board should be the following:

1. Sight the board's adjacent surface to determine the grain's direction.
2. Plane in the direction of grain where the grain is rising toward the surface away from you.
3. Stop your plane's travel the instant you observe that you are planing against the grain.

These procedures apply both to planing a board's edge and planing its wide surface. Planing a board's edge is easily performed if the plane's blade is wider than the board's thickness. One pass of the blade cuts the full width. If, however, the thickness of the board exceeds the blade's width, several passes of the plane must be made. You must at all times attempt to *dress down* the full width surface an equal amount. Do this

by making one pass, move your plane right or left, and make a second pass. Do this as often as is necessary to complete the job.

This same method is used to plane the flat surface of a board. There must be many passes of the plane along the board's surface. Each one should be slightly offset from the previous one. Your plane's edge must be slightly convex, as shown in Fig. 1-38, to allow for cutting of flat surfaces while preventing gouging by the corners of the blade. If the blade were perfectly straight across, its total surface would dig into the wood being planed. These gouges would be distinct lines where each corner cut.

Blades for jack and jointer planes (Fig. 1-39) are usually convex. Blades for smooth or block planes are usually straight but may be made convex if used for surface planing. A blade for any rabbet plane is always straight across.

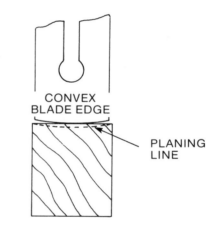

Fig. 1-38: *The convex shape of a plane blade prevents edge gouging.*

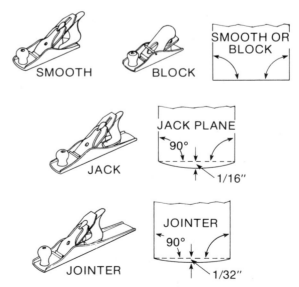

Fig. 1-39: *Unlike the smooth and block planes, the jack and jointer planes have convex blades.*

CHAPTER
— 2 —
SOFTWOOD LUMBER

Of the two types of woods—hardwood and softwood—most of your work as a do-it-yourselfer will be with softwood. Softwood is very versatile—it can be used for home construction, for remodeling work, and for exterior projects (Fig. 2-1), as well as for many interior jobs. Softwood lumber is a great deal easier to cut, fasten, and finish than hardwood. Softwoods are also much more available to the home craftsman and are generally less expensive than hardwoods. A little more than 50% of the total United States timber harvest goes to the production of lumber products (boards, dimensions, beams, and timbers). In 1976, the demand for lumber products in the United States was 13.3 billion cubic feet. Of that, 10.3 billion cubic feet was for softwood lumber. Because softwood lumber is used so extensively, you should have no trouble finding a softwood lumber source. Table 2-1 lists the species of softwoods commonly used in lumber making.

TABLE 2-1: SPECIES OF SOFTWOODS	
Cedar, Alaska	Larch, western
Cedar, incense	Pine, loblolly
Cedar, Port Orford	Pine, longleaf
Cedar, western red	Pine, ponderosa
Fir, Douglas	Pine, shortleaf
Fir, red	Pine, slash
Fir, silver	Pine, white
Fir, white	Pine, yellow
Hemlock, eastern	Redwood
Hemlock, western	Spruce, black
Larch, alpine	Spruce, Engelmann
Larch, American or black	Spruce, Sitka
Larch, Tamarack or Hackmatack	Spruce, white

SAWING SOFTWOOD LUMBER

As stated in Chapter 1, there are two basic methods of cutting logs into lumber: flat-grain and vertical-grain. The vast majority of softwood is cut by the flat-grain method. This method provides such advantages as:

- Lumber is easier to kiln dry.
- It is cheaper and less wasteful.
- Boards average greater widths.

Flat-grain sawing of softwood lumber is an art requiring highly skilled sawyers, edgermen, and re-sawyers with years of sawmill experience. After the bark is removed by mechanical or hydraulic means, the log is firmly fastened on a carriage with sufficient edge protruding to accommodate the first cut. The moveable carriage thrusts the log forward through a stationary band saw, then returns to begin a subsequent cut in its forward travel (Fig. 2-2).

Double-cut band saws, used in some mills, have teeth on both edges so a cut also can be made from the log as the carriage returns. The carriage and band saw together are called the headrig, operated by a sawyer. Sitting at a control panel where the log can be

Fig. 2-1: The uses of softwood lumber are many. Here a frame of softwood lumber for a gazebo is being erected.

Fig. 2-2: Most softwood lumber is plain sawn in the manner shown.

viewed clearly, the sawyer manipulates various button and lever controls. The sawyer may also utilize a computer. These regulate the carriage movement, the thickness of each piece removed by the saw, and the rotation of the log for subsequent cuts. The quality and variety of lumber produced by the mill are governed by the judgment and skill of the headrig sawyer. The sawyer must work swiftly and efficiently to slice the log into the best possible assortment of lumber grades, thicknesses, and widths, and previous experience with tens of thousands of logs allows the sawyer to know how to proceed. It's not an easy task as no two logs are alike, even though they may come from the same tree and have the same outward appearance.

The sawyer must know the kind of lumber customers have ordered from the mill when considering the size and quality of the logs which pass by on the carriage. The first cut of the saw produces a slab, generally reduced to chips for making pulp and paper. The second cut is usually 1" thick and reveals more clearly the interior quality of the log as well as the grades of lumber to be expected from the next cut. After additional cuts, the unique interior features of the log become visible.

As a tree grows, its upper limbs and those of surrounding trees cast shade upon the lower limbs which die, decay, and fall away. Subsequent growth covers the remaining limb structure with new wood fiber. The old limb growth remains near the center of the log, revealed as knots as the saw cuts deeper into the log. After five or six cuts, the sawyer rotates the log to cut into a face adjacent or opposite to the face first opened by the saw. The log is turned and sawn repeatedly until the highest valued pieces are removed and the log has been reduced to a heavy square or rectangular piece. This may be marketed as is or it may be cut into smaller pieces by edgermen and resawyers operating other saws in the mill. Illustrated here are

three different ways logs may be sawn into lumber. Each of these, and others with similar external characteristics, could have been sawn to produce lumber of different dimensions than those illustrated in Fig. 2-3. However, not all logs are turned before sawing. The type and size of the log, the kind of mill equipment, and the products desired all help determine the method of sawing. The three typical flat-grain sequences are:

Method #1 (Fig. 2-3A). The sawyer opened the log marked Side 1 and sawed off five thicknesses before turning the log and sawing Side 2. The sawyer then removed five pieces of lumber before turning the log and sawing Side 3. After removing eight cuts, he rotated the log and took five cuts from Side 4. By this time, the sawyer had reduced the log to a timber 12" square and had the choice of reducing it further or transferring the timber to other saws in the mill. The square could have been cut as shown or reduced further to produce other grades and sizes to meet the mill's cutting orders and customer orders.

Method #2 (Fig. 2-3B). This method is used by mills specializing in sawing small logs. The whole log was passed in one motion through a series of circular or band saws and wood chippers, which reduced it to 2" or 4" thick pieces. These pieces were then turned flat and transported through a series of saws which cut them in one operation into 2 × 2's, 2 × 3's, or 2 × 4's. Such pieces, when cut 10' or shorter, may be specially graded and called studs. Frequently, 1" thick boards can be obtained from the outside cuts on small logs.

Method #3 (Fig. 2-3C). This method is called "sawing around the log." The sawyer took six cuts from Side 1, then turned the log to begin sawing Side 2. The sawyer followed the same procedure with Sides 3 and 4 until a 16" square timber remained. He then had the same choices available as he had with Log No. 1 to reduce it as shown or market it as a timber 16" square.

The lumber yield of a softwood log can be generally classified as follows:

Dimension (2" to 4" thick, 2" and wider). Dimension lumber is used in nearly all types of construction and is graded for strength rather than appearance. Characteristics such as knots, splits, and slope of grain are taken into account as each has an effect on the strength of the piece.

Boards or Commons (all widths, all thicknesses). Boards are used for the exterior finish on homes, cabinets, shelving, crating, and many other applications (Fig. 2-4). Boards are generally graded for appearance rather than strength and are classified into grades according to the visible characteristics exhibited by each piece.

Timbers and Beams (5″ by 5″ and larger). These large structural members are used in the supporting framework of home, industrial, and farm buildings, and in engineered construction such as bridges, auditoriums, and stadiums. Although most grades are designed for strength and serviceability, some grades require both strength and good appearance, such as those used in an open beam ceiling (Fig. 2-5).

Shop (all widths, all thicknesses). Shop lumber is cut from log sections with numerous areas of clear wood containing usually large, but well-spaced characteristics, such as knots and knotholes. The lumber is transported to a millwork plant where saws remove the undesirable characteristics, leaving clear pieces of high value. These are later manufactured into doors, window frames, moulding, and other specialty items.

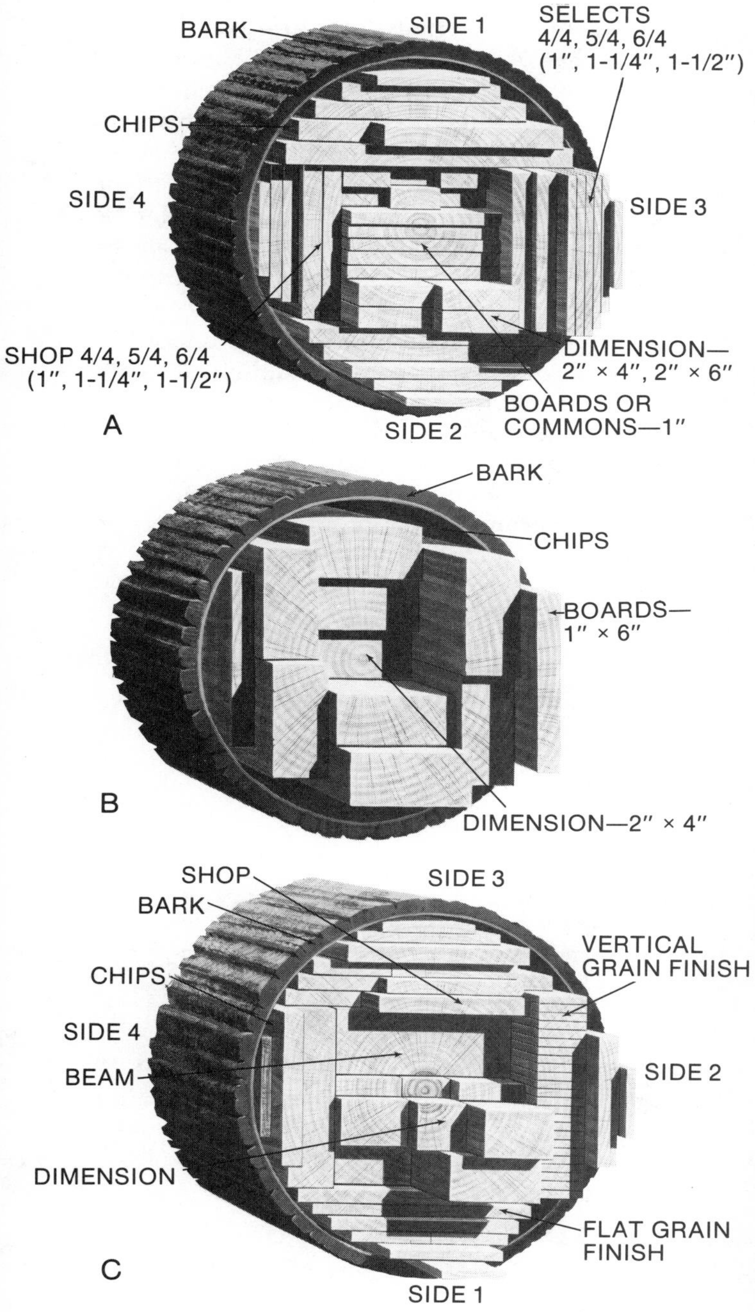

Fig. 2-4: Pine boards make excellent shelving material.

Fig. 2-5: Exposed timbers and beams add a rustic flavor to an interior decor.

Fig. 2-3: Three typical variations of plain sawing to produce flat-grain lumber: (A) sawing alternate sides, (B) sawing "through and through," and (C) "sawing around the log."

Selects and Finish (all widths, all thicknesses). Selects and finish lumber are usually found nearest the outside surface of a log. It is virtually free of knots and other characteristics which detract from appearance. These are the finest grades of lumber available and are used for interior finishing, cabinet work, and other uses where appearance is of primary importance.

Bark and Chips. Bark, chips, and sawdust are very much a part of the yield of a log. Bark is used as cattle litter, garden mulch, and in the production of hardboard. Wood chips become raw material for such items as paper, chipboard, hardboard, and particleboard. Even sawdust is utilized in the production of certain kinds of paper, hardboard, and particleboard.

CHARACTERISTICS OF SOFTWOOD LUMBER

Lumber comes from various species of softwood trees, all of which have certain characteristics that determine the suitability of particular woods for particular uses. Table 2-2 shows some of the characteristics to take into consideration when selecting a particular wood for a specific application. The most prevalent characteristics are rated A; the least prevalent C.

Strength. Of all the demands placed on wood in home remodeling, strength is the most important. The strength required of each piece of lumber depends not only on the purpose it is to serve, but also on the way the load (or stress) is distributed on the piece, and the length of time the piece must support the load. In turn, the strength of each piece of lumber itself depends on (1) the kind and quality of wood, (2) the way the piece is loaded in relation to the direction of its grain, and (3) its size.

Quality and strength of wood are affected by grain, by defects, and indirectly by moisture content. The last two points were fully covered in Chapter 1. All softwood lumber should be seasoned by either air-dried (AD) or kiln-dried (KD) seasoning. Both are effective means of seasoning lumber which should be dried to a moisture content that approximates the average humidity levels of where it is expected to be used. For this reason, KD lumber should generally be used indoors where it will be subjected to artificial heat. Grading rules call for proper moisture contents for the end use. This ranges from a maximum of 19% for most west coast woods to 15% maximum for southern pine, and 12% or less for factory lumber, finish grades, and other special use grades.

Grain. Grain, the arrangement of fibers or cells in the wood, is sometimes the basis for selecting lumber. Boards chosen for beauty often have fibers arranged in a wavy or curly pattern. In some softwoods, the fibers form a pronounced pattern due to differences in the size of the cells.

TABLE 2-2: CHARACTERISTICS OF SOFTWOOD LUMBER

Softwoods	Bending Strength	Strength as a Post	Hardness	Toughness	Freedom from Warping	Nail Holding	Paint Holding	Decay Resistance	Ease of Working	Freedom from Odor	Typical Use
Cedar, eastern red	B	B	B	B	A	B	A	A	B	C	Posts, paneling, chests
Cedar, western red	C	B	C	C	A	C	A	A	A	C	Shingles, siding, decks
Fir, Douglas	A	A	B	B	B	A	B	B	B	C	Construction, flooring
Fir, white	B	B	C	C	B	C	C	C	B	A	Light construction, containers
Hemlock, eastern	B	B	B	C	B	B	B	C	B	A	Construction, containers
Hemlock, western	B	B	B	B	B	B	B	C	B	A	Construction, doors
Larch, western	A	A	B	B	B	A	C	B	C	C	Construction, poles
Pine, Idaho white	B	B	C	C	A	C	A	C	A	C	Millwork, construction
Pine, lodgepole	B	B	C	C	C	B	C	C	B	C	Poles, lumber, ties
Pine, eastern white	C	C	C	C	A	C	A	B	A	C	Millwork, furniture
Pine, ponderosa	C	C	C	C	A	B	B	C	A	C	Millwork, construction
Pine, sugar	C	C	C	C	A	C	A	C	A	C	Millwork, patterns
Pine, yellow southern	A	A	B	B	B	A	C	B	B	C	Construction, poles, siding
Redwood	B	A	B	C	A	B	A	A	B	A	Siding, decks, millwork
Spruce, eastern	B	B	C	C	A	B	B	C	B	A	Construction, millwork
Spruce, Engelmann	C	C	C	C	A	C	B	C	B	A	Light construction, poles
Spruce, Sitka	B	B	C	B	A	B	B	C	B	A	Construction, millwork

For strength, boards should have a grain that is straight; that is, the wood fibers should run neatly parallel to the sides of the board.

When the fibers deviate from the parallel, the board is said to have cross grain. A small amount of cross grain is generally acceptable. Cross grain is the result of (1) the fibers following a spiral pattern in the tree's growth or (2) the sawmill operator not sawing the board parallel to the bark surface.

Grain pattern varies according to the way the board is sawn—flat-sawn or edge-sawn (vertical grained). Flat-sawn boards are more apt to warp or shrink than edge-sawn boards and, thus, are less desirable for some uses.

Toughness and Stiffness. Two other important characteristics are toughness and stiffness. Toughness is the ability to resist shock loading—an impact that momentarily stresses the piece to the breaking point, yet without breaking. Stiffness is the ability not to bend when loaded for a long period of time and is especially important in rafters, beams, and joists. Usually strength and stiffness are parallel, but two medium strength woods—western hemlock and Sitka spruce—are noted for their high degree of stiffness.

Dimensional Stability. Another factor that is always important when working with wood is dimensional stability. Wood cells act much like a sponge, swelling and shrinking as they absorb or lose moisture. Some species change much more radically than others and should be avoided in some applications. For example, lumber with an uneven grain pattern is subject to more swelling and shrinkage than wood with an even grain pattern and thus will not hold paint as well.

Exposure to weather, such as precipitation, temperature changes, and variations in humidity, will be harmful to most untreated wood. This process of deterioration is referred to as weathering. Weathering results in warping, cupping, splitting, checking, dis-coloring, and eventually decaying. Table 2-3 records the effect weather has on several species of softwoods. Nearly all species of softwoods will turn a grayish color when exposed to the weather for an extended period of time. To avoid the effects of weathering, either use a species that weathers well or buy treated wood. Both of these alternatives are discussed in the following chapters.

Hardness. An additional characteristic that is important when choosing a species for some building projects is the ability to hold nails. The harder species tend to grip nails more firmly and maintain their grip longer than softer woods. For example, southern pine has a tightly knit cell structure and closely spaced growth rings. Thus, it has excellent nail-holding abilities. On the other hand, nailing into southern pine is much more difficult than nailing into white pine or fir. If nail holding strength is not important to your project, use a "soft" species of lumber.

One of the most important considerations for the do-it-yourselfer is the ease of working. The easier it is to work with a wood, the easier the project will go together.

SOFTWOOD LUMBER SIZES

Dimensions of softwood lumber pieces are specified in inches; this is called *nominal* lumber size. This inch designation is given to the lumber before it's dried (seasoned) and planed smooth. The *actual* or true lumber size depends upon whether the pieces are rough or planed smooth, moist or dry. Rough lumber is usually very close to the nominal size; dressed or finished lumber is always considerably less.

Rough lumber is generally unacceptable for use with most of the projects described in this book. It

TABLE 2-3: CHANGES DUE TO WEATHERING

Wood	Resistance to Decay	Amount of Shrinkage	Color becomes	Conspicuous Checking	Cupping
Cedar, red	very high	low	dark gray	no	low
Fir, Douglas	medium	medium	dark gray	yes	medium
Fir, white	low	medium	dark gray	yes	medium
Hemlock, eastern	low	medium	light gray	yes	medium
Hemlock, western	low	medium	light gray	yes	medium
Larch	medium	medium high	dark gray	yes	medium
Pine, eastern white	medium	low	light gray	yes	medium
Pine, ponderosa	low	medium low	light gray	yes	medium
Pine, sugar	medium	low	light gray	yes	medium
Pine, western white	medium	medium high	light gray	yes	medium
Pine, yellow	medium	medium high	dark gray	yes	medium
Redwood	very high	medium low	dark gray	no	low
Spruce	low	medium	light gray	yes	medium

is splintery and often too moist. To get a rough effect you can have lumber resawn, giving it one smooth side and one saw-textured side, but the cost of having it specially cut is usually high. Many lumberyards keep a small stock of reasonably-priced resawn lumber on hand which can be used for rustic projects.

Lumber is surfaced or dressed by passing each piece through a planer (Fig. 2-6). The planer removes the rough surface and gives the wood a smooth surface. The lumber may be surfaced on one side (S1S), two sides (S2S), one edge (S1E), two edges (S2E), or a com-

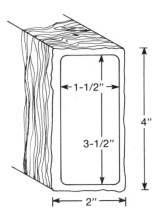

Fig. 2-7: After drying and planing, a nominal 2 × 4 is reduced in size to 1-1/2" × 3-1/2".

TABLE 2-4: DIMENSIONAL LUMBER SIZES

Nominal Size Original cut size in inches	Actual Size (Dry) Minimum cut size in inches	Actual Size (Unseasoned) Minimum cut size in inches
1 × 2	3/4 × 1-1/2	25/32 × 1-9/16
1 × 3	3/4 × 2-1/2	25/32 × 2-9/16
1 × 4	3/4 × 3-1/2	25/32 × 3-9/16
1 × 5	3/4 × 4-1/2	25/32 × 4-5/8
1 × 6	3/4 × 5-1/2	25/32 × 5-5/8
1 × 8	3/4 × 7-1/4	25/32 × 7-1/2
1 × 10	3/4 × 9-1/4	25/32 × 9-1/2
1 × 12	3/4 × 11-1/4	25/32 × 11-1/2
2 × 2	1-1/2 × 1-1/2	1-9/16 × 1-9/16
2 × 3	1-1/2 × 2-1/2	1-9/16 × 2-9/16
2 × 4	1-1/2 × 3-1/2	1-9/16 × 3-9/16
2 × 6	1-1/2 × 5-1/2	1-9/16 × 5-5/8
2 × 8	1-1/2 × 7-1/4	1-9/16 × 7-1/2
2 × 10	1-1/2 × 9-1/4	1-9/16 × 9-1/2
2 × 12	1-1/2 × 11-1/4	1-9/16 × 11-1/2
4 × 4	3-1/2 × 3-1/2	3-9/16 × 3-9/16
4 × 6	3-1/2 × 5-1/2	3-9/16 × 5-5/8
4 × 10	3-1/2 × 9-1/4	3-9/16 × 9-1/2
6 × 6	5-1/2 × 5-1/2	5-1/2 × 5-1/2

Fig. 2-6: Pieces of lumber are passed through a planer to give them smooth surfaces.

bination of sides and edges (S1S1E or S1S2E). The softwood lumber you will normally use will be dressed on four sides (S4S). When run through the planer, the surface dwindles in size by the amount of wood removed. A nominal 2 × 4 surfaced on four sides (S4S) thus shrinks to 1-1/2" × 3-1/2" in cross section (Fig. 2-7), a 1 × 6 board to 3/4" × 5-1/2". Table 2-4 lists some of the nominal and actual sizes of both dry and unseasoned lumber. The dimensions were established as standard by the American Softwood Standards. When planing a project, keep these dimensional changes in mind.

GRADING SOFTWOOD LUMBER

When buying lumber, you don't have to depend on guesswork as to the quality of wood you get. Most lumber sold in the United States is inspected and graded according to the number and sizes of defects present on the surfaces of the piece. Clearly, the grading of lumber is not an exact science because of its dependence upon visual inspection and the judgment of individuals, or individual judgment com-

bined with a mechanical measurement to determine the stiffness of the piece. Nonetheless, highly trained people and explicit grade rules make possible the establishment of 5% below grade as a reasonable variation between graders.

A number of lumber groups—Southern Pine Inspection Bureau (SPIB), Western Wood Products Association (WWPA), West Coast Lumber Inspection Bureau, Canadian Lumber Standards Grading Rule, and California Redwood Inspection Service—have grading rules and marks that comply with the United States Department of Commerce's National Grading Rule for Softwood Dimension Lumber.

Most softwood lumber sold through building supply retailers is divided into major grade categories based on where the trees are grown. The major lumber producing states are in the southern and western regions of the United States. There are differences between the species of trees grown in the two areas, but since all lumber is graded under comparable rules, the differences are not critical in selecting lumber for a particular project.

All softwoods produced in the South are grouped under a single category—southern pine. Included are such species as shortleaf, loblolly, slash, and longleaf pine, but because the physical properties of these species are so similar they can be graded under the same rules. The grading agency for southern pine is the Southern Pine Inspection Bureau (SPIB).

A number of different species grow in mixed stands in western forests and are harvested, manufactured, and marketed together. Some species, because they have similar performance and structural properties, can be graded together. Western lumber is graded by the Western Wood Products Association (WWPA) and the West Coast Lumber Inspection Bureau (WCLIB).

Douglas fir and larch lumber are nearly identical in appearance and strength properties. Often ponderosa pine and sugar pine also are shipped in mixed lots. Other prinicipal western species that are marketed include lodgepole pine and Engelmann spruce, western white spruce, hemlock, white fir, western red cedar, incense cedar, and Idaho white pine (Fig. 2-8). There are two general grade categories: white woods (Engelmann spruce, any true firs, any hemlocks, and any pines) and western woods (any combination of western species).

The various elements of the grade stamps issued by two grading agencies, Southern Pine Inspection Bureau and Western Wood Products Association, are illustrated in Fig. 2-9 and can be explained as follows:

A—Is the mark that identifies the grading agency (SPIB or WWPA) under whose rules the piece was inspected.

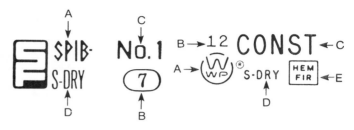

Fig. 2-9: Typical grading stamps of the Southern Pine Inspection Bureau and the Western Wood Products Association.

B—Is a permanent number assigned to each mill for grade purposes. Some mills are identified by mill name or abbreviation instead of by mill number.

C—Is an example of an official grade name abbreviation. Its appearance in a grade mark identifies the grade of a piece of lumber.

D—Indicates the moisture content of the lumber when manufactured. "S-DRY" indicates a moisture content not exceeding 19% in western woods, and 15% for woods under SPIB control. "MC 15" indicates a moisture content not exceeding 15% in western woods. "S-GRN" indicates that the moisture content exceeded 19%.

E—Identifies the wood species in the case of lumber graded under WWPA rules (Fig. 2-10). No species mark is indicated on SPIB grade stamps since all southern pine is graded under common rules.

Fig. 2-10: The species of wood—in this case, Engelmann spruce, lodgepole pine and alpine fir—is indicated on WWPA grade stamps.

Because of the differences in wood species, the quality of individual logs, and the ways lumber is manufactured, it is impossible to grade a natural material like lumber precisely. Grading rules do, however, set up ranges which apply to the utility, appearance, and strength of individual pieces of lumber. Most softwood lumber sold today is graded visually under grading rules that classify lumber in three broad categories based on usage and size. Of the categories of wood yielded by logs, boards, dimension lumber, and timbers are the ones used most often by the do-it-yourselfer (Table 2-5).

DOUGLAS FIR   **LODGEPOLE PINE**

WESTERN LARCH   **ENGELMANN SPRUCE**

PONDEROSA PINE   **WESTERN HEMLOCK-WHITE FIR**

SUGAR PINE   **WHITE FIR**

Fig. 2-8: Western softwood lumber is often graded into categories of mixed species having similar appearance and strength properties.

TABLE 2-5:   LUMBER GRADES

Boards	Grade	Characteristics of Grade
Select	B & Better	Top recognized grade of finish; generally clear with minimum number of knots.
	C	Reasonably clear but limited number of surface checks, small knots permitted.
	D	Economical, serviceable grade for natural or painted finish.
Commons	No. 1	High quality with good appearance. Sound and tight knotted; can be used for shelving.
	No. 2	High quality material, may be used for sheathing. Tight knots, generally free of holes.
	No. 3	Good quality material, may be used for a number of applications without waste.
	No. 4	Pieces with a minimum of waste that contain usable portions at least 24″ long.

Dimension Lumber	Grade	Characteristics of Grade
Structural Light Framing 2″ to 4″ thick 2″ to 4″ wide	Select Struct.	High quality, relatively free of defects which impair strength or stiffness. For use where high strength, stiffness, and good appearance are desired.
	No. 1	High strength, recommended for general utility and construction usage. Good appearance, especially useful for exposed applications due to minimum knots.
	No. 2	Specified number of tight knots are permitted. Suitable for all types of construction.
	No. 3	Recommended for general construction where appearance is not a controlling factor. Provides high quality and low cost construction.
Studs 2″ to 4″ thick 2″ to 6″ wide 10″ & shorter	Stud	Stringent requirements for straightness, strength, and stiffness permit this grade to be used for all stud uses, including load-bearing walls. Rules govern amount of crook and wane permitted.
Light Framing 2″ to 4″ thick 4″ wide	Construction	Recommended for general framing usage. Good appearance, strong, and serviceable.
	Standard	Recommended for general framing usage. Allows larger defects than in Construction Grade.
	Utility	Recommended where a combination of strength and economy is desired. Good for blocking, bracing.
	Economy	Usable lengths are suitable for bracing, blocking, other uses where strength, appearance not important.
Structural Joists & Planks 2″ to 4″ thick 6″ & wider	Select Struct.	High quality, free of characteristics that impair strength or stiffness. Recommended for uses where high strength, stiffness, appearance are required.
	No. 1	Provide high strength, recommended for general utility and construction usage. Good appearance, especially where exposed due to knot limitations.
	No. 2	Suitable for all types of construction, although not as tightly restricted as Grade No. 1. Has tight knots.

TABLE 2-5: LUMBER GRADES (Continued)

Dimension Lumber	Grade	Characteristics of Grade
	No. 3	Recommended for general construction where appearance is not a controlling factor. Provides high quality and low cost construction.

Timbers	Grade	Characteristics of Grade
Timbers, Beams, Posts 5" × 5" & larger	Select Struct. No. 1	High strength characteristics, recommended for general utility and construction usage. Good appearance, especially suitable for exposed use because of knot limitations.

Boards. Boards are nominally less than 2" thick and of varying widths of 4" or more. (Narrower boards are usually called *strips*.) Boards, as already stated, are graded primarily on the basis of appearance (not strength) into two broad categories: *select* and *common*. Select boards are those with the best appearance and which can be finished with the best results. Common boards allow more blemishes and knots than selects, and therefore are better suited for general utility and construction uses.

Boards are also available with edges that have been worked to provide a special fit. For example, pine floor boards usually have a tongue-and-groove fit. Fir siding may be shiplapped or beveled. Worked lumber is divided into three categories: matched, shiplapped, or patterned. Figure 2-11 shows several

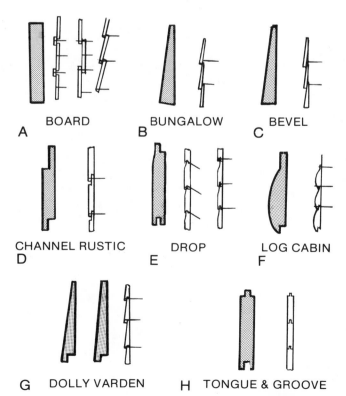

A BOARD   B BUNGALOW   C BEVEL

D CHANNEL RUSTIC   E DROP   F LOG CABIN

G DOLLY VARDEN   H TONGUE & GROOVE

Fig. 2-11: Types of siding.

types of worked lumber used as siding. Lumber or boards worked in these ways are used as exterior siding, interior paneling, and flooring. Some of the softwoods used in these applications are eastern white pine, western white pine, sugar pine, western hemlock, ponderosa pine, southern pine, and spruce.

Matched Lumber. Matched lumber is lumber that has been worked with a tongue on one edge of each piece and a groove on the opposite edge to provide a close tongue-and-groove joint by fitting two pieces together. When end-matched, the tongue and groove are worked in the ends. Figures 2-11E and H are examples of tongue-and-groove matched lumber.

Shiplapped Lumber. Shiplapped lumber is lumber that has been worked or rabbeted on both edges of each piece to provide a close-lapped joint by fitting two pieces together. Figure 2-11D is an example of shiplapped lumber.

Patterned Lumber. Patterned lumber is lumber that is shaped to a pattern or to a molded form in addition to being dressed, matched, or shiplapped, or any combinations of these workings. Some common patterns of siding are shown in Fig. 2-11B through G.

Dimension Lumber. Dimension lumber is commonly used in house framing and ranges from 2" to 5" in thickness. It is graded primarily on the basis of strength and is divided into two width categories: up to 4" wide, which may be called *structural light framing, light framing,* or *studs;* and lumber over 6" wide, which is termed *structural joists* or *planks.*

Studs are framing members that are 10' or shorter and are graded on the basis of vertical strength since they will be used for wall framing. Light framing grades usually are sold in two groups: *standard and better,* and *utility.* Structural joists and planks are sold in the same way, except the two groups are called *No. 2 and Better,* and *No. 3.* Structural light framing lumber is graded for both appearance and strength.

Timbers. Timbers are 5" thick or more. While they are graded on the basis of strength, select structural and No. 1 grades can be used for exposed applications. There are many varieties, sizes and shapes of timbers available.

In some applications, such as trussed rafters, floor and ceiling joists, specific strength values may be the primary consideration. All visually-graded lumber has stress ratings, but sometimes more precise ratings are needed. Also available is lumber that has been evaluated by mechanical stress rating (MSR) equipment. Each piece of MSR lumber is tested and marked with its modulus of elasticity as a part of the grade stamp.

Stress-rated lumber is normally used only in situations where precisely engineered loads must be calculated. Few do-it-yourself customers need MSR lumber. Special stress-rating tables and literature are available from lumber manufacturers and grading agencies.

BUYING SOFTWOOD LUMBER

Softwood lumber is usually sold by the board-foot measure. A board foot is equal to a piece 1" thick and 12" square. (All figures used in determining the board feet are nominal dimensions.) If you know the board-foot price, you can find the cost of any size or shape of lumber by using this formula (thickness and width are in inches and length is in feet):

$$\frac{\text{Thickness} \times \text{width} \times \text{length}}{12} = \text{board feet}$$

Thus, a 2 × 4 piece of lumber that is 12' long would contain 8 board feet:

$$\frac{2 \times 4 \times 12}{12} = 8$$

Lumber is always quoted at a specified price per M (thousand) board feet. For example, if it was quoted at $220 per M board feet, it would be charged for at the rate of $.22 per foot $\left(\frac{\$220}{1000} = \$.22\right)$. Thus, the 8' from the previous formula would be multiplied times $.22 for a cost of $1.76. While some home centers sell lumber at single 2" × 4" × 8' price (say $1.76 a piece), this price is based on a board-foot rate. The number of board feet in lumber of various sizes and lengths is given in Table 2-6.

It must be remembered, however, that prices are based on *nominal* or original rough sizes rather than *actual* dimensions as sold. In the case of softwoods, the actual thickness and width depend upon whether the pieces are rough-sawn or planed smooth, green or dry. For instance, a green, rough-sawn board 1" thick is actually 3/4" thick if dry and dressed; it is 25/32" thick if it is green (above 19% moisture content) and dressed. If the lumber is grade-marked, the stamp will indicate whether the piece was green or dry when it was dressed to size.

TABLE 2-6: BOARD-FOOT CONTENT

Size (inches)	Length (feet)								
	8	10	12	14	16	18	20	22	24
1 × 2	1-1/2	1-2/3	2	2-1/3	2-2/3	3	3-1/3	3-2/3	4
1 × 3	2	2-1/2	3	3-1/2	4	4-1/2	5	5-1/2	6
1 × 4	2-3/4	3-1/3	4	4-2/3	5-1/3	6	6-2/3	7-1/3	8
1 × 5	3-1/3	4-1/6	5	5-5/6	6-2/3	7-1/2	8-1/3	9-1/6	10
1 × 6	4	5	6	7	8	9	10	11	12
1 × 8	5-1/3	6-2/3	8	9-1/3	10-2/3	12	13-1/3	14-2/3	14
1 × 10	6-2/3	8-1/3	10	11-2/3	13-1/2	15	16-2/3	18-1/3	16
1 × 12	8	10	12	14	16	18	20	22	20
2 × 4	5-1/3	6-2/3	8	9-1/3	10-2/3	12	13-1/3	14-2/3	16
2 × 6	8	10	12	14	16	18	20	22	24
2 × 8	10-2/3	13-1/3	16	18-2/3	21-1/3	24	26-2/3	29-1/3	32
2 × 10	13-1/3	16-2/3	20	23-1/2	26-2/3	30	33-1/3	36-2/3	40
2 × 12	16	20	24	28	32	36	40	44	48
4 × 4	10-2/3	13-1/3	16	18-2/3	21-1/3	24	26-2/3	29-1/3	32
4 × 6	16	20	24	28	32	36	40	44	48
4 × 8	21-1/3	26-2/3	32	37-1/3	42-2/3	48	53-1/3	58-2/3	64
4 × 10	26-2/3	33-1/3	40	46-2/3	53-1/3	60	66-2/3	73-1/3	80
4 × 12	32	40	48	56	64	72	80	88	96
6 × 6	24	30	36	42	48	54	60	66	72
6 × 8	32	40	48	56	64	72	80	88	96

When ordering rough-sawn lumber, it is wise to order 10% more than you need to make up the difference between *nominal* and *actual* dimensions. When ordering lumber that is surfaced on four sides, order 15% extra when the width is 4″ or less and 10% extra when the width is over 4″. Order 30% more when buying 4″ wide tongue-and-groove lumber and 20% more when the worked lumber is wider than 4″.

Standard lengths of lumber are multiples of 2′ running from 8′ to 24′. Don't order pieces in nonstandard lengths or widths. When you order lumber that has to be culled or ripped from larger pieces, the dealer usually charges for the standard size of material. You pay for waste stock as well as for the labor of cutting. If you need several 5′ pieces, order 10′ stock and cut them to length yourself. If you need a 7-1/2′ piece, order the next largest size. The leftover will come in handy on some other project.

There is no denying the importance of being choosy when you purchase lumber. Most lumberyards and home centers will allow you to pick through a bin or stack if you ask permission. Many lumberyards that cater to the home craftsman have a serve-yourself policy; but be considerate, don't leave the bins in disarray. Sometimes by looking through a stack of, let's say, No. 2 Common, you can find pieces as good as a select grade. The only other way to be sure you get quality in every piece you order is to spend more money for a higher grade.

When you place an order, be specific about the kinds of wood, grade, seasoning, and finish. Your order should read something like this: 20 pieces of 2″ × 4″ × 8′, No. 2, kiln-dried, surfaced white pine. Your shipping ticket will likely read: *20-8 2 × 4 S4S No2 com pine 106-2/3 bd ft.*

SOFTWOOD LUMBER PROJECTS

The following projects will give you the opportunity to put into practice some of the wood working tips we've discussed so far. There's a project for outdoors, your workshop, a child's room, the den, and your living room. Make sure you understand the instructions completely before beginning any project and double-check every dimension before cutting.

Patio Table and Benches

This 52″ circular table can seat six adults or nine youngsters on its three benches. This project can be easily constructed by the average home craftsman and will cost far less than comparable units available in

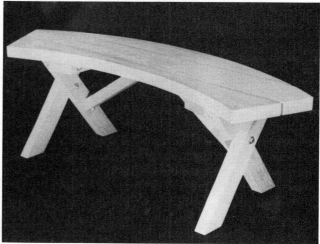

retail outlets. Make sure you understand all instructions and dimensions before beginning.

First, cut out and notch the rail pieces. Drill all holes in rail pieces before nailing to top pieces. Holes should be 7/16″ in diameter to allow clearance for 3/8″ bolts.

Next, cut pieces for the top. Cut 2 × 6's to length: five 5′ pieces, two 4′ pieces, and two 3′ pieces. Place the best side down, after marking the centers of these boards, and space them 1/4″ apart. Now line up centers and position rail pieces 8-1/2″ from the center line. Glue and nail with 8d galvanized box nails. Turn the top over and drive a small finish nail in the center of the top. By using a string and pencil, mark the circular outside edge. Cut on this line and then remove the finish nail. Finish making the top by drilling a 1-5/8″ hole in the center for an umbrella shaft.

To make the table legs, cut a 48.7° angle on the end of a 2 × 6 and then measure 36-3/4″ (long point to short point) to the other end which is the same angle. The legs can then be clamped or lightly nailed in posi-

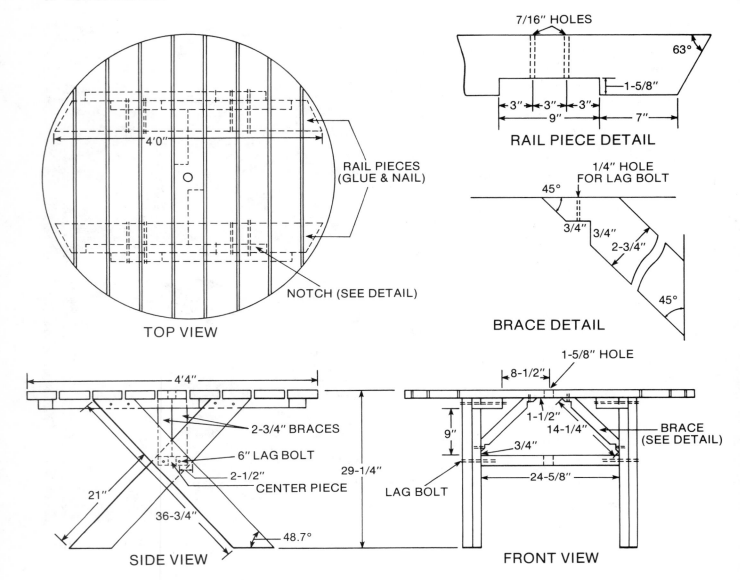

TOP VIEW

RAIL PIECE DETAIL

BRACE DETAIL

SIDE VIEW

FRONT VIEW

tion on rail pieces, making sure that they are crossed properly and that the bottoms of the legs are parallel to the top. Mark holes and drill.

The center piece is a 2 × 6 that is 24-5/8" long. Drill two 1/4" holes that are 1-1/2" in from each edge and drill a 1-5/8" hole in the center of the piece for an umbrella shaft.

Using bolts with washers on each end, attach the legs. Fasten the center piece with four lag bolts. Next, rip a 2 × 6 in half (2-3/4") and cut two braces 14-1/4" long with a 45° angle on each end. Notch and drill a 1/4" hole through the brace and a 3/16" hole into leg and top.

To make a bench, lay out two pieces of 2" × 6" × 4' and space 1/4" apart. Using string and pencil, swing an arc from a 4' radius that is 1-1/2" inside the edge of the far 2 × 6. Cut on this line. The piece that is cut off will be used for the other side of the bench. With the same radius point, mark pieces along the string for end cuts.

Next, cut rail pieces that are 10" long (long point to short point) with a 77° angle on each end. Notch and drill, and then glue and nail to top pieces 10" from center.

Legs are cut from a 2 × 6 that has been ripped in half (2-3/4"). Cut legs 18" long with 56° angles on the ends. Position on rail pieces and mark holes. Drill a 7/16" hole for a 3/8" bolt. Now bolt legs to rail pieces. Then, clamp legs together at crossing, and drill and bolt at 5-1/4" from bottom side of top.

To complete the bench, make braces cut from a 2 × 6 that is ripped in quarters—1-3/8". The braces are 17" long overall. Cut a 55° angle on the end that fastens to the leg and a 35° angle on the end that goes to the center on the bench. Attach legs with 1/4" × 2" lag bolts (put in on an angle).

Although patio furniture of softwood species does not require preservative treatment, a brush coat of a penta formula would be an inexpensive insurance

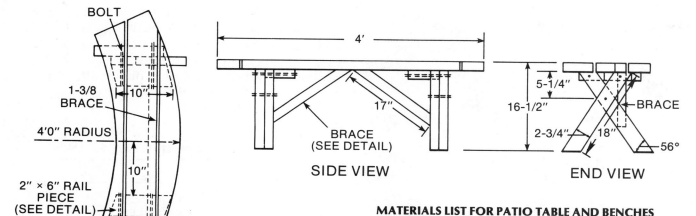

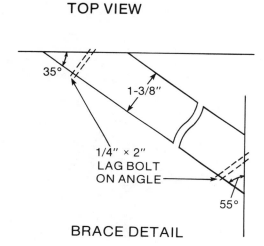

BOLT

1-3/8 BRACE

10"

4'0" RADIUS

10"

2" × 6" RAIL PIECE (SEE DETAIL)

BOLT

TOP VIEW

4'

17"

BRACE (SEE DETAIL)

SIDE VIEW

5-1/4"

16-1/2"

BRACE

2-3/4"

18"

56°

END VIEW

35°

1-3/8"

1/4" × 2" LAG BOLT ON ANGLE

55°

BRACE DETAIL

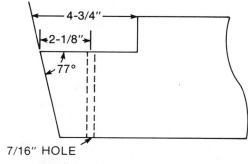

4-3/4"

2-1/8"

77°

7/16" HOLE

BENCH RAIL PIECE DETAIL

MATERIALS LIST FOR PATIO TABLE AND BENCHES

Quantity	Description
	Patio Table
1	2" × 6" × 8' lumber (table top)
2	2" × 6" × 10' lumber (table top)
1	2" × 6" × 12' lumber (table top)
1	2" × 6" × 8' lumber (rail pieces)
2	2" × 6" × 8' lumber (legs)
1	2" × 6" × 24-5/8" lumber (legs)
1	2" × 6" × 16" lumber (braces)
4	3/8" × 8" machine bolts
4	3/8" × 6" machine bolts
32	3/8" washers
4	1/4" × 2" lag bolts
4	5/16" × 6" lag bolts
	Benches
3	2" × 6" × 8' (tops)
1	2" × 6" × 6' (rail pieces)
1	2" × 6" × 10' (legs)
1	2" × 6" × 3' (braces)
6	3/8" × 8" machine bolts
6	3/8" × 6" machine bolts
6	3/8" × 4" machine bolts
36	3/8" washers
12	1/4" × 2" lag bolts
3 lbs	8d box nails
—	glue

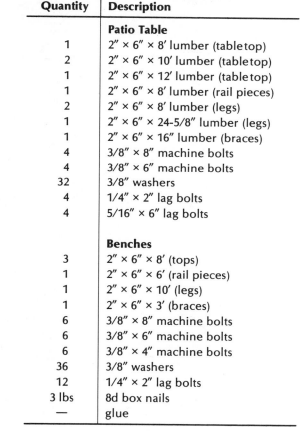

against weathering. Many good formulas for applying color to the lighter woods are available. With these formulas, you can stain the table and benches to match your decor. Darker colored woods can either be bleached or painted with a clear preservative. It might even be advisable to apply a low gloss sealer to the surface to resist food stains and provide a satin smooth surface for cleaning.

Portable Workbench

This sawhorse is a handy aid in any workshop. Not only is it a good height for hand sawing, but its lightweight and wide shelf turns it into a portable workbench. And when it is not in use, it can serve as a mini-storage counter or bench. Follow the dimensions shown in the exploded view.

Start by cutting the four 24" legs from a 8' long 2 × 4. Bevel each end 20°. Cut the 30" top cap from a 2 × 6 and bevel the sides 20°. Attach the legs to the cap with

Attach the sides first by gluing and nailing into the legs from the inside and then glue and nail the ends to the legs. Cut the 14" × 24" tray from 3/4" plywood. You may bevel the edges to match the angle of the legs, but this is unnecessary since the bottom of the tray will not be visible. Glue the shelf to the sides and ends, and nail to the ends with 8d nails.

MATERIALS LIST FOR PORTABLE WORKBENCH

Quantity	Description
1	2" × 4" × 8' pine or fir
1	2" × 6" × 30" pine or fir
1	1" × 3" × 8' pine or fir
1	3/4" × 14" × 24" exterior plywood
—	1/4" × 2-1/2" lag bolts and washers
—	#8 common nails
—	#8 finish nails
—	glue

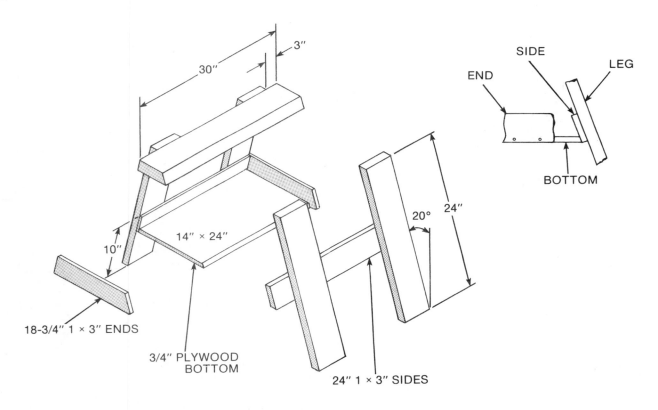

EXPLODED VIEW

glue and countersunk lag bolts 1/4" in diameter and 2-1/2" long. Predrill the holes before installing.

Cut the sides and ends of the tray from 1 × 3 stock. The ends should be 18-3/4" long, the sides 24" long. Bevel the end pieces to match the angle of the legs.

Butcher Block Tables

You can alter the dimensions of these two popular tables to fit your particular needs, but the basic 18" cube or 15" cube variation will function as end table, bedside table, or chess and checker table. The longer table will do well as a cocktail table. The only lumber required for these tables is 2" × 2", graded standard or better. This is inexpensive wood; so, it is no financial hardship to buy 25% more than you need to compensate for flaws. Before you begin any construction, inspect all lumber and choose the best boards—those with the most attractive grain and fewest imperfections.

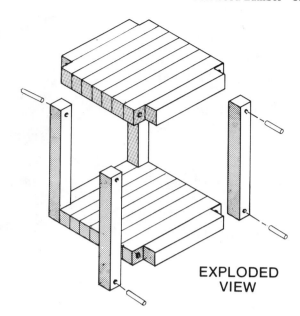

EXPLODED VIEW

Butcher block type tables are easy to build. While these instructions deal with the cocktail table in detail, they can be applied to cube type tables as well. Each cocktail table requires eleven 8' 2 × 2's of standard grade or better. (Cube tables of 15" or 18" size both require six 2 × 2's.) Cut twenty 36" long pieces for the top and base, eight 15-3/4" pieces for side sections, and six 15" legs. (For each 18" cube table, cut twenty-four 18" pieces for the top, base, and four legs, and four 15" side sections. The 15" cubes require twenty-four 15" top, base, and leg pieces, and four 12" sides.)

Select the ten best 36" pieces for the tabletop and prenail one side of nine with six 8d finishing nails in each. Stagger nails in alternating boards. Apply an even coat of aliphatic adhesive to one side of the unnailed piece and to the side opposite the nails on the first prenailed 2 × 2. Join the two together and drive in the two end nails, making sure the pieces are aligned properly.

Drive in the remaining four nails and countersink them with a nailset. Laminate the remaining 2 × 2's in this fashion, wiping away excess glue with a damp cloth. Assemble the base in the same manner. Glue two 15-3/4" side pieces to each side of the top and base, leaving 1-1/2" leg notches at the corners and between the two section pieces. Fasten them in place with pipe clamps, and before tightening, check the corners for a flush fit with a scrap piece of 2 × 2. (Cube tables have only one section piece to a side and no

center notch or leg, but assembly is basically the same.)

After allowing the glue to dry overnight, sand the top, base, and table legs to a smooth, even finish. Use coarse, then medium, and finally fine-grit abrasive paper. Apply aliphatic adhesive to the corner notches of the base, top, and the last 1-1/2" of the leg ends.

Secure the base and top in place with a web strap clamp, and adjust the legs to a flush fit before letting dry overnight. Glue the center legs into place and clamp them fast with pipe clamps.

Drill a 3" deep 3/8" diameter hole through each leg and into the side of the table top and base. Insert a 3-1/2" piece of dowel for added leg support. Use a piece of scrap wood as a pounding block to avoid damaging the dowel. Trim it flush to the leg surface.

Final finish is a matter of personal choice. Tables can be stained to any shade desired or left natural. They can be varnished, plasticized with polyurethane, or oiled and waxed. If you like the rich, satin luster of an oiled and waxed finish, use a dark walnut stain and Danish oil and paste wax for a hand-rubbed finish.

Study Center

This project will provide a place to study with plenty of room to keep things organized. To save space, the study center can be hung on a wall. It is built from softwood boards of various widths. Before beginning, cut all pieces to size.

Construct the desk unit as shown in the illustration, predrilling, gluing, and assembling with screws and grommets. Mount the desk to the wall with screws or

MATERIALS LIST FOR STUDY CENTER

Quantity	Description
	Coat rack
1	1" × 12" × 3'
6	3/4" × 6" dowel
	Shelves
5	1" × 12" × 3'
6	1" × 6" × 12"
2	1" × 12" × 12"
1	1" × 6" × 3'
	Desk
2	1" × 8" × 3'
2	1" × 10" × 3'
2	1" × 12" × 18"
1	1" × 12" × 3'
	Other Materials
2	54" shelf standard
8	brackets
—	1-1/2" #10 roundhead wood screws
—	2-1/2" #12 screws and grommets
—	36" × 30" corkboard

toggle bolts. The recommended clearance from the bottom of the lower shelves to the floor is: for children ages 5 to 12, 18" to 24"; for adults, 26" to 28".

Screw tracks to the wall approximately 32" apart (the width of two studs). To construct the shelves, simply glue and screw the end pieces as shown. To make the coat rack, drill six 3/4" holes in the backboard, spaced 4" up and 4" between for the dowel coat hangers. Mount the coat rack so that the top is the same distance from the floor as the top of the shelves.

To construct the bin, use a wooden yardstick to scribe an arc as illustrated and cut the bin front with a keyhole saw or jigsaw. Assemble the bin as shown in the illustration.

Mount the bulletin board on the wall using screws and grommets or strong adhesives. Glue and insert the dowel coat hangers. Install the light and insert adjustable shelves. Finish as desired.

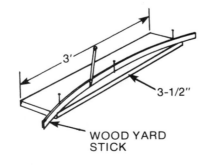

WOOD YARD STICK

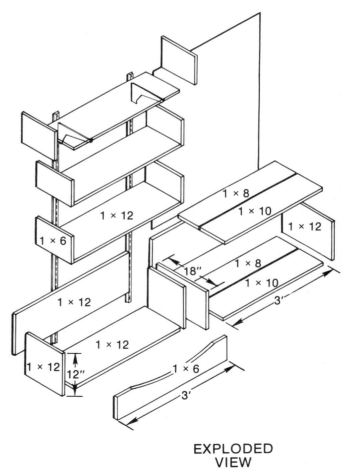

EXPLODED VIEW

Sofa

This handsome contemporary sofa project is designed for average woodworking skills. It is based on standard lumber sizes and grades available at the local lumberyard. Dimensions are planned to minimize extensive cutting and most lengths can be transported in the family car to save delivery charges. Basic construction is featured, with no tricky dovetail or mortise and tenon joints called for. Simple butt joints, secured with screws, are all that are necessary.

Steps in the construction of the modern roll-around wood sofa are shown in the following illustrations. When the project is completed, it must be finished to protect it from the soil and fingerprints of daily household activity. Clear finishes will show the natural grain to the best advantage and are available in dull, satin, or high gloss types.

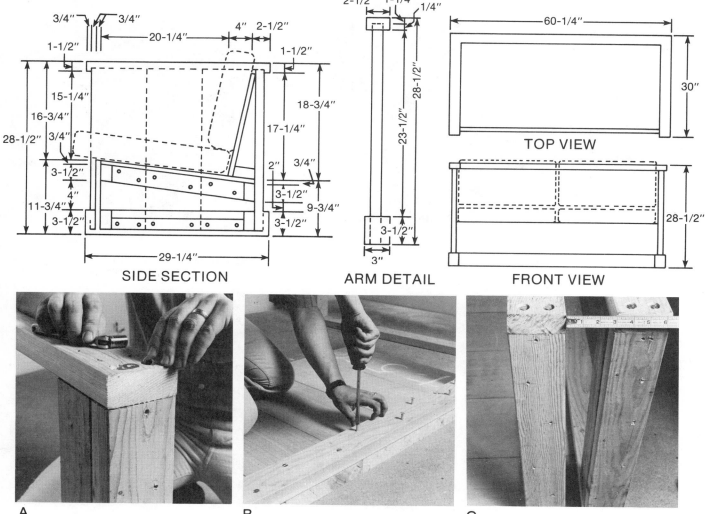

SIDE SECTION · ARM DETAIL · TOP VIEW · FRONT VIEW

(A) Begin by assembling the 2 × 4 framework with the countersunk lag bolts and washers. (B) Fasten the assembled frame to the 2 × 10 back pieces with 2-1/2" flathead wood screws. (C) Position the seat frame 2" from the bottom of the frame in the back, and 3" apart in the front.

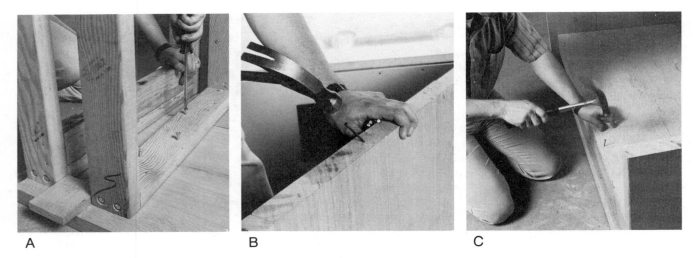

A   B   C

(A) Use a 3" spacer block while screwing the seat frame to the couch sides and back. (B) Drive the 16d finish nails at an angle to secure the 2 × 10 piece in place. (C) Cut the 3/4" plywood to size and apply the seat bottom to the frame with 8d box nails.

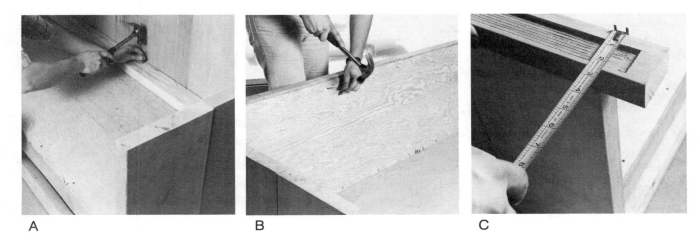

A   B   C

(A) Cut a 2 × 4 spacer, angling the front edge slightly, then nail it to the back of the seat. (B) After trimming the edge of the plywood seat back to a 30° angle, nail it in place with 8d nails. (C) Passes with a saw will create a 1-1/2" wide channel in the top of the trim. Chisel the ends square.

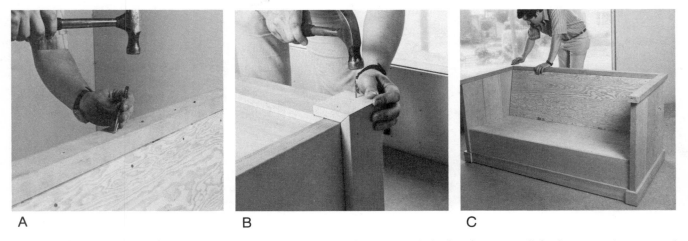

A   B   C

(A) Apply the 2 × 3 top trim to the sides and back with 8d nails and countersink the heads. (B) Install the front panel, miter, and apply the 1 × 4 base trim with 8d finish nails. (C) Fill all nail holes with wood putty and sand the completed sofa.

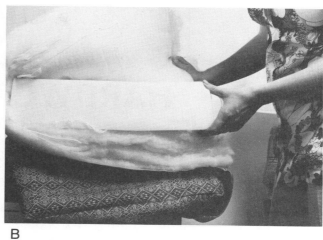

A   B

(A) Standard sewing techniques are used to create zippered seat covers. (B) Wrap the foam in Dacron padding material, and insert it in the completed seat covers.

MATERIALS LIST FOR SOFA

Quantity	Description
2	2″ × 10″ × 16′ lumber (sides)
1	2″ × 3″ × 10″ lumber (top trim)
1	1″ × 4″ × 16′ lumber (base trim)
6	2″ × 4″ × 10′ lumber (framing)
1	1″ × 12″ × 5′ lumber (front)
1	3/4″ × 4′ × 8′ plywood panel (A-C interior)
4	600 lb. ball casters
16	1/4″ × 4″ lag bolts/washers
48	2-1/2″ #9 flathead wood screws
—	wood putty
—	medium and fine abrasive paper
—	16d finish nails
—	8d finish nails
—	8d box nails
—	clear natural oil finish
—	white glue
	Seat Covers
2	24″ × 28″ × 4″ foam (seat)
2	16″ × 28″ × 3″ foam (back)
1	30″ × 30″ Dacron fiber fill (padding)

CHAPTER

—— 3 ——

HARDWOOD LUMBER

Fine, solid hardwood furniture (Fig. 3-1) is priced above many family paychecks. Many of us have settled for assembly line imitations that look good for a few years until the top comes unglued at one corner, the other corner crumples from a fall, and the dowels in the legs work loose. Instead of purchasing furniture, why not build the furniture yourself? You would not have to speculate about the quality of workmanship or the quality of the hardwood. You get exactly what you want and, in addition, gain the satisfaction of saying, "I built that myself."

Invariably, the best furniture is made of hardwoods. Most have all the necessary characteristics that are particularly desirable in wood used to make furniture:

- Stability, or the ability to maintain shape without shrinking, swelling, or warping.
- Suitable strength and grain characteristics.
- Ease of fabricating and finishing.
- Pleasing appearance.

Before taking a closer look at furniture projects, you should become familiar with the properties and characteristics of hardwoods.

SAWING OF HARDWOOD LUMBER

Like softwoods, hardwoods are plain-sawn and quarter-sawn. Hardwoods are also rift-sawn. When a log is to be quarter-sawn—one of the popular methods of cutting hardwoods—the log is cut in half, redogged on the carriage, and cut into quarters. Then, these quarters are resawn, either a board at a time or completely in one pass through a gang saw. The pattern made by the grain is a series of straight lines running down the length of the board's face.

Quarter-sawn stock has several characteristics that are superior to plain-sawn hardwood. It wears more evenly and is generally easier to finish. Because plain-sawn lumber will change almost twice as much in width as will quarter-sawn lumber, the latter is less

susceptible to checks or splits, is less affected by moisture, and holds finish better.

Quarter-sawn lumber does have disadvantages. Because quarter-sawing takes more time and results in more waste, lumber produced this way is more expensive. Spike knots, shakes, and pitch pockets that extend through the board are also common problems in the larger pieces. The clearest pieces are always the smallest pieces—those cut from the outside position of the log.

Fig. 3-1: The beauty of fine hardwoods ranks high among building materials.

CHARACTERISTICS OF HARDWOOD

Although the appearance of a species of wood may be the primary consideration in many projects, it is by no means of greater importance than its physical characteristics. In some projects resistance to breakage is critical. In others, resistance to dents and scratches is a prime factor in selection. In still others, you must guard as best you can against the chances of excessive shrinking and swelling that could cause splitting, spindle loosening, or other defects. Interlaced with all these characteristics is the ever-present consideration: How hard is it to work the wood—smooth it, turn it, and join it to itself or to other woods?

Hardness. The hardness of a wood is not only an important consideration in itself, but it is also a frequent indicator of other characteristics that may be desirable. For example, the extraordinary popularity of oak, birch, and maple for furniture is due not only to the hardness of these woods, but also to their strength and workability.

In practice, hardness means resistance to surface damage from rough treatment. Hardwoods are difficult to dent, scratch, or cut. Generally, they resist crushing under heavy loads. Most of the harder woods are easier to finish, mainly because they absorb less of the finishing liquids.

On the other hand, extreme hardness may produce related characteristics that are less than desirable. Hickory is hard and strong and resilient. But it is one of the most difficult woods to work with. It splits, splinters, shrinks, and swells. Also remember that actual hardness can vary from tree to tree, log to log, and board to board. The reasons may be moisture content, growing conditions that produced differing amounts of springwood vs. summerwood, and seasonal variations. Because of these differences, the listings in Table 3-1 are approximate, but can serve as a useful guide in wood selection.

Strength. The strength of wood used is, of course, important if the project must support heavy weights. Usually this isn't the case in most woodworking projects. The heaviest objects that furniture in your home usually holds include the television, stereo, and potted plants—things that won't overload most woods. For chairs, benches, and stools, stay away from soft, frail woods that might eventually break under repeated shock loading.

Weight. Weight, in itself, is not too important a consideration in the selection of hardwood. It's true, of course, that a stool or bench you might make for a small child would serve its purpose best if it were of a lightweight wood such as basswood or alder. On the other hand, it does not make any difference what a dining room table weighs; it isn't moved often enough for weight to be a factor. But for pure purposes of stability, it might be best to turn it out in maple or oak.

To a degree, weight and hardness parallel each other in woods. What is significant, however, is that weight and strength do run side by side in wood characteristics, for the most part. Given equal moisture content, the heavier of two woods will be stronger, since its weight is represented by a greater content of wood's strength-producing fibers.

Dimensional Stability. How well a wood resists shrinking and swelling, plus how well it maintains its shape without warping are primary considerations in the selection of a material. As has already been discussed, swell, shrink, and warp tendencies are of the greatest concern when you work with relatively wide stock or when you glue boards into wide elements. The amount of distortion is directly proportional to the width and, to a lesser degree, the thickness of the wood.

The tendency of a piece of wood to shrink or swell and to warp is not only a characteristic of the species, but also a tendency resulting from the way it was cut from the log. When you select material, take these factors into consideration.

Quarter-sawn stock is more stable than plain-sawn. This is because the maximum dimensional change is in the direction of the annual rings. Quarter-sawn stock will shrink more in thickness than will plain-sawn. But the difference is insignificant because of the dimensions. If a board shrinks a fraction of its 3/4" thickness, it is nothing compared to the same fraction of its 11-1/2" width. This is, in a sense, merely a magnification of your concern about the shrinkage and swelling in a very wide board or a wide glue-up.

There are other changes in the shape and stability of wood caused by the fact that flat members are cut from a material that grew naturally in the form of a cylinder or more accurately in the form of a tall, gently tapering cone. None of these changes can be avoided completely. For your purposes, you must try to select wood that shows the least distortion, using the most warp-free species when they are suitable for the project and picking quarter-sawn material whenever it is available.

Quite often you will find it possible to overcome the distortion in lumber. Sometimes it may be necessary—and this is often done—to rip the board down the middle, joint the sawn edges, and glue the two pieces together. This effectively cuts the distortion in half. The glue-up is not conspicuous, since the two edges were adjoining in the uncut stock. And, it is often possible to plane the surfaces to eliminate the unevenness entirely. Meanwhile, proper finishes will reduce changes in moisture content. Of course, all hard-

TABLE 3-1:   CHARACTERISTICS OF VARIOUS HARDWOODS

Name of Wood	Hardness	Strength	Stability	Weight	Decay Resistance	Split Resistance	Working Quality for Hand Tools	Shaping	Turning	Mortising	Planing and Jointing	Nailing	Gluing	Sanding	Cost
Alder	medium	weak	G	light	F	F	G	F	F	F	G	G	G	F	medium
Ash, white	medium	medium	E	medium-heavy	F	G	P	E	F	F	G	G	F	E	low
Balsa	soft	weak	G	light	P	E	E	P	P	P	G	E	E	P	low
Basswood	soft	weak	G	light	P	E	E	P	P	F	G	E	E	P	low
Beech	hard	medium	P	heavy	P	G	F	F	F	G	F	P	G	G	medium
Birch	hard	strong	G	heavy	P	G	P	E	G	E	G	P	F	F	high
Butternut	soft	weak	E	light	F	F	G	F	G	F	G	F	G	F	medium
Cherry	medium	medium	G	heavy	F	P	G	E	E	E	E	F	E	E	high
Chestnut	soft	weak	E	light	E	P	G	G	E	G	G	G	E	E	high
Cottonwood	soft	weak	G	light	P	E	E	P	P	P	G	E	E	P	low
Cypress	soft	medium	G	light	E	F	F	P	P	P	G	F	F	F	medium
Elm	medium	medium	P	medium-heavy	F	G	F	P	P	G	P	E	F	G	medium
Gum, red	medium	medium	P	medium	F	G	G	F	E	F	F	G	E	F	medium-high
Hickory	hard	strong	G	heavy	P	F	P	F	G	E	G	P	G	E	medium
Lauan	medium	medium	E	medium	G	P	G	F	G	F	G	G	E	P	low-medium
Magnolia	soft	weak	F	medium	F	G	G	G	F	P	G	E	E	G	medium
Mahogany	medium	medium	E	medium	F	P	G	E	E	E	G	G	E	G	high
Maple, hard	hard	strong	G	heavy	P	P	P	E	E	E	F	P	F	G	high
Maple, soft	medium	medium	F	medium	F	G	G	F	F	P	P	F	G	G	medium
Oak, red	hard	strong	E	heavy	P	F	P	F	G	E	E	G	G	E	medium
Oak, white	hard	strong	E	heavy	F	F	P	G	G	E	E	G	G	E	high
Poplar	soft	weak	G	medium	P	G	E	P	G	F	G	E	E	P	medium
Sycamore	medium	medium	P	heavy	F	G	G	P	G	E	P	E	G	P	low-medium
Walnut	medium	strong	E	heavy	G	F	G	G	E	E	G	F	E	E	high
Willow	soft	weak	G	light	G	G	G	F	F	F	F	G	G	G	low

(E = Excellent, G = Good, F = Fair, P = Poor)

woods used in cabinet and furniture work should be kiln-dried to cut down on warpage and shrinkage.

Working Qualities. There are many times that the workability is more important than actual appearance and even as important as the physical characteristics—hardness, strength, weight, and dimensional stability. If a complete shop of power tools is available to you, the problem of working qualities may be of little concern. But, working with hand tools is another story. With a hand saw, plane, chisel, and other cutting and shaping tools, the relative difficulty of working on a wood species should be taken into consideration.

Aesthetic Properties of Hardwood

Probably the most obvious trait of any wood used in a decorative fashion is the pattern or design created by the grain on the surface of the piece. The predom-inate contributor of this surface pattern is the growth rings of the tree.

As stated in Chapter 1, the earlywood (also called springwood) of a tree is usually composed of large cells that have very thin walls. Latewood (or summerwood) cells are smaller with thicker cell walls. In some species of trees the contrast between earlywood and latewood is prominent (Fig. 3-2). In others, the contrast is slight. The annual rings are quite conspicuous in such trees as ash but are relatively indistinct in woods such as maple.

The way the wood is cut, of course, affects the surface pattern. Plain-sawing produces V-shaped or U-shaped designs. Long lines running parallel to the length of the board decorate the face of quarter-sawn lumber.

The surface design of a piece of wood is also affected by knots, burls, crotches, buttresses, and swollen

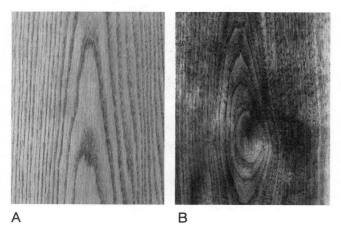

Fig. 3-2: *Examples of the contrast between earlywood and latewood: (A) conspicuous in white oak and (B) inconspicuous in black walnut.*

butts (Fig. 3-3). A burl is a mass of dormant bud growth that may protrude from the tree like a wart. Wood cut from burls has a swirly pattern that has been in demand since the Roman Empire. A buttress is the swollen part of the tree just above the ground. Wood cut from this part of the tree will have a crinkly, curly figure. The walnut tree is famous for this phenomenon.

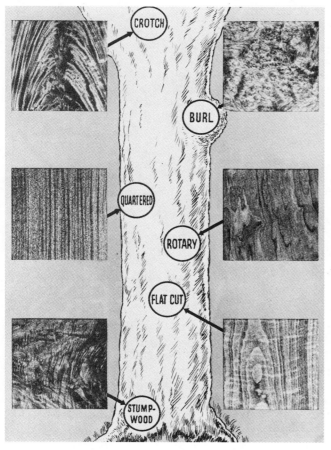

Fig. 3-3: *Various parts of a tree producing various grain patterns.*

To preserve this buttress, a walnut tree is dug out, the roots cut, and the tree pulled over. Logs are sent, base and all, to the mill in this condition.

Most spectacular patterns are cut into veneers and given names such as curly knot figure, bird's eye figure, feather crotch figure, etc. The price of such wood is higher than normal plain-sawn or quarter-sawn lumber. More will be said about veneers in the chapter covering hardwood plywood.

Texture. When most of us look at beautiful furniture, we aren't content to just look; we have to touch. Most of us will pull open a drawer, rap on the top, jiggle the legs, and run a hand over the surface. We expect the drawer to work, the rap to sound solid, the legs to be even, and the surface to feel glassy smooth. The glassy smoothness is a result of proper finishing—sanding, staining, filling, sealing, coating, polishing, and buffing. But underneath the varnish or lacquer the wood feels very different. The feel of the wood depends on its texture. Some woods are much smoother than others; some are very coarse. The texture of the wood is an important consideration in choosing a species for your project.

Two things affect a wood's surface smoothness. The major factor is the size and arrangement of pores. In hardwoods, nutrients pass from the roots to the leaves through large vessels created by open-ended cells arranged end to end. When the wood is cut across the grain, these nutrient pipe lines appear on the surface as tiny pores. If the diameters of these pores are relatively large, the wood will be coarsely textured and will feel rough, such as in the red oak. The pores of the red gum are much smaller in diameter. This wood is considered to be fine-textured and feels much smoother than red oak. Most trees fall somewhere between these two extremes. Some of the fine-textured woods are cherry, poplar, birch, gum, and maple. Oak, walnut, and pecan are coarse-textured woods.

Not only can the size of these pores affect the texture, but their arrangement among the other cells can as well. If the vessels are concentrated in the earlywood, the wood's surface will be alternately rough and smooth, creating the feel of ridges. Such wood is referred to as ring porous and has an uneven texture. On the other hand, if the pores are distributed evenly between earlywood and latewood, the wood is called diffuse porous and has an even texture. Again, there are trees which fit into categories between these two extremes.

Not only is the surface texture of the wood determined by the size and arrangement of pores, but texture is also affected by the presence of rays. Rays are passageways that conduct nutrients from the sapwood into the interior or heartwood of the tree. Instead of running parallel to the grain, they run across the grain. Rays appear on the surface of the wood as flecks.

In some trees such as the chestnut or aspen, these flecks may be invisible. The smallest rays are only one cell wide and may be visible only under a microscope. In other trees, the rays are very conspicuous. The white oak may have rays several inches in height.

Ray flecks often add to the beauty of a piece of wood. The sycamore, oak, and beech are especially noted for their speckled appearance. In some species, such as maple and sycamore, the ray flecks appear darker than the background wood; whereas in others, such as the cherry and yellow poplar, the flecks appear lighter.

The texture of a species affects the way the wood behaves when it is worked. A jointer or shaper may tear loose fibers of even chips from wood with uneven grain. On a lathe, coarse-grained woods tend to shred. The texture also determines the finishing techniques. Coarse-textured woods require a filler to close the pore before the top coat is applied.

Color. Very often a particular wood is chosen for its color more than any other characteristic. The heartwood of black walnut is, of course, dark brown; cherry is red; white oak, light brown; yellow poplar, yellowish-green; and willow, grayish-brown. The sapwood of many hardwoods is almost white in color. Table 3-2 lists several common hardwoods used in making furniture and the color of their heartwoods and sapwoods.

Heartwood and sapwood are not generally mixed in a piece of furniture; sapwood is weaker and softer than heartwood and the color contrast makes staining difficult. But very often a mixture of heartwood and sapwood makes very pleasing contrasts, especially in paneling.

HARDWOOD GRADES

Hardwood grading is complex. In fact, hardwood grading isn't consistent for all trees, nor in all parts of the country. On the whole, however, the National Hardwood Lumber Association's grading is generally accepted by most of the furniture and lumber industry. That is, the grade of each random sized piece of lumber is determined by the percentage of its surface that is free from defects and by how many defect-free pieces of a specific size can be cut from that one piece. For example, two sides of a board 6" wide and 12' long

TABLE 3-2:   COLOR CHARACTERISTICS OF HARDWOODS

Wood	Color of Heartwood	Color of Sapwood	Grain Figure
Alder	Light pinkish brown to white	Same	Obscure
Ash, white	Light grayish brown	White	Pronounced
Basswood	White to cream	Same	Mild grain figure
Beech	White to slightly reddish	Same	Obscure
Birch	Light to dark reddish brown	White	Varying from a stripe to curly
Butternut	Amber to cream	White	Like walnut
Cherry	Light to dark reddish brown	White	Obscure
Chestnut	Grayish brown	White	Conspicuous
Cottonwood	White to cream	White	Obscure
Elm	Light grayish brown, often tinted with red	White	Conspicuous
Gum, red	Reddish brown	Pinkish white	Obscure to figured
Hickory	White to light brown	White	Straight
Lauan	Brown to red brown	Light brown	Stripe
Mahogany	Brown to red brown	Pale reddish brown	Stripe
Maple, hard and soft	Light reddish brown	White	Obscure to figured
Oak, red and white	Grayish brown	White	Conspicuous
Poplar	Light yellow to dark olive	White	Obscure
Sycamore	Reddish brown	Pale reddish brown	Obscure to flake
Walnut	Light to dark brown	Cream	Obscure to figured

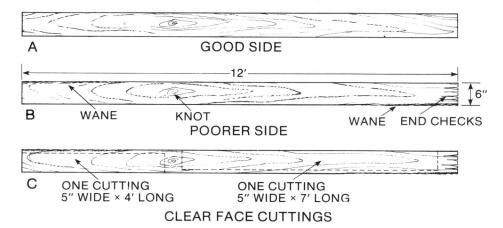

A
GOOD SIDE

B
WANE   KNOT   WANE   END CHECKS
POORER SIDE

12'
6"

C
ONE CUTTING
5" WIDE × 4' LONG
ONE CUTTING
5" WIDE × 7' LONG
CLEAR FACE CUTTINGS

Fig. 3-4: A typical hardwood board is graded according to the number of clear cuttings that can be obtained from its poorer side.

are shown in Figs. 3-4A and B. One side has only one defect: a knot. The other side, in addition to the knot, has wanes on both ends and end checks. The lumber grader grades this board from the poorer face by visualizing the size and number of clear cuttings that can be made from it, as seen in Fig. 3-4C. The minimum size of each cutting and the number of cuttings allowed on boards of a particular size qualify a board for a particular grade. Although the cutting that is 5" wide and 7' long would qualify our example board for a First or Second grade, the short cutting that is 5" wide and 4' long disqualifies the board for any grade above No. 1 Common.

Allowable defects vary with each grade. *Firsts* and *Seconds,* the top two grades, usually combine into one grade called FAS (Firsts and Seconds). Unless specified otherwise, orders are usually filled with FAS. *Selects* is the third grade of hardwood lumber, followed by lower grades that are generally undesirable. These, from fair to poor, are Number 1 Common, Number 2 Common, Sound Wormy, Number 3A Common, and Number 3B Common. Both sides of a board are graded; a board having only one side meeting FAS standards is "FAS 1 face." Choose this grade if only one side of your project will be visible.

Because of their expense, hardwoods are not cut to predetermined size like softwoods. They are cut to produce as much usable wood as possible. You'll find pieces of odd lengths in fractional widths and in a variety of thicknesses. In other words, each board is sawn as wide and long as the log allows, then trimmed just enough to make the edges and ends square. This method of sawing yields the maximum amount of usable material with the least amount of waste, thus reducing the cost of the operation. This is acceptable to the furniture industry because the buyer will further plane, cut, and shape the wood into a variety of forms and dimensions. Often the thicknesses are referred to

as so many quarters of an inch. For example 1" = four-quarters, 1-1/4" = five-quarters, 1-1/2" = six-quarters.

Hardwood lumber is planed only on one or both flat surfaces, but not on the edges. The reason for this is that such lumber is nearly always milled in some manner on the edges, and planing would be of little value. Actually, many furniture factories purchase their hardwoods rough on all four sides and run the stock through planers to bring it to the thickness desired for a given piece of furniture. This procedure is cheaper in material cost, plus it saves time. In fact, if you have a jointer or planer in your workshop, you can do the same thing and save money (Fig. 3-5). But, if you don't have a jointer or planer, it's best to purchase surfaced stock. As a general rule, it costs less to buy the surfaced stock from a hardwood dealer than to buy it rough and have the material finished in a cabinet shop. Of course, some suppliers don't have surfacing facilities so they must have the finishing done by an outside source and charge you extra. Custom surfacing can frequently cost more than the original price of the hardwood lumber.

Fig. 3-5: If you have access to a planer or jointer, unsurfaced hardwood lumber is cheaper to buy.

Like softwood, hardwood that has been planed on only one or both faces is referred to as S1S (surfaced 1 side) or S2S (surfaced 2 sides). When it is planed on all four sides, it's called S4S. Table 3-3 lists nominal and actual sizes of hardwood that is surfaced on one and two faces.

TABLE 3-3:   NOMINAL AND ACTUAL SIZES OF HARDWOOD LUMBER

Thickness (Widths Vary with Grades)		
Nominal (Rough)	Surfaced 1 Side (S1S)	Surfaced 2 Sides (S2S)
3/8"	1/4"	3/16"
1/2"	3/8"	5/16"
5/8"	1/2"	7/16"
3/4"	5/8"	9/16"
1"	7/8"	13/16"
1-1/4"	1-1/8"	1-1/16"
1-1/2"	1-3/8"	1-5/16"
2"	1-13/16"	1-3/4"
3"	2-13/16"	2-3/4"
4"	3-13/16"	3-3/4"

BUYING HARDWOOD LUMBER

Buying hardwood lumber is a much more difficult task than obtaining softwood lumber. You can't generally go to your local lumberyard or home center and select the hardwood you want. In most large cities, there are dealers who sell hardwoods exclusively. Hardwood suppliers are usually listed under a separate heading in the yellow page lumber category.

Some local lumberyards and home centers have samples of hardwood that they can obtain from a supplier for you in a few days. Hardwoods can also be obtained from mail-order woodworking suppliers. Names of these firms can be obtained from advertisements in how-to and wood-working magazines. As indicated in Table 3-1, the price of hardwood varies considerably with the kind of wood.

Hardwoods are sold by the board foot (same as softwoods), by lineal measurement, and, in cases, by the pound. Wider hardwood boards are always more expensive than the narrow stock so that when plans are made for wide pieces, the cost and labor of gluing should be considered. Another cost factor in ordering any quantity of lumber is choice of width and length. Random width and length will be cheaper than the specified sizes. In most cases, the project will cost less if you simply specify the footage you'll need to the dealer. Then, the salesperson will sell you what is in stock that will give you what you need for your project with the least waste. In addition, it is rewarding to pay a visit to a hardwood dealer and become acquainted with the sizes, grades, types of wood, and methods of handling that you should consider.

TIPS ON WORKING WITH HARDWOODS

To edge glue random width hardwood boards to make lumber of a desired size requires a special gluing technique. (General gluing techniques of wood were mentioned in Chapter 1.) There are actually two methods of gluing: edge-to-edge and face-to-face.

Edge-to-Edge Gluing. There are times when a woodworker needs a board wider than he can purchase in the usual market. When this need arises, the wider board can be made by gluing it up from narrower stock placed edge to edge.

The arrangement of the boards for assembly is most important in edge-to-edge gluing. If you place them with all the sap sides at the top, all will cup in the same direction as they shrink and the wide board will be a trough (Fig. 3-6A). Alternate sap with heart sides produce a wavy board which will approximate flatness if warping has been slight or the pieces are narrow; here a little planing will take out the curl (Fig. 3-6B). If, in addition, you arrange the boards with the grain running in the same direction, planing will be easy when the work is removed from the clamps. If the lumber, when assembled, will be stiffened with supporting cleats, as in a tabletop, boards 6" to 10" wide are suitable, and in natural or stained finishes may even look better. Where extreme flatness is required,

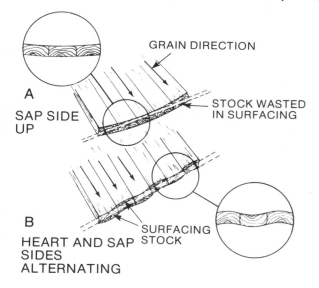

Fig. 3-6: Method of laying up boards for edge-to-edge gluing. When edge gluing boards of different widths, place the narrower boards in the center of the panel, with the wider boards at the edge. It is important that the clamping pressure be uniform over the entire glued area.

as in a drawing board, use narrow pieces. Since the piece must be surfaced, save time by planing all boards to flatness and the same thickness.

Cut pieces 1/2" longer than finished length, arranging them on sawhorses and marking them. After the pieces are test fitted, spread the adhesive on the edges being bonded. Then, apply the clamps (usually bar or pipe types) alternately, one from one side and one from the other, about every 10" to 15". A slight amount of glue should be visible along the glue line when the correct amount of pressure is applied. This excess can be wiped off with a damp cloth. If a board slips out of place while clamping, put a piece of scrap over the joint and knock it into position with a mallet. Carefully check when tightening the clamps to be sure that all corners of the workpiece ride down flat and secure against the clamps, so the surface will be flat with no warping or twisting. If the stock to be glued up is somewhat warped, it can frequently be straightened by clamping all four corners tightly against the bar of the bar clamp as shown in Fig. 3-7.

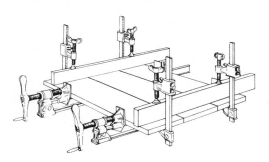

Fig. 3-7: Method of clamping warped boards.

Face-to-Face Gluing. Wood built up in thickness by face-to-face gluing is likely to be more stable than solid blocks; and by facing sap side to sap side, or the reverse, the tendency of one board to warp is offset by the opposite pull of the other board. Wide boards glued edge to edge can be joined face to face to increase thickness. Match up boards of about the same grain characteristics; gluing a board having wide annular rings to one with narrow, or a plain-sawn or flat-grain board with one quarter-sawn invites warping as soon as moisture content changes.

As pressure must be applied uniformly, clamps working at the center are necessary. Hand screws are standard for this work, and the maple jaws are adaptable to many conditions of use. Open or close the clamp by holding the handles tightly and rotating it like a crank. For first clamping, set the jaws slightly wide, draw them together with the nearest screw, and then tighten the rear screw. This applies pressure at the point, squeezing surplus glue out from the center

toward the edges of the assembly, thus driving out air bubbles. Then, loosen one of the clamps, tighten it toward the back, and apply to the work. This will place pressure on the edges, closing them tightly. Further turning of the rear screw will parallel the jaws, applying pressure full-length. Do this with all the clamps. Glued boards, when the adhesive is dry, can be surfaced and squared like solid hardwood.

Joints

The satisfaction obtained from any woodworking project comes not only from its initial appeal, but also from its continued attractiveness with use. Both its durability and its pristine appearance are important. The integrity of the joints is important to both of these aspects. This is particularly true in hardwood furniture making.

The term *joint* generally means the close securing or fastening together of two or more smooth, even surfaces. The construction quality of any wood project depends primarily on the quality of the joints. They must be neat, strong, and rigid to give the finished piece its necessary instant appeal and long-lasting durability. Keep in mind that destructive forces may be applied from the exterior of a joint or induced by internal forces. External forces may be those applied by sitting on a chair or racking caused by pushing a case across a rough floor. Internal forces may be from shrinking of wood parts or the steady pull of poorly mated parts forced together by clamping pressure. Proper joint selection will alleviate the first type while correction for the second type may be concerned with good manufacturing practice, such as selection of wood species, uniformity of moisture content, and joint accuracy.

There is a wide variation possible in joint design between a plain butt joint and a joint designed for maximum strength and durability. Some of these may even cause little or no change in external appearance. In other instances, considerable breadth in joint selection is possible if it does not show in the finished item. As a general rule, it is best to select the simplest joints that will do the job satisfactorily.

An assembly joint should be designed so that the majority of the glued area is either tangential or radial grain. It should be kept in mind that with most wood species, joints between side-grain (Fig. 3-8A) and flat-grain (Fig. 3-8B) surfaces can be made as strong as the wood itself in shear parallel to the grain, tension across the grain, and cleavage. Side-grain can be held to prevent any movement by using dowels (Fig. 3-8C), splines (Fig. 3-8D), or milled surfaces (Fig. 3-8E). The tongue-and-groove joint (Fig. 3-8F) and other shaped

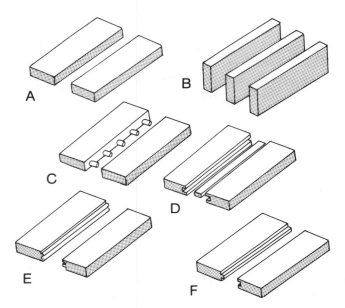

Fig. 3-8: Edge glued and face glued joints are strong, but they can be made stronger by using dowels, splines, and milled surfaces.

joints have the theoretical advantage of larger gluing surfaces than the straight joints, but in practice they do not give higher strength with most woods. Furthermore, the theoretical advantage is often lost, wholly or partly, because the shaped joints are more difficult to machine than straight, plain joints so as to obtain a perfect fit of the parts. Tongue-and-groove joints are, however, frequently used on side panels or in raised panel doors. If the panel insert is allowed to float, that is, if it is smaller than the encompassing frame, there will be less tendency for the expansion and contraction (from moisture changes) of the panel to stress the joints in the enclosing frame.

It is practically impossible to make end-butt joints (Fig. 3-9A) sufficiently strong or permanent to meet the normal requirements of furniture jointing. With the most careful gluing possible, not more than about 25% of the tensile strength of the wood parallel with the grain can be obtained in butt joints. In order to approximate the tensile strength of certain species, a scarf, serrated, or other form of joint that approaches a side-grain surface must be used. The plain scarf (Fig. 3-9B) is perhaps the easiest to glue and entails fewer machining difficulties than the many-angle forms.

It is also difficult to obtain the proper joint strength in end-to-side joints (Fig. 3-9C), which are further subjected in use to unusually severe stresses as a result of unequal dimensional changes in the two members of the joint as their moisture content changes. It is therefore necessary to use irregular shapes of joints, dowels (Fig. 3-9D), tenons, glue blocks (Fig. 3-9E), or other devices to reinforce such a joint in order to bring side

grain into contact with side grain or to secure larger gluing surfaces.

While there are well over 100 kinds of joints used in woodworking, they can be grouped into the following several basic types.

Butt Joints. The butt joint is the simplest of all joints. Though it is extremely simple to make, the edges to be joined must be tested for *absolute* squareness before the pieces are fitted together. But, even then the plain butt end grain to end grain or plain butt end grain to side grain joints have little strength, unless the joints are strengthened by either dowels, wood glue blocks, or mechanical fasteners such as nails or screws.

Dowel rods are made of hardwood—generally maple or birch—and are sold in 36″ lengths and diameters from 1/8″ to 3″, including the common 1-1/2″ clothes pole dowel. The sizes most often used for cabinetwork are 3/8″ and 1/2″ diameters. The dowel's hardness and the fact that it is used with grain at right angles to materials joined are the reasons for this added strength.

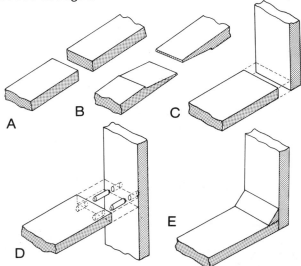

Fig. 3-9: End-to-end and end-to-side butt joints and methods of reinforcing them.

Actually, there are two methods used in doweling, the open method and the blind method. In the open method (Fig. 3-10A), a hole is drilled completely through one piece of wood and deeply into or through the piece to be joined. The dowel is coated with glue and pushed completely through the drilled holes, joining the pieces. The remainder is then sawn off flush with the outer surface. Thus, dowel stock for open doweling is kept long to allow for a flush cut after the joint is made.

In the blind method (Fig. 3-10B), holes are drilled part of the way into each piece from the joined faces. A rule of thumb is to drill the holes in each piece to

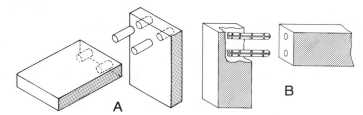

Fig. 3-10: (A) An open dowel joint; (B) a blind dowel joint.

a depth of approximately four times the diameter of the dowel. A dowel is then glue-coated and inserted in one hole, and the second piece is pressed onto the protruding dowel end. The length of the dowel rod should always be cut about 1/8″ to 1/4″ shorter than the total of the two holes. Chamfer the dowel at each end to aid in location during assembly. The fit of the dowel should not be so tight that the glue is all pushed to the bottom of the hole. Optimum size is a snug fit, such that the dowel, spline, or tenon can be pushed in with a finger, but not loose enough to wobble in the hole. A 1/64″ clearance is a good fit to obtain.

Consistency of dowel and hole diameter is difficult to obtain, as is the location of dowels and dowel holes (Fig. 3-11). Holes and dowels should be checked frequently for uniformity of diameter. Gluing should be done soon after machining to prevent change of size by change of moisture content.

Glue blocks are small square or triangular pieces of wood used to strengthen and support the two adjoining surfaces of a butt joint. Remember that while this joint reinforcement features a strong face-to-face gluing surface, varying moisture content will cause a differential wood movement, since the grain direction of the block and the substrate are at right angles to each other. This will highly stress the joint. Because of this, a number of short blocks is preferable to one long one.

Mortise-and-Tenon Joints. The mortise-and-tenon is a very good joint, stronger and more widely used than the butt joint. It is one of the best techniques used in fine furniture making. All enclosed mortises (those with material on four sides) should be cut with a mortising attachment on a drill press (Fig. 3-12A), with a router, or by hand with a chisel.

The tenon for the mortise-and-tenon joint can be cut in a number of different ways depending on the equipment available and the nature of the joint. In Fig. 3-12B, a tenon is being cut on a table saw. In any case, thickness of the tenon should not exceed one-third the thickness of the mortised member. Some of the more popular variations of the simple mortise-and-tenon (Fig. 3-13) are described in the following paragraphs.

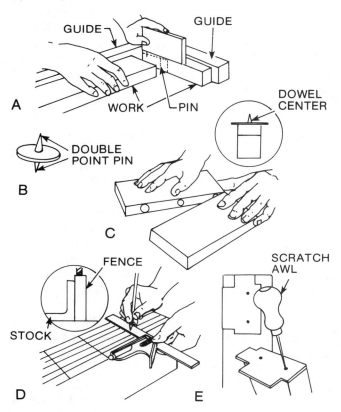

Fig. 3-11: Methods of laying dowel holes.

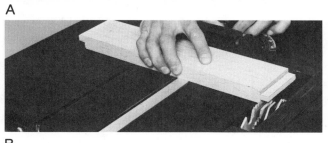

Fig. 3-12: Making a mortise-and-tenon joint: (A) drilling out the mortise and (B) cutting the tenon.

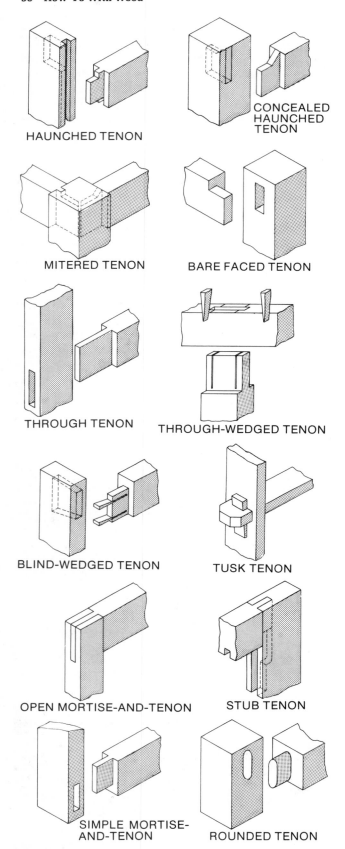

HAUNCHED TENON

CONCEALED HAUNCHED TENON

MITERED TENON

BARE FACED TENON

THROUGH TENON

THROUGH-WEDGED TENON

BLIND-WEDGED TENON

TUSK TENON

OPEN MORTISE-AND-TENON

STUB TENON

SIMPLE MORTISE-AND-TENON

ROUNDED TENON

Fig. 3-13: Common mortise-and-tenon joints.

The *haunched tenon* is employed where added tenon strength is needed and where partial exposure on top is not objectionable.

The *concealed haunched tenon* gives the needed extra strength to the joint without showing a break at the end.

The *mitered tenon*, frequently utilized in table construction, is used to secure the maximum length of tenon. Each joint is a simple mortise-and-tenon with the tenon end mitered at 45°. The two mortises meet at 90° inside the vertical (leg) member. Mitering of the tenon ends allows for deeper tenons.

The *bare-faced tenon* has but one shoulder and it is used when a tenoned piece is thinner than a mortised piece.

A *through tenon* is a useful joint in some types of furniture. Where added strength and resistance to pulling apart are required, wedges can be used. The two ends of the mortise are sloped outward to provide room for the wedges, which are about half the tenon in length.

The *blind-wedged tenon* is used in the same way as the through-wedged tenon but can be employed in locations where the through-wedged cannot.

The *tusk tenon*, that goes right through and is locked with a key, peg, or wedge, goes back to medieval days. They were more common in some middle European countries than in Great Britain, but they may be found in some Colonial furniture. The use of a wedged or keyed tenon would improve an ordinary tenon, where the fit is not good.

The *open mortise-and-tenon* is most commonly used in simple frame construction where an exposed tenon end is not objectionable.

Although not a true mortise-and-tenon joint, the *stub tenon* is sometimes used in frame construction and is made with a short tenon that fits into the groove of the frame.

Dovetail Joints. The interlocking of two pieces of wood by special fan-shaped cutting is called a dovetail joint. It is used extensively in making fine furniture, drawers, and in projects where good appearance and strength are desired. A dovetail joint has considerable strength because of the flare of the projections, technically known as pins, on the ends of the boards, which fit exactly into similarly shaped dovetails.

There are four basic dovetail joints (Fig. 3-14):

1. Through or lap dovetails are joints where the dovetail and pin are both clearly visible from two sides of the joint.

2. Stopped-lap dovetails or half-blind dovetails are joints where the face of one board is perfectly smooth and the pins and dovetails are visible on the face of the other.

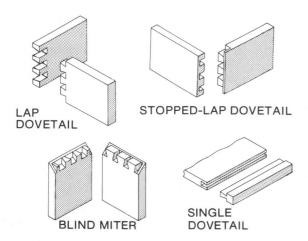

A

B

LAP DOVETAIL

STOPPED-LAP DOVETAIL

BLIND MITER

SINGLE DOVETAIL

Fig. 3-14: Common dovetail joints.

3. Blind dovetail joints are those where all the cutting is done without marring the outside face of either of the two pieces.

4. A single dovetail (Fig. 3-15), as its name implies, is just one dovetail cut into a corresponding frame. It is useful in making a table base in which multiple legs are attached to a central post.

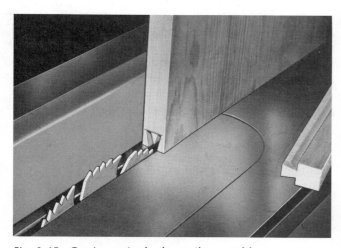

Fig. 3-15: Cutting a single dovetail on a table saw.

Dovetails can be cut by hand using a dovetail saw and small chisel or with a special template or pattern with a drill press or router (Fig. 3-16). The latter two methods are highly accurate and considerably faster than cutting by hand.

Dado Joints. A dado joint is formed when one piece of wood is set into a groove or dado cut into another. There are many variations of a dado joint (Fig. 3-17) used in cabinetwork and furniture making. For instance, a standard or housed dado joint is a groove that is cut in one piece of wood to the exact thickness of the second piece to be joined. Sometimes a dado is stopped on one or both sides.

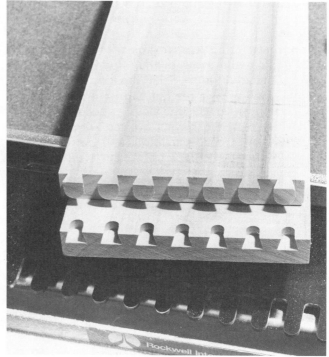

C

Fig. 3-16: Steps in making a dovetail joint with a router: (A) putting the template in place; (B) cutting with the router; and (C) the results.

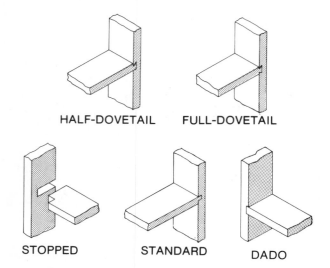

HALF-DOVETAIL   FULL-DOVETAIL

STOPPED   STANDARD   DADO

Fig. 3-17: Common dado joints.

The shouldered dado is generally employed for drawer joints, but is also used extensively in shelf construction. The full-dovetail dado is made by first cutting a mortise or slot. Then, the dado is cut to the narrowest width. The half-dovetail dado is cut the same way except that the angle cuts are made on only one side of the joint. Actually, a dado is a poor joint for gluing as it has the same deficiency as an end-to-side grain joint—low glue joint strength. The dovetail dado does have more strength than a plain dado, as the shear strength of the wood prevents the rupture of the joint.

Lap Joints. Bring two workpieces together, notch them equally where they overlap, and you have either a cross or middle-joint, a half-lap joint (end-to-end, at right angles), or a tee half-lap joint (end-to-side, at right angles). The desired visual effect of such joints is that the two thicknesses overlap within a single thickness. A well-made lap joint is a strong joint in that the glued surface is a face-to-face surface (Fig. 3-18).

The end or corner-lap joint is made by halving and shouldering the opposite sides of the ends of the workpieces and then joining them at right angles. When one of the cuts is made at a point other than the end of the workpiece, you have a center, or middle, lap. This joint is used most commonly when joining a rail to an upright.

The edgewise cross lap or middle lap is another joint that is made by halving the two pieces at right angles, but in this case the notches are cut in the edges rather than the surfaces of the two members. This is particularly useful when making framing or partitioning, and often both cuts can be made at the same time.

The full-dovetail half lap and the half-dovetail half lap are fancier versions of the corner and cross lap which are often seen in old cabinetwork. In both these joints the dovetail is half-lapped into a rail, crosspiece, or upright, and the two pieces are joined at right angles. The main difference between the two is that the half-dovetail half lap is not as difficult to make.

Miter Joints. The miter joint is primarily for show. For example, it may be used for an uninterrupted wood grain around edges (side to top to side of a cabinet) or at corners (a picture frame). The joining ends or edges are usually cut at angles of 45°, then glued and clamped (Fig. 3-19). The 45° glued miter joint is stronger than the end-to-end or end-to-side joint, but not nearly as strong as a face-to-face glued joint. For a high quality mitered joint, various modifications are possible which contribute to the strength of this construction. These include splines, feathers (or keys), or dowels (Fig. 3-20).

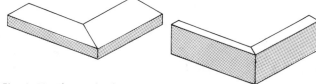

Fig. 3-19: Flat and edge miter joints.

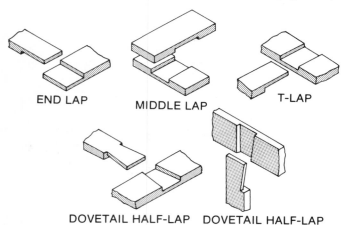

END LAP   MIDDLE LAP   T-LAP

DOVETAIL HALF-LAP   DOVETAIL HALF-LAP (ONE SIDE)

Fig. 3-18: Common lap joints.

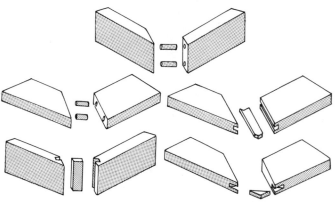

Fig. 3-20: Flat and edge miters with dowels, splines, and feathers.

Splines are used to strengthen all types of joints from plain butt to fancy miters. The spline itself is a thin strip of hardwood or plywood inserted in a groove cut in the two adjoining surfaces of a joint. The groove is cut with a saw blade or dado head to a specific width and depth. (The groove for the spline is commonly run in with the dado head, 1/4" being usual for 3/4" to 1" stock, although a 1/8" spline, a single saw cut, is sometimes used, especially for miters.) A thin piece of stock is then cut to fit into this groove. The spline stock should be cut so that the grain runs at right angles to the grain of the joint.

A very simple way to produce splines is to cut up scrap pieces of 1/8" plywood or hardboard. A supply of these can be kept on hand. The advantages of the plywood are its strength in each direction and its constant thickness. Quite probably your saw blade cuts a 1/8" kerf which is just right.

A key is a small piece of wood inserted in a joint to hold it firmly together. The key is sometimes called a *feather*. It is often placed across the corners of miter joints.

Lapped miter joints (Fig. 3-21) are generally used only if it is desirable to have the miter show on one side. This joint will give the appearance of a conventional miter from one side, yet will be considerably stronger because of the increase in the area of contacting surfaces.

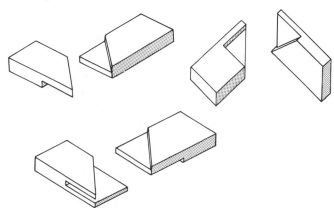

Fig. 3-21: Lapped miter joints.

Corner Joints. Various types of corner joints (Fig. 3-22) can be used in woodworking, ranging from a simple rabbet to the complex lock miter joint. A rabbet is an L-shaped groove cut across the edge or end of one piece. The joint is made by fitting the other piece into it. The width of the rabbet should equal the thickness of the material, and its depth should be one-half to two-thirds the thickness. The rabbet joint conceals one end grain and also reduces the twisting tendency of a joint. The backs of most cases, cabinets, and chests are joined with the end grain facing the back.

The lock-corner joint is one of the better joints to use on chests and special boxes. Allow a little tolerance between tongues and grooves so that you can assemble the joint by sliding the pieces together.

Although the illustrations and explanations in this chapter might make the joints appear simple, it is extremely easy to spoil expensive hardwood material by making such common mistakes as cutting through or on the wrong side of the layout lines, not properly identifying mating surfaces, and/or not following the proper sequence of steps. Therefore, when attempting a joint for the first time, it is wise to practice on scrap material or with softwood of the same size to check settings, fits, and final results. Sometimes it might be necessary to make the same joint several times before obtaining satisfactory results. Remember, when woodworking, "practice makes perfect." All the joints described here, as well as edge-to-edge and face-to-face gluing techniques, work equally as well when using softwoods.

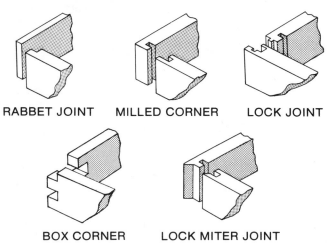

RABBET JOINT   MILLED CORNER   LOCK JOINT

BOX CORNER   LOCK MITER JOINT

Fig. 3-22: Common corner joints.

HARDWOOD PROJECTS

Some of the furniture shown in these projects will give you experience in making the joints discussed in this chapter. Measure each dimension carefully before cutting, and work carefully to give each joint a tight, professional look. Study the material in Chapter 12 before finishing your projects.

Shaker Bench

For hard to reach places, a Shaker foot stool comes in handy. The ingenious simplicity of Shaker joinery is well illustrated by the half-dovetail joints on this small bench. This construction results in a finished product that is both light and strong. It is made of hard maple and can easily be built.

Cut the boards to the sizes shown and cut half-circles in the legs. Cut 1/4" × 1/2" dadoes in the top to fit the legs. Miter the ends of the braces and cut notches. Glue a full-size template to one of the braces and use it to position a stopblock for each cut.

Assemble one leg into the top without glue, lay a brace in position, and mark the cuts to be made in the top and leg. Repeat for the other braces. Make the initial cuts with a dovetail saw or backsaw.

Clean out the cuts using a dado blade with the miter gauge at 90° and then at 45°. Finish-sand all the pieces before assembly. Assemble the bench with white glue and nails. The Shakers used square cut nails and left the heads exposed, which made an attractive detail. If ordinary brads are used, countersink them and fill the holes. Trim the ends of the braces flush. A router with a self piloting bit will do this very quickly, but a block plane and/or rasp will also do a satisfactory job. Break all sharp edges with a block sander and very fine abrasive paper. Finish as desired.

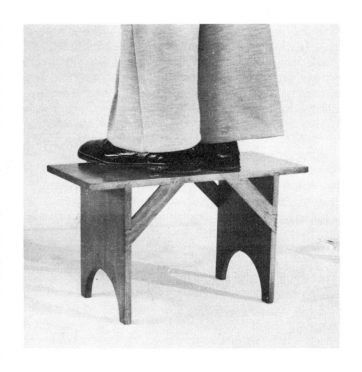

MATERIALS LIST FOR SHAKER BENCH

Quantity	Description
1	1/2" × 8" × 17" pine
2	1/2" × 8" × 9-15/16" hard maple
4	3/16" × 1-1/4" × 7-1/4" hard maple
8	cut nails or 1" brads
—	white glue
—	finishing materials

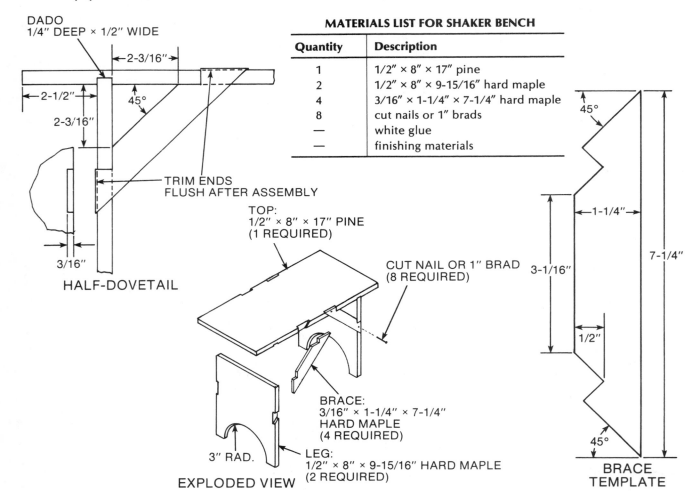

DADO
1/4" DEEP × 1/2" WIDE
2-3/16"
2-1/2"
45°
2-3/16"
TRIM ENDS FLUSH AFTER ASSEMBLY
3/16"
HALF-DOVETAIL

TOP:
1/2" × 8" × 17" PINE
(1 REQUIRED)

CUT NAIL OR 1" BRAD
(8 REQUIRED)

BRACE:
3/16" × 1-1/4" × 7-1/4"
HARD MAPLE
(4 REQUIRED)

3" RAD.

LEG:
1/2" × 8" × 9-15/16" HARD MAPLE
(2 REQUIRED)

EXPLODED VIEW

45°
1-1/4"
7-1/4"
3-1/16"
1/2"
45°
BRACE TEMPLATE

Oak Plant Stand

Simple construction and a clean design highlight the distinctive, natural oak grain characteristics of this plant stand. The overall size is 14-1/2" square × 42" high. Red or white oak stock in 6/4 dimension when sanded will be approximately 1-1/4" thick. Follow the assembly instruction given below.

Cut all parts to length and sand flat sides (do not round edges at this time). On all the 14-1/2" long frame pieces, drill 3/4" diameter holes approximately 5/16" deep and centered 5/8" from end and edges. Holes are drilled on top and outside edge. On top hole, drill a 3/16" hole in the center for a single leg screw. On side hole, drill two 3/16" holes offset to clear the vertical center hole.

On the 14-1/2" long pieces, drill 3/8" diameter hole, 3/4" deep for glass top support. Center the holes 3" from each end and 1/2" down from the top surface. Glue pegs in place and slightly round tip ends.

Assemble top and bottom square frames using clamps, glue, and double screw joints. Wipe off any excess glue with a damp cloth. Check for square construction.

Attach top and bottom square frames to vertical legs with glue and screws. Clamp in place or weight top to provide pressure while glue dries. Glue 3/4" oak plugs or roundhead buttons into holes.

Round all edges slightly with sandpaper. Sand unit carefully with particular attention to smoothing exposed end grain. Finish plant stand with walnut or other color stain or oil finish to complement your existing room furnishings. Cut 1/4" thick glass top to size and drop into place on support pegs.

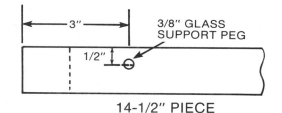

14-1/2" PIECE

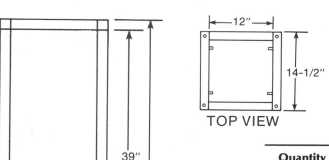

TOP VIEW

SIDE VIEW

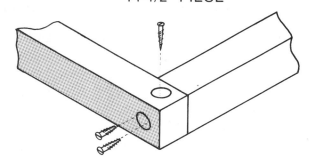

MATERIALS LIST FOR OAK PLANT STAND

Quantity	Description
4	1-1/4" × 1-1/4" × 14-1/2" top square frames
4	1-1/4" × 1-1/4" × 12" bottom square frames
4	1-1/4" × 1-1/4" × 39" legs
16	3/8" × 3/4" oak dowel plugs or 3/4" oak buttons
4	3/8" × 1-1/2" oak dowels (glass top supports)
1	1/4" × 12" × 12" plate glass, clear or smoke tint
24	#8 × 2" flathead wood screws
1 pt.	glue
1 pt.	walnut stain or oil finish

Walnut Tray and Folding Stand

Classic design and rich, solid walnut fits comfortably with either contemporary or traditional furnishing. This generously sized tray may be used separately or placed permanently on the folding walnut stand. Follow these procedures to assemble the tray and stand.

Tray. Edge joint and glue 1/2" thick walnut boards to make the tray bottom slightly oversized. When the glue is dry, sand with 180 grit paper on both sides and trim to the final 16" × 29" size. Trim front edge of left and right side pieces as shown in the plan, and run a 1/4" × 1/2" rabbet on the inside bottom edge of sides and back.

Drill and cut out hand holes as indicated on the side pieces. Bevel inside tray frame surfaces 3/8" × 4" on a jointer; resaw on band saw or plane by hand. Then, miter inside corners to 45° angles.

Sand all tray frame parts with fine 180 grit paper including the edges of the hand holes. Assemble tray using glue and 6d finish nails at the corners and 2d finish nails through the bottom into the sides. Wipe off excess glue immediately with a damp cloth. Countersink and fill nail holes with matching walnut wood putty.

Folding Stand. Trim all parts to length and angle-cut the top rails as indicated in the plan. Assemble the inside or narrow frame first; locate and drill 1/4" diameter dowel holes 1" deep at leg and rail joint.

On the *outside* of the narrow frame legs, drill 1/4" diameter holes 1" deep exactly 17" from the leg bottom. This is the location of the pivot pins for folding the stand. Glue the 1/4" pins in place. Assemble the narrow frame, gluing the dowel joints, and clamp until dry. Check for square construction.

Drill 1/4" diameter holes 1" deep, 17" from the bottom of the *inside* of the large frame legs. Assemble the top and bottom rail and one side of the large frame.

Insert the narrow frame inside the larger frame, lining up the pivot pins in the frame holes. *Do not glue pins in the large frame legs.* Position and glue the remaining outside frame leg in place. Sand all stand parts at the joints and the surface, and ease edges slightly.

Your walnut tray and folding stand can be finished with a clear polyurethane or polymer oil finish to complement other interior furnishings. Follow the finish manufacturer's recommendations for best results. When the finish is completely dry, tack or staple the strapping to the underside of the frame top rails so that the frame opens to approximately 24" in width.

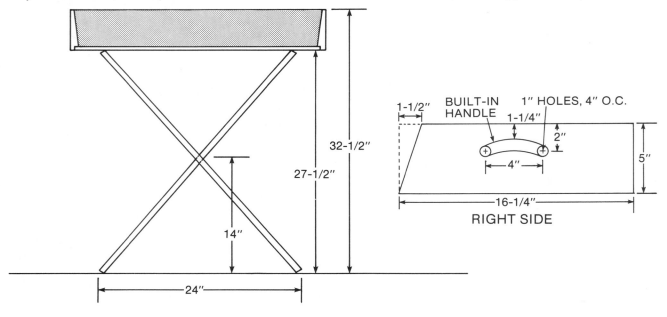

RIGHT SIDE

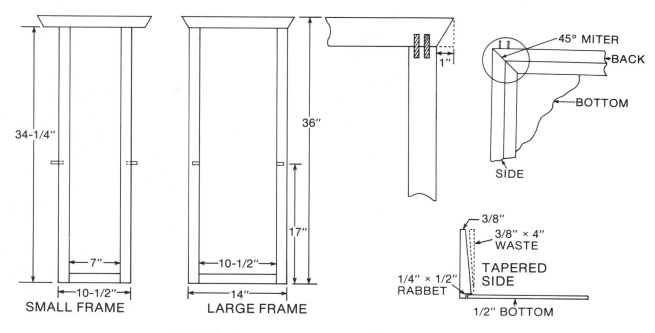

34-1/4"

7"

10-1/2"

SMALL FRAME

36"

17"

10-1/2"

14"

LARGE FRAME

45° MITER

BACK

BOTTOM

1"

SIDE

3/8"

3/8" × 4" WASTE

TAPERED SIDE

1/4" × 1/2" RABBET

1/2" BOTTOM

MATERIALS LIST FOR WALNUT TRAY AND FOLDING STAND

Quantity	Description
1	3/4" × 5" × 30" tray back
2	3/4" × 5" × 16-1/2" tray sides
3—5	1/2" random width—tray bottom (enough material to produce finished 1/2" × 16-1/2" × 29" bottom)
4	3/4" × 1-3/4" × 34-1/4" legs
2	3/4" × 1-3/4" × 16" top rails
1	3/4" × 1-3/4" × 10-1/2" large bottom rail
1	3/4" × 1-3/4" × 7" small bottom rail
18	1/4" × 1-3/4" grooved dowel pins
1 pt.	glue
1/2 lb.	2d finish nails
1/2 lb.	6d finish nails
2 pcs.	1-1/2" × 2" × 32" long fabric strapping

Cheese Cutting Board

A very attractive cheese cutting board or a party server can be made of maple or cherry wood and finished with a dark cherry stain. The wire bladed knife is designed to fit right into the board. A bright colored ceramic round tile makes a perfect cutting surface.

The cutting board is made of two pieces of stock, 5/16" thick, which are cut to size and shape.

Use a fine jeweler's blade on a scroll saw for cutting the finger opening in the knife. To start the cut, drill a hole on a drill press and then insert the jeweler's blade. The opening for the ceramic tile insert is cut the same way. Be sure to check the diameter of the tile when marking off the cutout opening, making sure

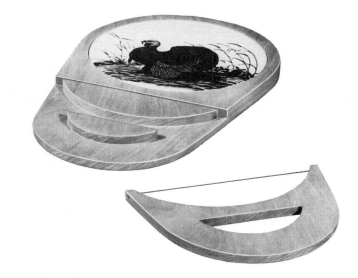

the tile fits tightly. When all of the parts are cut and properly fitted, mark off the outline position of each piece with a pencil. Glue the pieces to the bottom board using wood hand screws. If a veneer press is available, use it instead. Glue all of the pieces to the board except the cutting knife. Holes for fastening the steel wire to the knife are bored at an angle.

Allow the glue to set overnight before doing any further work on the board. Sand all the parts with a fine abrasive paper, breaking all sharp corners. Finish with a desired wood colored stain. When dry, apply two coats of satin polyurethane finish or another synthetic varnish. Incidentally, a penetrating oil resin finish may be substituted as a top coat. Attach three small rubber-headed nails to the bottom of the board to prevent it from sliding while in use.

Early American Wall Planter

The uses for this attractive wall shelf are almost limitless—it can be hung in practically any downstairs room and used to hold anything from an ivy plant to your fancy herb and spice containers.

The wall shelf is made entirely of 3/8″ thick solid cherry (except for the 1/8″ hardboard drawer bottoms) and is an easy project to build. Verify each measurement before you begin to cut. After laying out one side piece and drawing the curves with a compass, tack the other side piece to it and cut both simultaneously. Separate the pieces and dado each one in three places with a 3/8″ wide × 1/8″ deep groove. The same size groove is also made in the center of the two lower cross members.

The drawers have conventional tongue and groove joint construction. Assemble the project with glue and either 1-1/4″ brads of No. 4 × 1″ flathead wood screws. Finish with polyurethane finish. Highly polished 1/2″ brass knobs add the final touch.

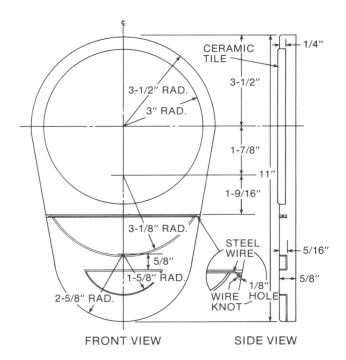

FRONT VIEW   SIDE VIEW

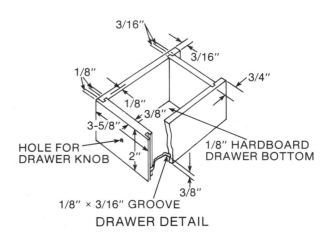

DRAWER DETAIL

MATERIALS LIST FOR EARLY AMERICAN WALL PLANTER

Quantity	Description
2	3/8″ × 6-1/2″ × 13-1/2″ sides
3	3/8″ × 6-1/2 × 7-1/2″ shelf boards
1	3/8″ × 6-1/2″ × 2-1/4″ separator
1	3/8″ × 8″ × 15-5/8″ back
2	3/8″ × 2″ × 3-7/16″ drawer fronts
4	3/8″ × 2″ × 6-3/8″ drawer sides
2	3/8″ × 1-1/2″ × 3-1/16″ drawer backs
2	1/8″ × 3-1/16″ × 6-5/16″ hardboard (drawer bottoms)
2	1/2″ dia. brass drawer knobs
—	white glue
—	1-1/4″ brads and/or No. 4 × 1″ flathead wood screws
—	fine abrasive paper
—	polyurethane finish

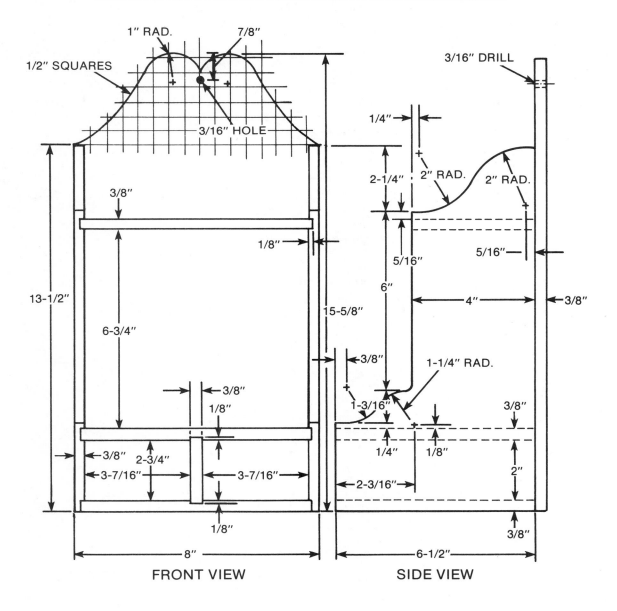

FRONT VIEW

SIDE VIEW

CHAPTER
— 4 —

WEATHER AND DECAY RESISTANT WOODS

Wood can be used out-of-doors in many ways (Fig. 4-1), but as was discussed in the previous chapter, wood used in exterior applications is subject to weathering. With most lumbers, unless painted or otherwise preserved, constantly changing temperatures and humidity will cause splitting, warping, discoloring, and eventually decaying. Weathering should not have such adverse effects if the right wood is used.

Some woods are naturally decay resistant. The heartwood in these species contains natural extractives that inhibit the growth of fungi and insects. Table 4-1 categorizes many hardwoods and softwoods according to their resistance to decay. A species high in natural resistance—for example, redwood—would be a much better choice as a fence post than would a less resistant species—say, white pine. But if the white pine was treated with a chemical preservative, its life as a fence post would be greatly lengthened. So, you have two choices of wood for outside projects—naturally resistant woods and treated woods. Let's first look at the naturally resistant woods, then at those which can be treated.

TABLE 4-1: COMPARATIVE RESISTANCE OF HEARTWOOD TO DECAY

Resistant or Very Resistant	Moderately Resistant	Slightly or Nonresistant
Bald cypress (old growth)	Bald cypress (young growth)	Alder
Catalpa	Douglas fir	Ashes
Cedars	Honeylocust**	Aspens
Cherry, black	Larch, western	Basswood
Chestnut	Oak, swamp chestnut	Beech
Cypress, Arizona	Pine, eastern white	Birches
Junipers	Pine, longleaf	Buckeye**
Locust, black*	Pine, slash	Butternut
Mesquite	Tamarack	Cottonwood
Mulberry, red*		Elms
Oak, bur		Hackberry
Oak, chestnut		Hemlocks
Oak, Gambel		Hickories
Oak, Oregon white		Magnolia
Oak, post		Maples
Oak, white		Oak (red and black species)**
Osage-orange*		Pines (most other species)**
Redwood		Poplar
Sassafras		Spruces
Walnut, black		Sweetgum**
Yew, Pacific		Sycamore
		Willows
		Yellow poplar

*These woods have exceptionally high decay resistance.
**These species, or certain species within the groups shown, have higher decay resistance than most of the other woods in their respective categories.

Fig. 4-1: This wood deck is an example of the outdoor uses for weather and decay resistant lumber.

REDWOOD, CEDAR AND CYPRESS

Of the species listed in Table 4-1 as being resistant or very resistant to decay, only three are economically feasible for outdoor uses. Some, like the white oak or black walnut, are valued for decorative uses and as such are far too expensive. Other woods listed in this category are not available commercially in most areas. The three species most commonly used when durability is demanded are redwood, cedar, and bald cypress.

The durability of these three are rated according to their ability to resist deterioration. Table 4-2 compares these with other woods commonly used for construction from the standpoint of their resistance to decay, to termite infestation, and to effects of weathering.

The heartwood of two—redwood and cypress—can resist all three of these despoilers. Cedar is rated high in resistance to decay and weather erosion but is not termite resistant. Given the distinctive color, texture, and grain characteristics of redwood, it is probably the most popular of the three.

Redwood

For 500 miles along the Pacific Coast from southwestern Oregon to a point just south of California's Big Sur, the lofty California redwood grows. This tallest of all living things hugs the foggy, mountainous coastline in disconnected groves and forests that rarely stretch inland for more than 30 miles. This evergreen is so in need of moisture that the fog is actually a clue to the redwood's whereabouts.

This coastal redwood is often confused with its high mountain relative, the Sierra redwood, although they differ in several ways. The Sierra, for example, is much heftier, but shorter than the coastal variety. It lives longer, grows at higher altitudes and the species is almost entirely protected within parks and reserves in the Sierra Nevada Mountains. The coastal redwood, on the other hand, is much taller (one specimen soars to 367.8'); it is rarely found above 3,000' elevation and yields one of the world's best performing and most naturally beautiful building materials.

Commercial redwood forests yield an endless supply of building materials. After harvesting, the red-

TABLE 4-2: DURABILITY COMPARISON OF WOODS COMMONLY USED FOR CONSTRUCTION

	Durability of Heartwood		Weather Resistance		
	Decay Resistance	**Termite Resistance**	**Tendency to Weather Check**	**Tendency to Cup and Pull Nails Loose**	**Volumetric Shrinkage to 10% Moisture Content**
Redwood	high	resistant	inconspicuous	slight	4.5
Bald cypress	high	resistant	inconspicuous	slight	7.0
Western red cedar	high	nonresistant	inconspicuous	slight	4.5
Douglas fir	moderate to low	nonresistant	conspicuous	distinct	7.9
Pine western white	moderate to low	nonresistant	conspicuous	distinct	7.9
eastern white	moderate to low	nonresistant	conspicuous	distinct	5.5
ponderosa	moderate to low	resistant	conspicuous	distinct	6.4
southern yellow	moderate to low	resistant (very resinous heartwood only)	conspicuous	distinct	8.2
sugar	moderate to low	nonresistant	conspicuous	distinct	5.3
Sitka spruce	moderate to low	nonresistant	conspicuous	distinct	7.7
Western hemlock	moderate to low	nonresistant	conspicuous	distinct	8.0

wood bounces back like no other tree in the world. The coastal redwood reproduces by seeding *and* by sprouting from the stump and root system of the parent tree—something no other commercial softwood can do. In fact, it is not unusual to find three to five, and sometimes more, mature redwoods growing from a single aged stump. This characteristic has led the Society of American Foresters to estimate that there are more coastal redwoods in existence today than when logging first began. And once a seedling or sprout is on its way, it proves that redwood is the fastest growing commercial softwood in the United States, producing more board feet per acre per year than any other species. Producing seedlings has been refined to a science. Redwood farms such as the one in Fig. 4-2 are producing thousands of new trees. The growth of young redwood trees in commercial forests has doubled since World War II and is expected to double again by the year 2001. There is evidently no danger of exhausting the supply of redwood in the foreseeable future.

If the redwood forests and the harvesting and manufacturing processes seem remarkable, so too is the end product: California redwood lumber. Redwood's unique natural characteristics assure outstanding performance for widely varied building conditions and distinctive designs—from industrial storage tanks and cooling towers to fine interior paneling, trim and cabinetry, exterior siding and fascia, and rugged landscape and outdoor living structures (Fig. 4-3); from decks, fences, and planters to hot tubs and garden shelters.

Fig. 4-3: A deck constructed with California redwood.

Natural extractives give redwood heartwood outstanding resistance to decay and insects, while redwood's lack of pitch or resins and open cellular structure enhance its workability for sawing, nailing, and machining to almost any degree of detail; a wide variety of stains and paints also performs well on redwood.

Table 4-3 compares average physical properties of clear redwood with a number of other species. In physical strength properties, redwood ranks equal to or above many western woods in various categories, while falling below the strength values of coastal Douglas fir and southern pines. Although the hardness of redwood is somewhat higher than would be expected of a wood of its weight, its shock resistance is somewhat lower. Overall, redwood is well qualified for construction purposes, although its price usually restricts it to applications demanding resistance to decay and weathering.

Grades of Redwood. Redwood lumber is graded by appearance and durability, with criteria defined by grading rules of the Redwood Inspection Service. Figure 4-4 illustrates redwood grade stamps. These stamps give the grade name, the amount of seasoning, and the symbol of the authorized grading agency. The CRA trademark is only on products of member mills of the California Redwood Association.

Fig. 4-2: Raising redwood trees is a thriving farm enterprise on the West Coast.

Fig. 4-4: The California Redwood Association/Redwood Inspection Service stamps of quality.

TABLE 4-3: AVERAGE PROPERTIES OF CLEAR REDWOOD COMPARED WITH A NUMBER OF OTHER SPECIES

Commercial species	Trees tested	Specific gravity, oven-dry, based on volume when green	Weight per cubic foot		Composite strength values				
			Green	At 12 percent moisture content	Bending strength	Compressive strength (endwise)	Stiffness	Hardness	Shock resistance
1	2	3	4	5	9	10	11	12	13
	Number		Pounds	Pounds	Percent	Percent	Percent	Percent	Percent
Cedar, Port Orford*	14	0.40	36	29	99	87	123	89	122
Cedar, eastern red*	5	.44	37	33	81	84	58	150	175
Cedar, western red*	15	.31	27	23	72	72	79	70	80
Cedar, northern white*	5	.29	28	22	60	50	57	56	72
Cypress, southern*	26	.42	50	32	95	89	99	96	117
Douglas fir (Coast type)	34	.45	38	34	108	104	132	109	125
Douglas fir (Rocky Mountain type)	10	.40	35	30	90	81	104	96	103
Fir, lowland white	10	.37	44	28	87	80	114	80	111
Fir, noble	9	.35	30	26	89	74	109	72	105
Fir, silver	6	.35	36	27	84	74	107	69	108
Fir, white	20	.35	47	26	87	71	93	78	92
Firs, white (average of four species)	45	.35	41	26	87	74	103	76	102
Hemlock, western	18	.38	41	29	89	82	105	93	112
Pine, loblolly	10	.50	54	38	112	101	121	115	143
Pine, longleaf	34	.55	50	41	128	119	138	141	158
Pine, northern white	18	.34	36	25	76	65	87	65	85
Pine, short leaf	12	.49	51	38	117	101	124	126	171
Pine, sugar	9	.35	51	25	77	66	82	70	85
Pine, western white	14	.36	35	27	83	73	100	65	100
Pine, ponderosa	31	.38	45	28	78	67	82	76	89
Redwood*	16	.39	52	28	100	100	100	100	100
Spruce, Sitka	25	.37	33	28	87	73	105	81	117

*Naturally resistant species.

Appearance. Excellence of appearance, clearness, and freedom from knots are the determinants for the highest grades. Other grades are categorized by number, size, and nature of knots, and other characteristics that may occur in each piece of lumber.

Durability. For durability—resistance against insects and decay—redwood is graded by its color and other factors. Reddish-brown heartwood from the inner portion of the tree contains extractives that render it resistant.

The cream-colored sapwood that develops in the outer growth layer of the tree, like most whitewood, does not possess the heartwood's resistance to decay and insects. Lumber containing streaks of both sapwood and heartwood is often preferred, however, for visual interest where durability is not a factor.

The all-heartwood grades are Clear All Heart, Select Heart, Construction Heart, and Merchantable Heart. Grades containing sapwood are Clear, B Grade, Select, Construction Common, and Merchantable. Table 4-4 describes each grade and gives common uses for each.

Cedar

Second only to redwood among decay resistant species are the cedar trees. Actually, there are no true cedars native to North America, but since the early explorers gave these trees the name cedar, we will not break with tradition here. There are several different cedar trees in North America. The more familiar names are northern white cedar, western red cedar, Port Orford cedar, California incense cedar, eastern red cedar, and Atlantic white cedar. The two most familiar, if for no other reasons than their greater range and availability, are the western red cedar and the eastern red cedar.

The western red cedar and the eastern red cedar are not closely related aside from their names. The western red cedar is related to the northern white cedar, and the eastern red cedar is a member of the juniper family. Of the two, the western red cedar is the larger and is one of the four most important timber trees of

TABLE 4-4: REDWOOD LUMBER GRADES AND USES

Heartwood Grades

Grade	Description	Uses
Clear All Heart	Finest architectural heartwood grade, normally kiln-dried, (also available unseasoned), well manufactured, free of defects one face (reverse may have slight imperfections). Surfaced or saw-textured.	Siding, paneling, trim, cabinetry, moulding, fascia, soffits, millwork. Also fine decks, hot tubs, garden structures.
Select Heart	A tight-knotted heartwood grade resistant to insects and decay, with face free of splits or shake. It is suitable for high quality construction without waste. Usually unseasoned. This durable grade is available surfaced or rough.	Decks, posts, garden structures, curbing, retaining walls, industrial uses, farm structures.
Construction Heart	A heartwood grade containing knots of varying sizes and other slight imperfections. Usually unseasoned, (also available seasoned). This highly useful grade can be ordered surfaced or rough.	Decks, posts, retaining walls, fences, garden structures, stairs, or other outdoor uses, especially on or near soil.
Merchantable Heart	This economical heartwood grade allows slightly larger knots than construction grades, holes limited to size of knots. Allows checks, some splits, and some manufacturing flaws. Unseasoned, surfaced, or rough.	Fences, retaining walls, garden structures, especially on or near soil.

Sapwood Grades

Grade	Description	Uses
Clear	Same general quality as Clear All Heart except contains sapwood in varying amounts. Normally kiln-dried (also available unseasoned). Some imperfections not permitted in Clear All Heart. Available surfaced or saw-textured.	Siding, paneling, trim, cabinetry, moulding, fascia, soffits. Also quality decking, garden shelters, and other aboveground outdoor applications.
B Grade	Quality grade containing sapwood limited knots and other characteristics not permitted in Clear All Heart and Clear. Available kiln-dried or unseasoned. This grade can be surfaced or saw-textured.	Siding, paneling, fascia, moulding, and other architectural uses. Quality decking, garden shelters, and other aboveground outdoor applications.
Select	Same general characteristics as Select Heart, but contains sapwood in varying amounts, some imperfections on the back side not permitted in Select Heart. Usually unseasoned. This economical grade is available surfaced or rough.	Decking, fence boards, garden structures, and other aboveground uses where durability is not a factor.
Construction Common	Same general characteristics as Construction Heart, but permits sapwood in varying amounts. Unseasoned or seasoned, it can be surfaced or rough. Also available saw-textured.	Unseasoned—decking, fence boards, and other aboveground garden uses that do not require heartwood's insect and decay resistance. Seasoned—rustic sidings.
Merchantable	Has same characteristics as Merchantable Heart, but contains sapwood in varying amounts. This economical grade is available unseasoned, can be ordered surfaced or rough.	Fence boards, railings, and other aboveground outdoor and garden uses. Also subflooring, and temporary construction.

the Pacific Northwest, ranging from Alaska to California and from the Pacific to Montana. It grows to a height of 150' to 200', occasionally reaching 250' high and 18-1/2' in diameter. The older trees are estimated to be 700 to 1,000 years old.

The western red cedar gets its name from its cinnamon-red bark. The wood is also reddish brown when it is first cut and has an aromatic smell. The lightweight wood is soft and brittle and not particularly strong, as you can see in Table 4-3. The wood has a medium to coarse grain texture and is free of pitch; thus, it is easy to work. There is very little shrinkage, swelling, or warping in the wood. Paints, varnish, and lacquers adhere to it readily. The wood also glues easily.

The eastern red cedar, covering most of the eastern half of the United States, is much smaller and grows much slower than its western namesake. It ordinarily reaches a height of only 20' to 50' and a girth of 1' to 2' in diameter. It is noted not only for its decay resistance but for its fragrant aroma and moth repellant properties. The wood is heavier than most other cedars, a fact that is responsible for its finer texture and higher composite strength values than those of the western red cedar.

Eastern red cedar has the excellent dimensional stability and easy workability common to cedars. Cedars find application as shingles, exterior siding, interior paneling, sashes and doors, greenhouse furniture (Fig. 4-5), ship and boat construction, boxes, crates, poles, and posts. Its longevity qualifies it for any outdoor project you might have in mind.

Fig. 4-5: The potting tables in this greenhouse were constructed of red cedar.

A popular application of cedar is in exterior siding and roofing, especially in the form of shingles and shakes (Fig. 4-6). Shingles and shakes are made by sawing or splitting a block of cedar into thin rectangular slabs. These slabs placed in overlapping rows act as a sluice to remove rainfall, add to the structural strength of wall or roof, and last for decades without any maintenance.

Fig. 4-6: Cedar shingles used as roofing and siding.

In fact, cedar shakes and shingles weather so well that they are left unfinished. As the cedar weathers, it changes color. In moist areas of the country the first stage is darkening of the wood; in time this trend reverses and the wood gradually bleaches to a soft gray. The weathered effect will not be uniform. It will vary on different sides of the building, depending upon the amount of light and moisture to which the wood is exposed. In drier climates, unfinished cedar will gradually turn tan and then pass through progressively lighter shades of tan. Numerous cedar buildings that have never had a finish application are in good condition after 150 to 200 years of exposure.

Cypress

Another wood high in durability properties is the bald or southern cypress (Fig. 4-7). This tree is less familiar than the redwood or cedar, preferring the dark water of southern swamps and riverbeds to the plains, hills, and mountains, Covered by Spanish moss, the cypress conveys an air of tropical splendor. The three remaining species of cypress in North America seem determined not to be extinguished. In fact, the oldest living thing on earth is believed to be a cypress tree, which is estimated to be between 5,000 and 7,000 years old, at Rio del Tulle, Mexico. It is this kind of durability that makes cypress valuable as a lumber product.

Fig. 4-7: Bald cypress trees have a natural resistance to decay and weathering.

Cypress trees are found from Delaware to Texas and northward up the Mississippi to southern Indiana and Illinois. Most virgin forests have been cut, and the trees that now stand average 100' to 150' in height and measure 5' to 15' in diameter.

Cypress wood is so decay resistant that it has been called "the wood eternal." But aside from being naturally decay resistant, the wood of the cypress is moderate in weight, strength, and hardness. From Table 4-3 you can see that cypress ranks closer to redwood in structural properties than any of the cedars. Yet, it is less stable dimensionally than most cedars mentioned. Cypress contains no resin ducts and is easily worked. It feels slightly waxy when cut and has a peculiar swampy odor.

In spite of their high level of resistance to decay and insect attack, cypress trees are susceptible to a type of heart-decay fungus which fills the heartwood with holes. Lumber cut from such wood is known as *pecky cypress* and is valued in interior paneling.

Cypress wood finds use today as shingles, exterior siding, interior paneling, and in the construction of coffins, tanks, vats, ships, greenhouses, stadium seats, boxes, and crates. You can use it anywhere you desire without fear of decay.

TREATED WOOD

The same decomposers that attack dead trees in the forest will ruin every piece of wood you place outside unless you practice some simple conservation. Decomposition can be prevented by eliminating any of the four elements necessary for the growth of fungi: moisture, favorable temperatures, oxygen, and food.

Fungi exist best in a temperature range of 75°F to 90°F. Unfortunately, that is the comfort range for humans, as well. Below 40°F and above 105°F, fungi development ceases. Temperature control is not a practical means of preserving outdoor wood projects.

By minimizing the moisture content of lumber, you can greatly reduce the possibility of decay damage. When wood has a moisture content of approximately 30%, the cell walls are saturated with water and the cell cavities are empty (full of air). Given the proper temperature, this is the ideal condition for fungal development. To avoid this situation, lumber is dried to a moisture content below 20%, at which point there is insufficient moisture for fungi to exist. Sheltering the wood in a relatively dry environment maintains this moisture content level and prevents decay. Your backyard probably gets more than enough precipitation to encourage fungal growth. Wood that is in contact with the soil or that suffers continuous wetting from rain seepage, splashing, plumbing leaks, and condensation is prime decay material.

Too much moisture can be just as unhealthy for the fungus plant as too little. The little decomposers drown if submerged in water; they need oxygen to survive. Wooden ships that sank hundreds of years ago are still sound due to the fact that decay causing fungi cannot survive underwater. Obviously, drowning the fungi is not the solution to your problem.

Fungi also need food; that's where your wood may come in. Sapwood, with its storage cells full of carbohydrates, is a fungal delicacy. For this reason, untreated sapwood—even that of a decay resistant species—is never recommended in applications where the wood makes contact with the ground.

The heartwood of many species contains varying amounts of extractives that are toxic or repellent to fungi. The use of such wood was discussed earlier in this chapter. Unless you use a wood high in decay resistance, do not place untreated wood out-of-doors (especially in contact with the ground).

Aside from naturally resistant species, pressure-treated lumber is the only way to beat decay. Your local lumber company or home center carries a complete line of pressure treated products in anything from 2 × 4's to timbers. The housing industry requires pressure treated lumber for sills, plates, and furring strips in contact with masonry foundations or fascia, and all-weather wood foundations. Treated lumber finds application in marinas, houseboats, bridges, bleacher seats, open decks, tanks, cooling towers, and pole frame buildings, to name just a few examples. The same lumber is available to you for sandboxes, cold frames, planter boxes, fences (Fig. 4-8), lawn furniture, dog houses, and many other outdoor projects.

Types of Preservatives

Wood preservatives are not a new innovation. Pitch is similar to the creosote used today to seal telephone poles, railroad ties, and marina installations (piers, docks, etc). Both are derived from the distillation of

Fig. 4-8: Treated lumber finds popular application in fences.

coal tar. Today, additional means of wood preservation are available. The two most common are pentachlorophenol and chromated copper arsenite (CCA).

Creosote. Creosote, the oldest of wood preservatives, is familiar to most people. For decades, telephone poles have been coated with creosote.

But creosote is messy to handle, has a repugnant odor, and is toxic to plants that come in contact with it. Wood coated with it can't be painted and for a few days after the creosote is applied, it is easily ignited. So, freshly coated lumber which is creosote treated is seldom used around the house. The undesirable qualities dissipate with time. Discarded railroad ties or telephone poles can be purchased and used as flower borders, retaining walls, stairways, etc.

Pentachlorophenol. A more recent development in preservatives is a petroleum-based solution called pentachlorophenol. Some "penta" solutions are borne in heavy oil; others in lighter volatile oils. Penta preservatives are not as messy to handle and some of the lighter oil-based solutions may be painted. But pentachlorophenol tends to leach out of the wood, poisoning any plants around it. Wood treated this way also has ill effects on animals. It can't safely be used as either planting boxes or feed boxes until the leaching ceases. Penta lumber ranges in color from light brown to black, depending on the type of carrier oil.

Waterborne Salt-Type Preservatives. The most common waterborne preservative is chromated copper arsenite (CCA). You will probably find that lumber treated with CCA is the best choice for use around the house. Such wood is leach resistant, is not toxic to plants, has no increased combustibility, has no odor, has no messy surface residues, can be painted and glued, and is relatively low in cost.

Without worry, use it for anything from wood foundations to tree houses, or from raised gardens (Fig. 4-9) to picket gates. It will outlast most other treated

wood. In fact, one major chemical preservative company is now issuing a 30-year guarantee on its CCA treated wood products.

Traditionally, most pressure treated woods had a greenish color. Today, some manufacturers are featuring a so-called "cedar tone" which gives the wood a reddish cedar color.

Fig. 4-9: Pressure treated timbers can be used for garden borders and retaining walls.

Methods of Preserving Wood

The key to preserving wood is penetration. The wood will be protected only as deeply as the preservatives penetrate. To ensure the deepest penetration, most lumber treated with CCA is pressure treated. Less satisfactory methods are brushing and dipping. Usually, a combination of pressure treated lumber and brush applications is necessary in any project requiring treated lumber.

Pressure Treatments. To maximize the life of treated lumber, chemical preservatives are forced deep into the wood under pressure. This process takes place in a heavy steel pressure vessel such as that shown in Fig. 4-10. Pressures up to 180 pounds per square inch are used to force the chemical solution into the wood cells. There a reaction takes place with the wood sugars which results in an insoluble bond between the chemicals and the wood.

Coating Method. Most projects require some cutting of the lumber to size. When you cut pressure treated lumber, cutting will expose the untreated interior. These exposed areas undermine the effectiveness of the treatment and will allow decay to invade

Fig. 4-10: Lumber is treated with preservatives in a large cylindrical vessel.

Fig. 4-11: A typical AWPB quality mark.

the lumber. This danger is especially acute if the cut portion is butted to another piece in a joint. Moisture will be trapped in the joint, evaporation will be inhibited, absorption prolonged, and the decay process accelerated. To avoid such problems, coat the cut with a preservative. Brush or spray it on or dip the wood in the chemical. At least two coats should be applied, the second after the first is completely dried. Preservatives may be purchased from most hardware stores and building supply companies that sell other types of wood finishes.

Do not depend on coating, though, to do the whole job of preserving your wood. Coating does not impregnate the wood as pressure treatments do; it only covers it, and this covering will eventually leach off. When treated wood is necessary, buy it treated. The little you save by doing it yourself may eventually result in a big loss.

Quality Marks

The American Wood-Preservers Bureau (AWPB) has established the standards whereby lumber and plywood are pressure treated with preservatives. The AWPB quality mark is patterned after the lumber grade mark system. The AWPB quality mark on each piece of pressure-treated lumber and plywood is the consumer's assurance that the treatment complies with established standards. A typical AWPB quality mark is given and explained in Fig. 4-11.

FIRE-RETARDANT TREATED LUMBER

Fire-retardant treated lumber has been pressure treated to reduce the spread of flames and the rate of combustion. Chemicals forced into the wood will ignite at temperatures slightly below the ignition point of wood. As the chemicals burn, they release noncombustible vapors and produce a char on the surface of the wood that insulates the wood from the flames and reduces the amount of smoke and toxic fumes released by the fire.

While fire-retardant treatment of lumber does not change the color of the wood appreciably, a whitish powder will sometimes appear on the surface. This residue should be removed by light sanding before applying paint, stains, varnish, or sealers. Water-based paints or finishes should not be used on fire-retardant treated material. Fire-retardant treated material is so hard that carbide-tipped tools are required to work with it.

Fire-retardant treated lumber is used in construction as studs, plates, trusses, rafters, joists, roof decking, trim, paneling, and in other applications beyond the scope of this book. Not only is fire-retardant treated lumber available, but hardboard and plywood treated this way are also available. Such wood is used most often in commercial buildings where building codes require it. The average homeowner seldom has need for it.

WEATHER AND DECAY RESISTANT WOOD PROJECTS

The following projects can be constructed with either naturally resistant lumber—redwood, cedar, cypress—or pressure treated lumber. Although you will initially pay more for this kind of wood, the long life of your project will more than pay for itself. Make sure you understand each instruction before beginning actual construction.

Outdoor Utility Table

The small utility table shown here is an attractive outdoor project. Place it in your backyard or garden, or on your patio or deck; use it to display flowering plants or to hold a portable TV set. It makes a great snack table for outdoor barbecues and picnics.

After cutting the pieces to size and shape, assemble the feet around the bottom of the post. Predrill and nail as shown.

For the tabletop, predrill the face nail holes in both ends of the tabletop border pieces and nail the table border together. Space the remaining three interior pieces 1/4" apart, predrill, and nail.

Predrill two nail holes in both the 26° and 64° tapered ends of the four gussets to prevent splitting the tapered ends when nailing into the post and tabletop. Check the position of these holes which face the tabletop to make sure that the nails won't penetrate the tabletop when driven in.

Invert the tabletop on a flat, solid surface and place the top of the post (the end without the feet) in the center of the tabletop. Then, arrange the gussets symmetrically with the 90° angle at the intersection of the post and tabletop. While a helper holds the post in a plumb position, drive nails through the predrilled holes of the gussets into the undersurface of the tabletop. Complete the project by nailing the gussets to the post, again through predrilled holes.

MATERIALS LIST FOR OUTDOOR UTILITY TABLE

Quantity	Description
3	2" × 4" × 8'
1	4" × 4" × 25-1/2"
1 lb	10d galvanized nails

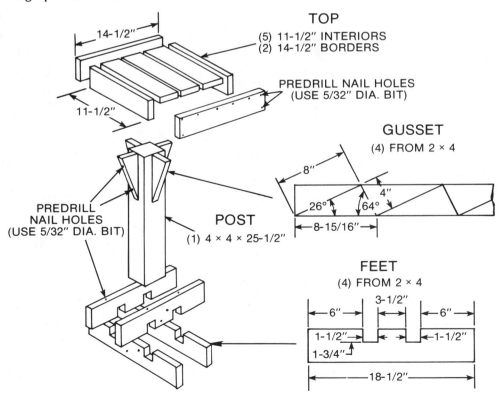

TOP
(5) 11-1/2" INTERIORS
(2) 14-1/2" BORDERS

14-1/2"
11-1/2"

PREDRILL NAIL HOLES
(USE 5/32" DIA. BIT)

GUSSET
(4) FROM 2 × 4

8"
4"
26° 64°
8-15/16"

PREDRILL
NAIL HOLES
(USE 5/32" DIA. BIT)

POST
(1) 4 × 4 × 25-1/2"

FEET
(4) FROM 2 × 4

3-1/2"
6"   6"
1-1/2"   1-1/2"
1-3/4"
18-1/2"

EXPLODED VIEW

Post Lamp

This post lamp can brighten your yard, deck, or entryway. Obtain the materials listed here and cut them to the sizes indicated. Make sure you understand the drawings and instructions before beginning actual construction. Follow the photos as you build.

MATERIALS LIST FOR POST LAMP

Quantity	Description
2	2" × 6" × 8'
2	2" × 3" × 8'
1	2" × 2" × 12'
1	1" × 3" × 5'
2	1/2" × 4" × 7'
2	1" × 4" × 8'
1	1" × 1" × 3'
1	2" × 12" × 1'
—	3d nails
—	5d nails

CUT SIZES FOR POST LAMP

2 × 6	2 pcs.	8' post sides
2 × 2-3/8	2 pcs.	8' post fillers
2 × 2	4 pcs.	2'8"
1 × 3	2 pcs.	1'4"
1 × 3	4 pcs.	5-1/2"
1/2 × 4	28 pcs.	5-1/2" louvers
1 × 4	8 pcs.	22-1/2" louver sides
1 × 1	4 pcs.	22-1/2"
1 × 6	4 pcs.	7" tops of louvers
2 × 10	1 pc.	9-1/2" sq. top of lamp

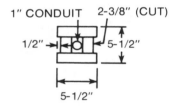

PLAN OF LIGHT POST

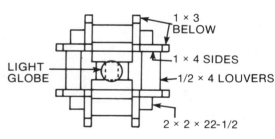

PLAN AT LAMP

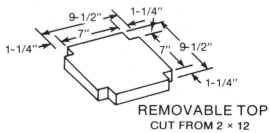

REMOVABLE TOP
CUT FROM 2 × 12

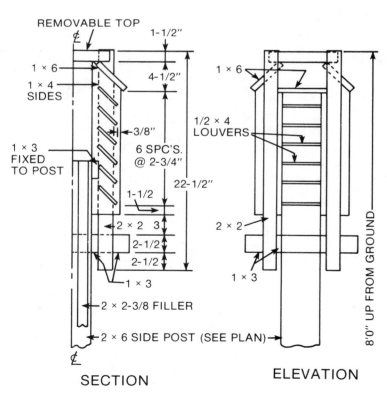

SECTION

ELEVATION

Spacing lines are marked and louvers are nailed to sides of four units.

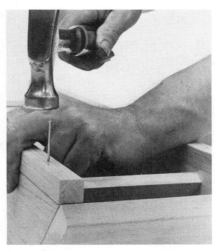

Filler strips of 1 × 1's are nailed to inside edges of two louver units.

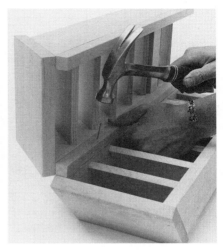

Filler strips are used to secure units to each other, aligned carefully.

Placing fourth unit requires careful nailing to assure lamp fits over post.

Lengths of 2 × 2's, 22-1/2" long, are toenailed into four corners formed by louver units.

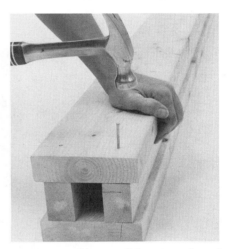

Lamp post, fabricated from 2 × 6's and filler pieces cut to 2-3/8", holds wire conduit.

Collar of 1 × 3's at top of post; 1 × 3 strips below help hold lamp assembly in place.

Lamp assembly is slipped over top of post; 2 × 2's are toenailed to 1 × 3 strips.

Removable top cut from 2 × 12, with corners notched, fits snugly into 2 × 2's.

Planter Boxes

Sometimes the simplest materials and techniques make the most appealing projects—as with the large planter box shown at right. Ordinary framing lumber and tongue and groove flooring are all you need. The metal liner shown in the exploded view is optional. Two or three coats of a good epoxy paint will protect the wood and seal the seams just as efficiently.

To make the large planter box, begin by nailing the 2 × 6 flooring to the three 2 × 2 cleats. Cut the tongue and groove boards 33" long to accommodate the side pieces. Next, nail 1' pieces of 2 × 2 to the 2 × 10 and 2 × 8 side boards. Miter the ends of each side and join with 8d nails. Nail sides to the floor. After the sides are joined, two 2 × 2's are added at each corner for a finished look.

Two other simple planter boxes are shown in following illustrations. The materials for all three planters are given in the materials list.

MATERIALS LIST FOR PLANTER BOXES

Quantity	Description
	Large Planter
1	2" × 10" × 12' lumber
1	2" × 8" × 12' lumber
1	2" × 6" × 12' T&G flooring
1	2" × 6" × 8' T&G flooring
6	2" × 2" × 10' lumber
6	8d galvanized nails
—	16d galvanized nails
—	finishing material
	Small Planter
1	2" × 8" × 12' lumber
1	3/4" × 13" × 13" exterior-type plywood
1	2" × 2" × 6" lumber
4	5/16" × 14-1/2" threaded rods
8	5/16" hex bolts to fit rod
8	5/16" dia. washers
—	finishing material
	Hexagonal Planter
6	2" × 2" × 12' lumber
1	2" × 2" × 8' lumber
1	3/4" × 24-3/4" × 30" exterior-type plywood
6	5/16" × 12" threaded rods
12	5/16" hex bolts to fit rod
12	5/16" dia. washers
—	finishing material

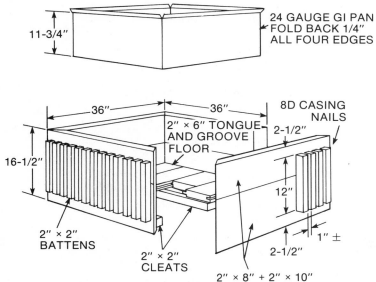

24 GAUGE GI PAN
FOLD BACK 1/4"
ALL FOUR EDGES

11-3/4"

36"   36"

8D CASING
NAILS

2" × 6" TONGUE
AND GROOVE
FLOOR

2-1/2"

16-1/2"

12"

2" × 2"
BATTENS

2" × 2"
CLEATS

2-1/2"

1" ±

2" × 8" + 2" × 10"

EXPLODED VIEW OF LARGE PLANTER

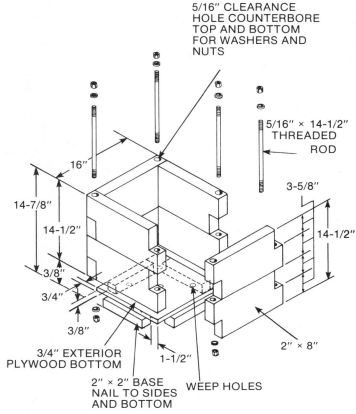

5/16" CLEARANCE
HOLE COUNTERBORE
TOP AND BOTTOM
FOR WASHERS AND
NUTS

5/16" × 14-1/2"
THREADED
ROD

16"

3-5/8"

14-7/8"

14-1/2"

14-1/2"

3/8"

3/4"

3/8"

3/4" EXTERIOR
PLYWOOD BOTTOM

2" × 2" BASE
NAIL TO SIDES
AND BOTTOM

1-1/2"

WEEP HOLES

2" × 8"

EXPLODED VIEW OF SMALL PLANTER

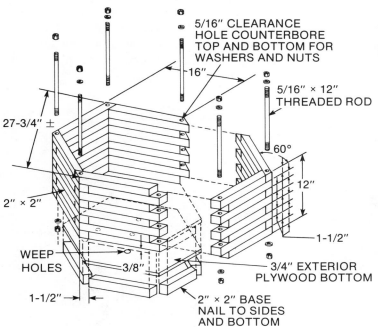

5/16" CLEARANCE
HOLE COUNTERBORE
TOP AND BOTTOM FOR
WASHERS AND NUTS

16"

5/16" × 12"
THREADED ROD

27-3/4" ±

60°

12"

2" × 2"

1-1/2"

WEEP
HOLES

3/8"

3/4" EXTERIOR
PLYWOOD BOTTOM

1-1/2"

2" × 2" BASE
NAIL TO SIDES
AND BOTTOM

EXPLODED VIEW OF HEXAGONAL PLANTER

Deck with Firepit

Here's a simply designed deck that provides the perfect spot for backyard entertaining. Equipped with a firepit and ringed with benches, it will provide years of enjoyment if built with treated or naturally resistant lumber. The materials you will need to buy and the proper sizes of each deck course, from the center out, are given for you. Study the accompanying drawings carefully before beginning.

Start by leveling a 10' × 10' area. Build the firepit in the middle of this area. The firepit has five courses of 4" × 4" × 16" concrete blocks. The girdle of mitered 2 × 6's is attached with carriage bolts. Set the 4 × 4 sleepers on a layer of 1-1/2"-minus gravel. After cutting the 2 × 4 deck courses to size, begin laying them starting with the course closest to the firepit. Toenail the decking to sleepers with 6d nails and face nail each one at the corners with 16d galvanized nails. Use pieces of 1/4" plywood to space each piece.

CUT SIZES FOR DECK

Treated 4 × 4 sleepers:

2 pcs. 10'	4 pcs. 4'6-1/2"
2 pcs. 3'	mitered 45°
4 pcs. 3'2-1/2"	4 pcs. 5-7/8"

2 × 4 deck courses from center out:

2 pcs. 3', 2 pcs. 3'3"
2 pcs. 3'3-3/4", 2 pcs. 3'6-3/4"
2 pcs. 3'7-3/8", 2 pcs. 3'10-3/8"
2 pcs. 3'11", 2 pcs. 4'2"
2 pcs. 4'2-3/4", 2 pcs. 4'5-3/4"
2 pcs. 4'6-1/4", 2 pcs. 4'9-1/4"
2 pcs. 4'9-7/8", 2 pcs. 5'7/8"
2 pcs. 5'1-5/8", 2 pcs. 5'4-5/8"
2 pcs. 5'5-1/8", 2 pcs. 5'8-1/8"
2 pcs. 5'8-7/8", 2 pcs. 5'11-7/8"
2 pcs. 6'3/8", 2 pcs. 6'3-3/8"
2 pcs. 6'4", 2 pcs. 6'7-1/4"
2 pcs. 6'7-3/4", 2 pcs. 6'10-7/8"
2 pcs. 11-3/8", 2 pcs. 7'2-3/8"
2 pcs. 7'3-1/8", 2 pcs. 7'6-1/8"
2 pcs. 7'6-3/4", 2 pcs. 7'9-3/4"
2 pcs. 7'10-3/8", 2 pcs. 8'1-3/8"
2 pcs. 8'2", 2 pcs. 8'1-3/8"
2 pcs. 8'2", 2 pcs. 8'5"
2 pcs. 8'5-5/8", 2 pcs. 8'8-5/8"
2 pcs. 8'9-3/8", 2 pcs. 9'3/8"
12 pcs. 9'3/8"

Finish the deck by constructing the benches and the cover/table for the firepit. The bench shown in this project is suitable for deck, lawn, or garden. It is easily built and will last years if built with treated or naturally resistant lumber. Follow the sequence of photos that illustrates construction of the bench.

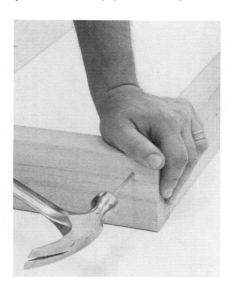

MATERIALS LIST FOR DECK WITH FIREPIT

Quantity	Description	Quantity	Description	Quantity	Description
	Deck		**Benches**		**Firepit**
4	4" × 4" × 10' (sleepers)	5	4" × 4" × 8'	40	4" × 4" × 16" concrete
1	4" × 4" × 8' (sleepers)	20	2" × 4" × 10'		blocks
1	4" × 4" × 14' (sleepers)	10	2" × 4" × 14'	—	bag mortar
13	2" × 4" × 8' (decking)	2	2" × 4" × 12'	4	2" × 6" × 3' 3-1/8"
17	2" × 4" × 10' (decking)	1	2" × 4" × 10'		mitered both ends
8	2" × 4" × 12' (decking)	20	3/8" × 7" carriage bolts,	8	3/8" × 6" carriage bolts,
8	2" × 4" × 14' (decking)		nuts, and washers		nuts, and washers
8	2" × 4" × 16' (decking)	—	6d galvanized nails		**Cover/Table**
—	6d galvanized nails	—	16d galvanized nails	16	2" × 2" × 8'
—	16d galvanized nails			1	2" × 2" × 4'
cubic yard	1-1/2"-minus gravel				

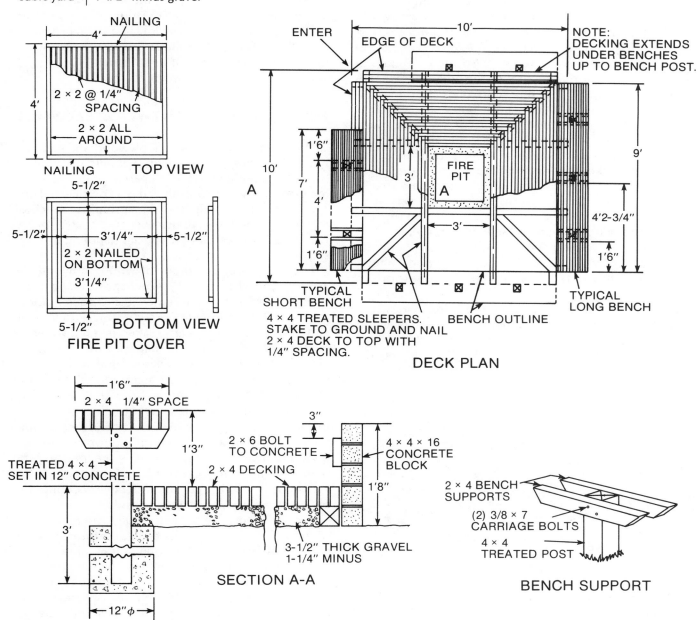

TOP VIEW

BOTTOM VIEW

FIRE PIT COVER

DECK PLAN

SECTION A-A

BENCH SUPPORT

CHAPTER
— 5 —

SOFTWOOD PLYWOOD

Plywood is strictly a modern 20th century wood product and is a valuable material for the home workshop as well as for general building purposes. Plywood is all wood and is made of several layers of veneers, or plies, glued together so that the grain of each layer is at right angles to the adjacent layers. A layer may consist of one or more plies. An odd number of layers is used (Fig. 5-1). The outer plies are called *faces*, and the inner plies are the *core*, which consists of a center and crossbands. The intermediate layers which run across the panel are called *crossbands*. This banding makes the panel strong along both the length and width of the panel and gives the material a greater dimensional stability and resistance to checking and splitting. The layers are usually arranged so that the surface grain pattern runs the length of the panel. In addition to strength and wear qualities, plywood has the great advantage of size over ordinary wood. Sheets are made in standard 4' widths and lengths from 6' to 12'.

The outer faces of the plywood are made from softwood or hardwood. Common hardwood plywood comes with an exterior face of oak, walnut, elm, cherry, maple, birch, gum, teak, rosewood, or mahogany.

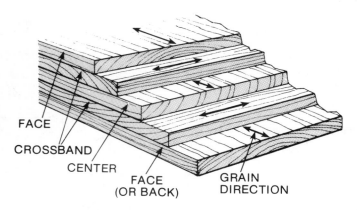

FACE

CROSSBAND

CENTER

FACE
(OR BACK)

GRAIN
DIRECTION

Fig. 5-1: Softwood plywood is made up of layers of wood veneers.

As described in this chapter, the most common softwood plywoods have a face of Douglas fir or southern pine. The better surface ply is called the *face veneer*. The other surface ply is called the *back veneer*. (Sometimes both surfaces are of equal quality.)

PRODUCTION OF SOFTWOOD PLYWOOD

The process of softwood plywood manufacture has six general steps: (1) peeling veneers, (2) trimming veneers, (3) veneer drying, (4) panel lay-up, (5) applying pressure, and (6) finishing. It is a complicated procedure, requiring skilled workmanship and precision machinery; and the unusual characteristics of the materials involved call for special handling at every step.

To produce veneer for the plywood, softwood logs are first sorted by length, wood species, and grade quality. Then, the bark is removed and *peeler blocks*, or *peeler logs* (8'4" long), are cut to fit into veneer-cutting lathes. The logs are soaked in a hot water vat or steamed to condition them for peeling. The peeler blocks are then rotated in a large lathe against a long knife blade which peels off a continuous ribbon of veneer in thicknesses ranging from 1/10" to 1/4".

From the lathe, the long sheets of veneer go through the automatic clipper, which consists of large blades that cut them to the width required for the ultimate plywood panels. Highly skilled is the person who regulates the cutting blades; his job is to scrutinize the veneer as it rolls by, cut out defective sections, and obtain as many clear sheets as possible.

Veneer sheets are then carefully dried in ovens where the wet wood is reduced to a uniform moisture content of less than 5% in only a few minutes. The next step is the *laying up* of panels on glue spreaders. These machines consist mainly of two huge steel or rubber rollers—resembling those on newspaper presses—which are covered with a liquid glue. As veneer is fed between the rollers, the adhesive is spread to a uniform coverage on both sides simultaneously. Then glue-carrying sheets are alternated with dry sheets to form panels of three or more plies.

The glued-up veneers, assembled into panels of odd numbers of layers, are placed in presses that make the veneers into plywood. These presses look much like giant accordions, stretched out and standing on one end. When the panels are in place between the openings, the plates of the machine come together under a pressure of 175 to 200 pounds to the square inch, while steam heat of 275° to 315°F pours through the plate walls to speed the bonding process. Pressing time is from four to 10 minutes, depending on panel thickness.

The plywood panels then come out of the presses for final trimming, sanding, grading, and preparation for shipment. The trimming is to precision dimensions and sanding is to exact thickness and satin smoothness.

There are many auxiliary operations along the assembly line. Most fascinating, perhaps, is the elimination of small knots and other blemishes in the veneer (Fig. 5-2). This is done by cutting them out and forcing into the openings boat-shaped patches which become, in effect, a part of the panel and which are not evident upon casual examination after the softwood plywood is manufactured.

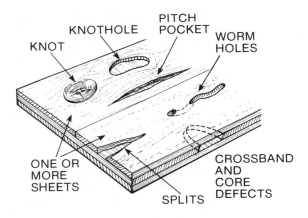

Fig. 5-2: Knots and other blemishes are eliminated in plywood veneers.

CHARACTERISTICS OF SOFTWOOD PLYWOOD

In addition to these qualities, softwood plywood has a number of properties that make possible its use for a wide variety of purposes where it must meet rigid tests of performance in everyday practice. Plywood has the characteristics outlined in the following paragraphs.

Strength. By actual test it has been proven that, pound for pound, plywood is stronger than solid steel. Because of the cross-ply lamination, plywood has great strength across the grain as well as lengthwise. This strength in both directions makes plywood a preferred product for covering large areas and for jobs which require maximum strength and minimum weight. As a general rule, the greater the density, the greater the strength. Maximum efficiency, however, is often obtained by using low density woods such as western pine as the center of the core, and high density woods such as Douglas fir, larch, and southern pine as faces. Highest strength-weight ratios are obtained in this manner.

Dimensional Stability. With approximately half of the wood grain in one direction and the other half at right angles, the tendency of wood to shrink or swell is counteracted and the panel is highly stable. Distortion because of moisture is at a minimum because the wood is carefully dried during the manufacturing process, making the moisture content as uniform as possible.

Resistance to Impact and Splitting. A prime factor in the use of plywood for many heavy-duty purposes is its resistance to splitting. The impact of a blow is dissipated over the entire area of the panel by its cross-grained construction. For the same reason, nails and screws can be placed in plywood, even near the edge of a panel, without causing the panel to split. Moreover, plywood has resiliency (ability to return to normal position after intermittent loads). For example, the only life raft which could withstand a 40' drop into the sea in military procedure tests was made of plywood; other materials buckled.

Smooth Surface. The manufacturing methods of cutting veneers and sanding plywood produce panels that have smooth surface without grain raise and which will readily take a final finish. Also, if abrasion resistance is a prerequisite, a plywood with a high density overlay can be used.

Workability. Plywood can be easily machined with ordinary woodworking tools. Its uniform texture and relative freedom from chipping and breaking make it ideal for the amateur craftsman as well as the professional carpenter. Wide panels save labor and money in prefabrication and assembly-line construction. Because plywood is stronger and lighter than conventional lumber, it is easier to handle than thicker and heavier lumber and can often accomplish the same task.

Product Standards

Most softwood plywood is produced according to the provisions of *United States Product Standard*

PS 1-74/ANSI A199.1 for Construction and Industrial Plywood. The plywood industry and the United States Department of Commerce developed PS 1 as a detailed specification of how plywood must be manufactured to qualify for grade marking. Therefore, with panels stamped with the PS 1 mark (Fig. 5-3), you can be assured that the plywood has been made in conformance with the minimum manufacturing requirements.

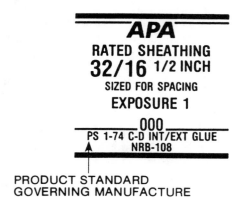

Fig. 5-3: The PS 1 mark is an assurance of quality.

APA Performance Standards

Today, most softwood plywood is manufactured by mills that are members of the American Plywood Association (APA). The grading rules and manufacturing standards used by APA were developed in cooperation with the federal government and prescribe panel characteristics for their usage.

APA rated panels are tested for *dimensional stability,* the product's resistance to expansion; *bond durability,* the ability of the adhesive system to retain bonding capability under adverse exposure; and *structural adequacy,* verification of the panel's ability to sustain uniform and concentrated static and impact loads, to hold fasteners, and to resist wall racking (distortion from its rectangular shape).

GRADES AND CLASSIFICATIONS

Many factors determine the grade of a softwood plywood panel. You'll need to be familiar with such subjects as veneer grades, group numbers, and exposure durability classifications in order to determine which panel would be best suited to your purpose. Once you have the basics down, you'll be able to refer to the tables given in this chapter and the grade stamps on plywood panels to confidently select the right panel for your particular project.

Veneer Grades

Veneer grade refers to the quality of the veneer used for the front and back. Veneer used for PS 1 plywood is graded on the basis of wood characteristics—knots, splits, and so on. The grade stamp will tell you the grade of veneer used for the face and back by the use of two capital letters (Fig. 5-4). The first refers to the panel face, the second refers to the back. The grades, in descending order of quality, are *N, A, B, C plugged, C,* and *D.* Table 5-1 lists various veneer grades and their specifications.

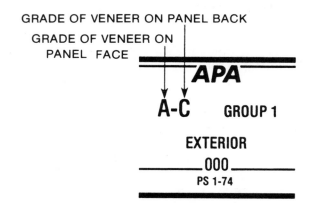

Fig. 5-4: The front and back faces of plywood are graded individually.

TABLE 5-1: SPECIFICATIONS OF VENEER GRADES

Grade	Specifications
N*	Very high quality appearance veneer. Smooth surface. All heartwood or all sapwood. Free of open defects, allowing no more than six repairs per (standard) panel. Repair patches of wood only, parallel to grain, and matched in grain and color.
A	Smooth and able to be painted with up to 18 neatly made repairs. May be used as natural finish in less demanding applications.
B	Solid surface. Minor splits, tight knots, and repair plugs permitted.
C plugged	Splits to 1/8" width, holes to 1/4" × 1/2", synthetic repairs, and some broken grain permitted.
C	Tight holes to 1-1/2" permitted. Knotholes to 1-1/2" if the total width of all knots and knotholes is within specified limits. Synthetic repairs, limited splits, and discoloration and sanding defects that do not impair strength allowed.
D	Knots and knotholes permitted to 2-1/2" across the grain, 3" under specified limits. Limited to interior-type panels.

*Not commonly available.

Plywood can be separated into two broad categories based on the intended use of the panels: construction quality panels and appearance quality panels. The first type is intended for applications where strength and durability are the main concern. As its name implies, construction grade plywood is typically used for construction jobs, such as sheathing and subflooring. Plywood of this type is normally unsanded since its intended usage does not require a smooth surface. In some instances, however, the panels are touch-sanded (lightly sanded) to make the panel thickness more uniform.

When the appearance of the panel is important, one or both of the face veneers will have a minimum of defects and will be sanded smooth. Normally, all grades with N, A, or B faces fall within this category. Sanded and touch-sanded panels possess nearly the structural properties of unsanded panels, but they have a more polished appearance. Even though these panels could be used as roof sheathing or subflooring, don't pay for appearance quality when you don't need it. Match grade with intended use when you buy plywood.

Group Numbers

Plywood is now manufactured from over 70 species of woods. These species are divided into five groups, with the strongest and stiffest in Group 1, the next strongest in Group 2, and so on. The American Plywood Association graded panels that do not have span ratings are given a group number from the weakest species used in the face and/or back ply (Fig. 5-5). Remember, the lower the number in the grade stamp, the stronger and stiffer the panel. Table 5-2 shows the classification of wood species.

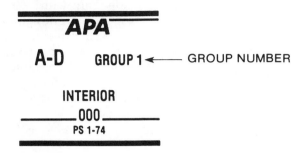

Fig. 5-5: The strength of a sheet of plywood depends on the species of wood used to make it.

Exposure Durability Classifications

The exposure durability classification on the grade stamp will tell you for what kind of conditions the plywood has been designed. The classification is based on the veneers, wood materials, adhesives and resin binders required in its production, and on the severity and duration of weather and moisture exposure the panel is designed to withstand.

Exposure durability is indicated in one of two ways on a grade stamp. If manufactured under PS 1 regu-

TABLE 5-2:   THE AMERICAN PLYWOOD ASSOCIATION'S CLASSIFICATION OF PLYWOOD BY GROUPS

Group 1	Group 2		Group 3	Group 4	Group 5
Apitong	Cedar, Port Orford	Maple, black	Alder, red	Aspen	Basswood
Beech, American	Cypress	Mengkulang	Birch, paper	bigtooth	Fir, balsam
Birch	Douglas fir 2*	Meranti, red	Cedar, Alaska	quaking	Poplar, balsam
sweet	Fir	Mersawa	Fir, subalpine	Cativo	
yellow	California red	Pine	Hemlock, eastern	Cedar	
Douglas fir 1*	grand	pond	Maple, bigleaf	incense	
Kapur	noble	red	Pine	western red	
Keruing	pacific silver	Virginia	jack	Cottonwood	
Larch, western	white	western white	lodgepole	eastern	
Maple, sugar	Hemlock, western	Spruce	ponderosa	black (western poplar)	
Pine	Lauan	red	spruce	Pine	
Caribbean	almon	Sitka	Redwood	eastern white	
ocote	bagtikan	Sweetgum	Spruce	sugar	
Pine, southern	mayapis	Tamarack	black		
loblolly	red lauan	Yellow poplar	Engelmann		
longleaf	tangile		white		
shortleaf	white lauan				
slash					
Tanoak					

*Douglas fir from trees grown in the states of Washington, Oregon, California, Idaho, Montana, Wyoming, and the Canadian Provinces of Alberta and British Columbia shall be classed as Douglas fir 1. Douglas fir from trees grown in the states of Nevada, Utah, Colorado, Arizona, and New Mexico shall be classed as Douglas fir 2.

lations, the panel will be labeled either *interior* or *exterior* (Fig. 5-6). Interior type plywood is recommended for use where no moisture will be present and the panels will be protected from the weather. Interior type plywood is almost always manufactured with moisture-resistant or waterproof exterior glue.

Exterior-type plywood is made *only* with 100% waterproof exterior glue and is specifically designed for use in permanently exposed applications. It is important that you never use interior-type plywood for exterior applications; but, remember that unless the project is going to be outside or in a moist area (such as a bath or laundry room), you can save money by purchasing interior-type plywood.

APA performance-rated panels are labeled as *Exterior, Exposure 1,* or *Exposure 2* (Fig. 5-7). Panels identified as Exterior are comparable to exterior-type panels under PS 1 and are designed for exterior

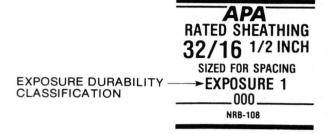

EXPOSURE DURABILITY ——→
CLASSIFICATION

Fig. 5-7: APA performance rated panels are labeled as Exterior, Exposure 1, or Exposure 2.

applications. Exposure 1 panels are intended for protected applications but can resist moisture and bad weather during construction delays. This type of panel is similar to interior panels with exterior glue. Exposure 2 panels are comparable to those designated as interior-type with intermediate glue under PS 1 and are, therefore, intended for protected applications. Table 5-3 summarizes panel exposure durability and appropriate uses.

Span Ratings

Span ratings indicate the maximum recommended center-to-center spacing of supports (in inches) over which a particular panel should be placed when used in construction. Center-to-center simply refers to the spacing from the center of one framing member (2 × 4, for example) to the center of the next (Fig. 5-8). It's important to always place the panel with the long dimension perpendicular to and across three or more supports to develop the greatest possible strength and stiffness.

Span ratings are carried in the trademarks of *APA Rated Sheathing, APA Rated Sturd-I-Floor,* and *APA 303 Siding* panels. On APA Rated Sheathing, the rating is written as two numbers separated by a slash, 32/16

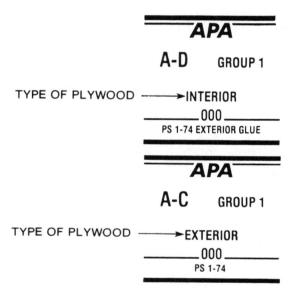

Fig. 5-6: Exposure durability is indicated by the labels exterior and interior.

TABLE 5-3:   PS 1/PERFORMANCE-RATED PANEL EXPOSURE DURABILITY DESIGNATIONS

PS 1 Designations	Performance-Rated Panel Designations	Recommended Use	Typical Applications
Exterior type	Exterior	permanent exposure to weather or moisture	exterior siding, soffits, fences, decks, planters, storage buildings, concrete forms
Interior type/exterior glue	Exposure 1	prolonged temporary exposure to weather or moisture	roof and wall sheathing, roof overhangs
Interior type/intermediate glue*	Exposure 2*	brief temporary exposure to weather or moisture	sheathing, if quickly covered
Interior type/interior glue*		protected from weather or moisture	cabinets, furniture, built-ins, shelving

*Not commonly available.

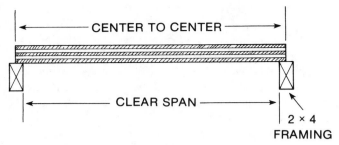

Fig. 5-8: Center-to-center framing.

and 48/24 for example (Fig. 5-9A). Refer to the left-hand number when the panel is to be used for roof sheathing and the right-hand number when using the panel for subflooring.

APA Rated Sturd-I-Floor panels use single span ratings (16, 20, 24, 48) (Fig. 5-9B) to help you install the panels in residential or other light-frame single-floor applications. Such panels function as both structural subflooring and smooth underlayment for direct application of finish flooring.

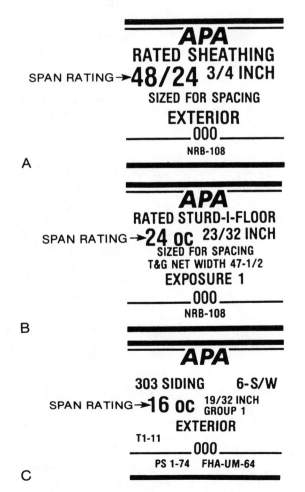

Fig. 5-9: Grade stamps for APA Rated Sheathing, APA Rated Sturd-I-Floor, and APA 303 Siding panels.

APA 303 Sidings have single span ratings of either 16″ or 24″ for spacing of studs (Fig. 5-9C) when panels are applied vertically to studs or over nonstructural wall sheathing (fiberboard, gypsum, or rigid foam insulation). The panels can be installed vertically (long dimension parallel to supports) because walls don't have to support the kinds of loads that floors and roofs do. If applied horizontally, the horizontal joints must be backed with lumber blocking. When applied over other structural panels or lumber sheathing, the rating refers to the maximum recommended spacing of vertical rows of *nails.*

Specialty Plywoods

APA Rated Sheathing, Sturd-I-Floor, and Sidings are discussed in other sections. Here, we'll look at specialty plywoods you may come across or choose for a future project. Remember that the grade stamp on a particular plywood panel will always tell you exactly what kind of panel you're purchasing.

C-D plugged and *C-C plugged* grades have touch-sanded C plugged face veneers. C-D plugged is an interior-type panel with exterior or interior glue, while C-C plugged is an exterior-type panel. C-C plugged can be used as floor underlayment, among other things. The veneer under the face ply of C-D plugged Interior, however, may contain large knotholes. C-D plugged, therefore, does not have the indentation resistance necessary for use as underlayment.

Underlayment grades are designed specifically for use as a base for finish flooring. These touch-sanded panels are installed over structural subflooring. Underlayment panels of interior and exterior types are available.

Plyform is a panel designed for concrete form applications and is not commonly available at local lumber dealers. Class I and II panels are manufactured, Class I being the stronger, stiffer, and more readily available of the two. Structural I Plyform is a special Plyform panel designed to be extra stiff and strong for engineered applications. Plyform is a reusable panel with both faces made of mill-oiled, sanded B-grade veneer. Plyform is also manufactured with high density overlaid surfaces, which are hard, smooth, and abrasion-resistant.

Plyron is an all-veneer panel with hardboard faces (see Chapter 7). Plyron provides an extra-smooth and long-wearing surface which is able to be painted. It is well-suited for projects such as cabinets, fixtures, and work benches. You can also use it for flooring that must hold up under heavy rolling loads. Interior

Plyron is manufactured with standard, tempered, smooth, or screened hardboard surfaces. The panel is made with D-grade veneer, except for the layer directly beneath the face which must be C-grade veneer. Exterior Plyron is made of C-grade veneer throughout and can be manufactured with either a tempered smooth or a treated surface.

Medium density overlay (MDO) and *high density overlay (HDO)* panels are all-veneer exterior panels with resin-treated fiber overlay bonded to the plywood. MDO can be purchased with overlay on one or both sides. This type of panel is ideal for painting, since the surface is ready to accept a rapid, even application. In most cases, a primer and single top coat layer are sufficient. HDO panels are overlaid on both sides, giving excellent resistance to abrasion, moisture penetration, and deterioration from common chemicals and solvents. Like Plyron, HDO is not easy to find at your local lumber dealer. This type of plywood is often used for concrete forms, highway signs, and industrial tanks. HDO is designed to be used without further finishing, although it is also a good base for paint after a slight roughening of the surface. Only paint products formulated for wood should be used to finish overlaid plywood.

Marine grade plywood is an exterior plywood that has A- or B-grade faces and no voids in the interior plies. The plies are supported and the edges are free from voids if the panel is cut. These panels are especially suitable in applications where bending is required, such as in boat hulls.

Shop cutting panels are panels which have been rejected for failure to conform to the requirements of PS 1. Such panels can sometimes be cut to eliminate the defect, and the remaining pieces can then be used for applications which are not governed by building codes.

Decorative panels are available in a wide variety for diverse applications. Softwood plywood is frequently used for paneling as well as siding. Paneling and siding panels are available in a wide variety of textures and come in panels of nearly any thickness. Most panels measure 4' × 8', 9', or 10'. Normally, panels are installed vertically, but they may be installed horizontally if horizontal joints are nailed to blocking. Always take into consideration the allowable stud spacing indicated on the grade stamp.

You can apply plywood panels with nails or with adhesives. You may also be interested to know that plywood paneling and siding provide good sound and thermal insulation, since the large size of the panels reduces the number of joints that can allow noise and air to pass. Plywood wall systems can also be insulated to improve the heat and sound insulation.

BUYING SOFTWOOD PLYWOOD

There is a kind of plywood for every use (Table 5-4), and the right selection will be not only most satisfactory but most economical as well. Unfortunately, too many plywood users buy grades that are more expensive than they need be for ordinary uses. For instance, plywood with both sides of top quality is sometimes put into cupboard walls and shelves where only one side could possibly show. Or exterior plywood is used for applications that will never come in contact with the weather. Familiarity with grade marks and what they mean will help you to select the right plywood. Sometimes it is possible, with a little extra work, to upgrade plywood. In other words, by purchasing a lower-grade plywood and filling defects and sanding, you may raise the grade to meet your requirements.

The species and grade, and consequently the price, will be governed by the nature of the project and the type of finish desired. For a paint finish, A- or B-grade plywood is adequate, but for a natural wood effect, N-grade will give better results. A savings can be noted by using C- and D-grade veneer panels for back and concealed construction. Therefore, before you attempt to buy the panels, jot down the thickness, grade, span rating, exposure durability classification, dimensions, and number of pieces you require. It's a good idea to have a second and even third choice in case your supplier does not carry the specific panel you have in mind.

Plywood is normally priced by the square foot of surface measure or by the standard 4' × 8' sheet. (A piece of plywood 4' × 8' is 32 square feet in area.) Often you won't need to buy a full sheet of plywood, and in such cases, you may find a suitable piece in the "handy panels" stocked by most dealers. Odd-sized pieces are available in this way. Also remember that you can save money by purchasing interior-type plywood rather than exterior on projects that will not be exposed to weather or excessive moisture.

When placing a plywood order, you can eliminate any confusion by stating all the necessary information in the correct sequence. The formula calls for number of panels, then the panel thickness, width, and length, followed by the grade, grading association, face and back veneer grades, plus type of glue. For instance, your order might read something like this: 5 panels 1/2" × 4' × 8' APA, A-B interior plywood, or 10 panels 3/4" × 4' × 8' APA underlayment C-C plugged exterior plywood.

Storing Plywood. Although you may seldom need to store a large quantity of plywood panels, there are some important guidelines for such a situation. Ply-

TABLE 5-4: CONDENSED GUIDE TO PLYWOOD GRADES AND USES

Interior Type

Grade Designation	Description and Most Common Uses	Typical Grade Trademarks	Veneer Grade			Most Common Thicknesses (inch)				
			Face	Inner Plies	Back					
APA A-A INT	For applications with both sides on view: built-ins, cabinets, furniture, partitions. Smooth face, suitable for painting.	A-A G-1 INT-APA PS1-74 000	A	D	A	1/4	3/8	1/2	5/8	3/4
APA A-B INT	Use where appearance of one side is less important but where two solid surfaces are necessary.	A-B G-1 INT-APA PS1-74 000	A	D	B	1/4	3/8	1/2	5/8	3/4
APA A-D INT	Use where appearance of only one side is important: paneling, built-ins, shelving, partitions, flow racks.	APA A-D GROUP 1 INTERIOR 000 PS 1-74 EXTERIOR GLUE	A	D	D	1/4	3/8	1/2	5/8	3/4
APA B-B INT	Utility panel with two solid sides. Permits circular plugs.	B-B G-2 INT-APA PS1-74 000	B	D	B	1/4	3/8	1/2	5/8	3/4
APA B-D INT	Utility panel with one solid side. Good for backing, sides of built-ins, industry shelving, slip sheets, separator boards, bins.	APA B-D GROUP 2 INTERIOR 000 PS 1-74 EXTERIOR GLUE	B	D	D	1/4	3/8	1/2	5/8	3/4
APA underlayment INT	For application over structural subfloor. Provides smooth surface for application of resilient floor coverings. Touch-sanded. Also available with exterior glue.	APA UNDERLAYMENT GROUP 1 INTERIOR 000 PS 1-74 EXTERIOR GLUE	C Plgd.	C & D	D		3/8	1/2	19/32 5/8	23/32 3/4
APA C-D plugged INT	For built-ins, wall and ceiling tile backing, cable reels, walkways, separator boards. Not a substitute for *Underlayment or Sturd-I-Floor* as it lacks their indentation resistance. Touch-sanded. Also made with exterior glue.	APA C-D PLUGGED GROUP 2 INTERIOR 000 PS 1-74 EXTERIOR GLUE	C Plgd.	D	D		3/8	1/2	19/32 5/8	23/32 3/4

Exterior Type

Grade Designation	Description and Most Common Uses	Typical Grade Trademarks	Veneer Grade			Most Common Thicknesses (inch)				
			Face	Inner Plies	Back					
APA A-C* EXT	Use where the appearance of only side is important: soffits, fences, structural uses, boxcar and truck linings, farm buildings, tanks, trays, commercial refrigerators.	APA A-C GROUP 1 EXTERIOR 000 PS 1-74	A	C	C	1/4	3/8	1/2	5/8	3/4
APA B-B EXT	Utility panel with solid faces.	B-B G-2 EXT-APA PS1-74 000	B	C	B	1/4	3/8	1/2	5/8	3/4
APA B-C* EXT	Utility panel for farm service and work buildings, boxcar and truck linings, containers, tanks, agricultural equipment. Also as a base for exterior coatings for walls, roofs.	APA B-C GROUP 1 EXTERIOR 000 PS 1-74	B	C	C	1/4	3/8	1/2	5/8	3/4
APA underlayment C-C plugged EXT	For application over structural subfloor. Provides smooth surface for application of resilient floor coverings where severe moisture conditions may be present. Touch-sanded.	APA C-C PLUGGED GROUP 2 EXTERIOR 000 PS 1-74	C Plgd.	C	C		3/8	1/2	19/32 5/8	23/32 3/4

*Not a substitute for *Underlayment* or *Sturd-I-Floor* as it lacks their indentation resistance.

TABLE 5-4: CONDENSED GUIDE TO PLYWOOD GRADES AND USES (Continued)

Grade Designation	Description and Most Common Uses	Typical Grade Trademarks	Veneer Grade			Most Common Thicknesses (inch)				
			Face	Inner Plies	Back					
APA C-C plugged EXT	For use as tile backing where severe moisture conditions exist. For refrigerated or controlled atmosphere rooms, pallet fruit bins, tanks, boxcar and truck floors and linings, open soffits. Touch-sanded.	APA C-C PLUGGED GROUP 2 EXTERIOR 000 PS 1-74	C Plgd.	C	C		3/8	1/2	5/8	19/32 23/32 3/4
APA HDO EXT	High Density Overlay. Has a hard semi-opaque resin-fiber overlay both faces. Abrasion resistant. For concrete forms, cabinets, countertops, signs, tanks. Also available with skid-resistant screen-grid surface.	HDO A-A G-1 EXT-APA PS1-74 000	A or B	C or C Plgd.	A or B		3/8	1/2	5/8	3/4
APA MDO EXT	Medium Density Overlay. Smooth, opaque, resin-fiber overlay one or both faces. Ideal base for paint, both indoors and outdoors. Also available as a 303 Siding.	MDO B-B G-2 EXT-APA PS1-74 000	B	C	B or C		3/8	1/2	5/8	3/4
APA marine EXT	Ideal for boat hulls. Made only with Douglas fir or western larch. Special solid jointed core construction. Subject to special limitations on core gaps and number of face repairs. Also available with HDO or MDO faces.	MARINE A-A EXT-APA PS1-74 000	A or B	B	A or B	1/4	3/8	1/2	5/8	3/4
APA B-B Plyform Class I and Class II EXT	Concrete form grades with high reuse factor. Sanded both sides and mill-oiled unless otherwise specified. Special restrictions on species. Class I panels are stiffest, strongest, and most commonly available. Also available in HDO for very smooth concrete finish, in STRUCTURAL I (all plies limited to Group 1 species) and with special overlays.	APA PLYFORM B-B CLASS I EXTERIOR 000 PS 1 74	B	C	B				5/8	3/4

wood is durable, but must be protected from prolonged exposure to moisture. Therefore, you should store panels under cover, if at all possible. If moisture absorption is expected and cannot be prevented, the steel banding on panel bundles should be cut to prevent edge damage due to expansion.

If you must store panels outside, stack them on a level platform so that they are never in direct contact with the ground; don't store them on end. The stack should be covered loosely with tarps or plastic, keeping the covering open and away from the sides and bottom. The coverings should be loose to assure good circulation of air around the panels. Tight coverings, when exposed to sunlight, create a greenhouse effect which encourages mold formation. Also, be careful to select a high, dry location for the stack.

If the panels will be exposed to repeated wetting and drying, a sealant should be applied to the edges of the stacked panels to reduce water absorption into the panel. Remember, the faces may darken if exposed to direct sunlight for any length of time, so cover the top panel.

When handling the panels, be especially careful not to damage the edges. Plywood splits easily along the plane of the panel, so avoid dropping the panels on edge, which may splinter or chip the corners, adding to repair costs. Tongue and groove edges are especially fragile.

TIPS ON WORKING WITH SOFTWOOD PLYWOOD

Softwood plywood can be cut, formed, and put together with conventional tools. However, in this kind of material, the grain of the wood goes in two directions. If the cutting edges of the tools are dull or if you try to cut too fast, the work will tear and splinter.

Sawing. Plywood's large size simplifies almost every step of construction; the only step that must precede actual construction is laying out the panels for cutting. It will reduce waste and simplify your work if you do this with care. When many pieces are to be cut from one panel, it is easiest to plan if you sketch the arrangement on a piece of paper before marking the plywood for cutting. Be sure to allow for a saw kerf between adjacent pieces. Try to work it out so that your first cuts will result in pieces small enough for easy handling.

One of the most important points to watch in planning your sequence of operations is to cut all mating or matching parts with the same saw setting. Watch the direction of the face grain when cutting. Except where indicated otherwise in the plan, you will want this to run the long way of the piece. Make your markings on the better face of the plywood unless you are going to cut it with a portable power saw, in which case it should be marked on the back.

If you are using a handsaw, place plywood with the good face *up*. For most work, a 10-point crosscut saw is best. Be sure to support the plywood firmly on a bench or horses so that it won't sag. Cut the final inch or so with care so that the edge doesn't splinter. You can reduce splitting out of the underside by putting a piece of scrap lumber under it and sawing both together. It also helps to hold the saw at a low angle, and you can keep the wood from creeping by pressing down with one hand while sawing with the other. If the saw tends to bind when making a long cut, insert a screwdriver in the kerf.

Power sawing on a radial or table saw should be done with the good face of the plywood *up*. Use a sharp combination blade or a fine-toothed one without much set (Fig. 5-10). Let the blade protrude above the plywood just the height of the teeth (about 1/2" or less). It is easier to handle large panels alone if you build an extension support with a roller; such a support can have a base of its own or it can be clamped to a saw horse.

A portable power saw, circular or saber, should be used with the good face of the plywood *down*. Tack a strip of scrap lumber to the top of each saw horse and you can saw right through it without damaging the horse. The blade should not protrude more than 1/2".

Fig. 5-10: Use a sharp combination blade or a fine-toothed blade without much set to cut plywood on a table saw. Just the teeth of the blade should protrude above the plywood.

For sawing curves, use a sharp, fine-toothed coping saw or jigsaw. For inside cuts, start the hole with a drill; then insert the blade of a coping or jigsaw or use a keyhole saw to make the cut.

Planing. Planing plywood edges won't often be necessary if you make your cuts with a sharp saw. If you do any planing, carry the plane only about two-thirds of the way across the edge of the wood; then begin to work from the opposite end. Examine and check the wood frequently to make sure that you are cutting evenly and not making bumps or hollows. Pushing the plane off the end usually chips corners. Use a sharp blade with a shallow set. A jack plane is good for cutting, smoothing, and chamfering plywood edges. For curved surfaces or hard-to-get-to places and for light finishing cuts, easing edges, etc., use a shorter, more easily handled block plane.

Drilling. A brace and bit are best for cutting large holes in softwood plywood. Support the work well and back the spot you are boring with a piece of scrap wood to prevent splintering. As soon as the point of the bit appears, reverse the panel and complete the hole, working from the other side. Drilling for screws and nails or making other small diameter holes can be done with either hand or power drills. Again, support the plywood firmly and use a piece of wood behind the panel. Cut through slowly at the end to avoid splintering. In drill-press work, use a reasonably slow rate of feed with the drill turning at high speed.

Routing. The router is one of the most versatile of all home-workshop tools. It is a hand-operated power tool with a high-speed bit used to V-groove plywood, shiplap edges, or lip edges of panels for cabinet doors (Fig. 5-11). It also has special bits for moulding and chamfering. For safety and accuracy, always use a straight edge guide. Use sharp bits and take care when working across the panel or against

Fig. 5-11: A router is handy for cutting shiplap edges or lip edges in cabinet construction.

the grain. Deep cuts in the edge of the panel should be made in two stages. For specific operating instructions, see the literature of the manufacturer of your tool.

Fastenings. Softwood plywood can be held together or fastened by nails, screws, glue, or a combination of any of these. But softwood plywood has a great advantage over other woods when it comes to fastening in that it cannot split.

Not only can nails or screws be placed close to panel edges, but outside fastenings or clamps can be used. The crisscross arrangement of wood fibers also creates extraordinary resistance to the pull-through of the heads of the screws or nails.

Whether you fasten with nails, screws, bolts, or adhesives, three basic principles must be considered.

1. Fasteners must be strong enough to support both external and internal stresses.
2. Fasteners must be placed so as to overcome any panel tendency to bend, belly, or buckle.
3. Fasteners must be of a type to compensate for any potential movement. Movement must be anticipated where there are extreme fluctuations in moisture content or where panels are fastened to supporting members of different material. For example, large plywood panels riveted to metal frames or studs have a tendency to work loose because heat produces exactly opposite reactions in metal and wood: metal expands; wood contracts due to reductions in moisture content.

Nailing. Softwood plywood holds nails well. Nails can be placed near the edge of a panel without splitting it. For finish work, casing nails hold better than finish nails. The heads of the nails can be driven flush or slightly set and filled with wood filler, spackle, or putty. When this is done, the nail holes will be nearly invisible and the panels will be ready for finishing. If appearance isn't important, box or common nails should be used. Spiral or ring-barbed nails give extra holding power. For exterior work, use hot-dipped zinc-coated nails to avoid rust.

The thickness of the plywood you are using should determine the size of the nails. For 3/4" plywood, use 6d common or 8d finish nails; for 5/8", 6d or 8d finish nails; for 1/2", 4d or 6d; for 3/8", 3d or 4d; for 1/4", use 3/4" or 1" brads, 3d finish nails, or (for backs where there is no objection to heads showing) 1" blue lath nails. Although proper spacing depends on the job, as a rule nails at edges should be no more than 6" apart. Closer spacing is necessary only with thin plywood where there may be slight buckling between nails. Nails and glue together produce a strong, durable joint. When nails are placed in or very close to an edge, first drill a pilot hole slightly smaller than the nail diameter.

Screws have much greater holding power than nails. Moreover, screws can be removed and replaced again after work in which they are used has been put together without damaging the panel. Holes of slightly smaller diameter than the screws should be drilled beforehand; it also helps to soap the screws. Sizes given here are minimums; use longer screws when work permits. Table 5-5 gives plywood thickness, the smallest recommended diameter and length of the screws, and the size of the drill hole. Sheet-metal screws tend to hold better than ordinary wood screws and may be used where holding power is important. Glue should also be used if possible.

Screws should be countersunk and the holes filled with wood filler, dough, or surfacing putty. Apply the filler so it is slightly higher than the plywood and sand it level when it is dry.

TABLE 5-5:   MATCHING SCREW SIZE WITH PLYWOOD THICKNESS

Plywood Thickness	Smallest Recommended Diameter of the Screw	Length of the Screw	Size of the Drill Hole
3/4"	No. 8	1-1/2"	5/32"
5/8"	No. 8	1-1/4"	5/32"
1/2"	No. 6	1-1/4"	1/8"
3/8"	No. 6	1"	1/8"
1/4"	No. 4	3/4"	7/64"

It is often desirable to cover the head of the screw with a wood plug that matches the plywood, so that the plug is not noticeable. With a plug cutter, cut a small disc that will cover the head of the screw (plug cutters are available in various sizes). A hole 3/8" in diameter is satisfactory for most screws. Bore the hole 3/16" deep and drive the head of the screw to the bottom of the hole. Cut the plug from a thin piece of the same kind of wood, match the grain as nearly as possible, and glue the plug into the hole so that it follows the grain of the veneer (Fig. 5-12).

Other Fastenings. Corrugated fasteners can reinforce miter joints in 3/4" plywood and hold the joints together while glue sets. Bolts and washers are good for joining sectional units and for installing legs, hinges, or other hardware when great strength is required. If you use bolts, use washers as well to give ample bearing surface.

Gluing. Softwood plywood can be glued following the same techniques for gluing wood described in Chapter 1. But, when gluing softwood plywood, apply a preliminary coat of glue to the end grain and let it soak in for a few minutes since the end grain absorbs glue more quickly than face grain. When the end grain portion is tacky, apply glue to both the end and face grain pieces and join the parts.

Fig. 5-12: Wooden plugs can also be used to disguise countersunk screws.

SOFTWOOD PLYWOOD PROJECTS

The following projects will allow you to apply some of the knowledge and skills necessary for working with softwood plywood. Not only will the projects be learning experiences, but they will also provide you with useful items you can use in your home.

Weight Lifting Bench

With one sheet of 3/4" plywood, some miscellaneous hardware, and a little initiative, you can build your own weight lifting bench. The one pictured here has a leg lift, a curl bar, an adjustable seat, a squat rack, and a two-position incline back—all features of an expensive steel bench. The few hours it will take to construct it will provide your family with an inexpensive means of staying in shape.

Start by drawing and cutting out the plywood pieces as shown. The slots cut into the side pieces should be slanted 3° from vertical in the direction shown. Next, cut the steel pipe and rods to length. The steel pipe should then be cut into two lengths: 48" and 26-1/2". Thread the ends of the shorter sections and file away any burrs. After the steel bars are cut, they must be bent to shape with a hammer and vise.

Attach the slot pieces to the racks with glue and right-angle brackets. Remember to drill pilot holes before installing wood screws. Follow the same procedure in attaching slots to the leg lift braces.

The seat of the weight bench is divided into two sections, one longer than the other. These two seat sections are connected by hinges to a bench support. This part must be constructed by laminating two plywood sections together. When the support has dried, attach the bench back and bench seat to the bench support with hinges as shown. At the same time, attach the two incline supports to the bench back with glue and right-angle brackets.

At this point, the bench is ready to be assembled. The sides, the front and back crosses, and the incline rods must be slotted together simultaneously. Then, bolt on the racks and the leg lift braces. Next, add the bench seat and back assembly. Make sure that the bench support fits into the slots on the bench sides. Finally, the leg lifts can be installed. Sand, prime, and paint the entire assembly.

To make exercising a little more enjoyable, the bench seat, back, and leg lift bars should be padded. Upholster the bench seat and back with vinyl material over 1" thick foam. The vinyl can be tacked to the seat and back. Two-inch-thick foam should be used for the leg lift bars. Wrap the foam around 1-1/8" diameter cardboard tubing 26" long and capped with 4-1/2" diameter end discs with 1-1/4" diameter center holes. These discs can be cut from 1/4" scrap plywood or paneling. Machine stitch the vinyl cover sleeve, slip it over the foam, and staple the ends into the plywood discs. When both pads are finished, slide the sections of threaded pipe through the pads, collars (available at most sports stores), and leg lifts. Cap the ends of the shorter pipe with pipe caps.

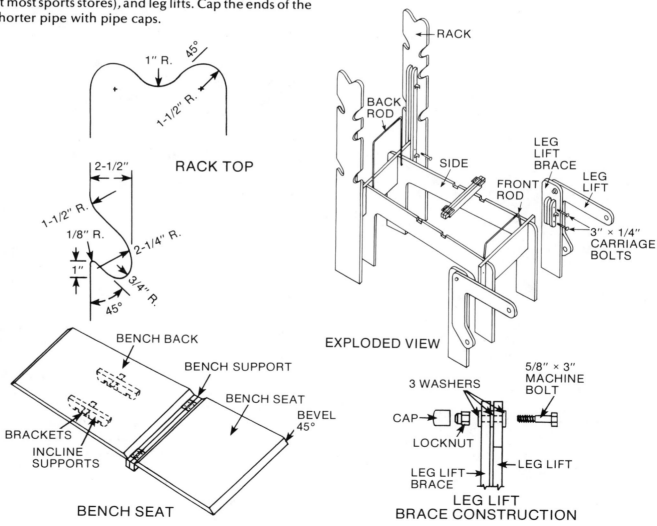

BACK ROD

FRONT ROD

GLUE 2 PIECES TOGETHER

SAME ANGLE AS BENCH

HINGES

BENCH SUPPORT

RACK TOP

RACK

BACK ROD

SIDE

FRONT ROD

LEG LIFT BRACE

LEG LIFT

3" × 1/4" CARRIAGE BOLTS

EXPLODED VIEW

BENCH BACK

BENCH SUPPORT

BENCH SEAT

BEVEL 45°

BRACKETS

INCLINE SUPPORTS

BENCH SEAT

3 WASHERS

5/8" × 3" MACHINE BOLT

CAP

LOCKNUT

LEG LIFT BRACE

LEG LIFT

LEG LIFT BRACE CONSTRUCTION

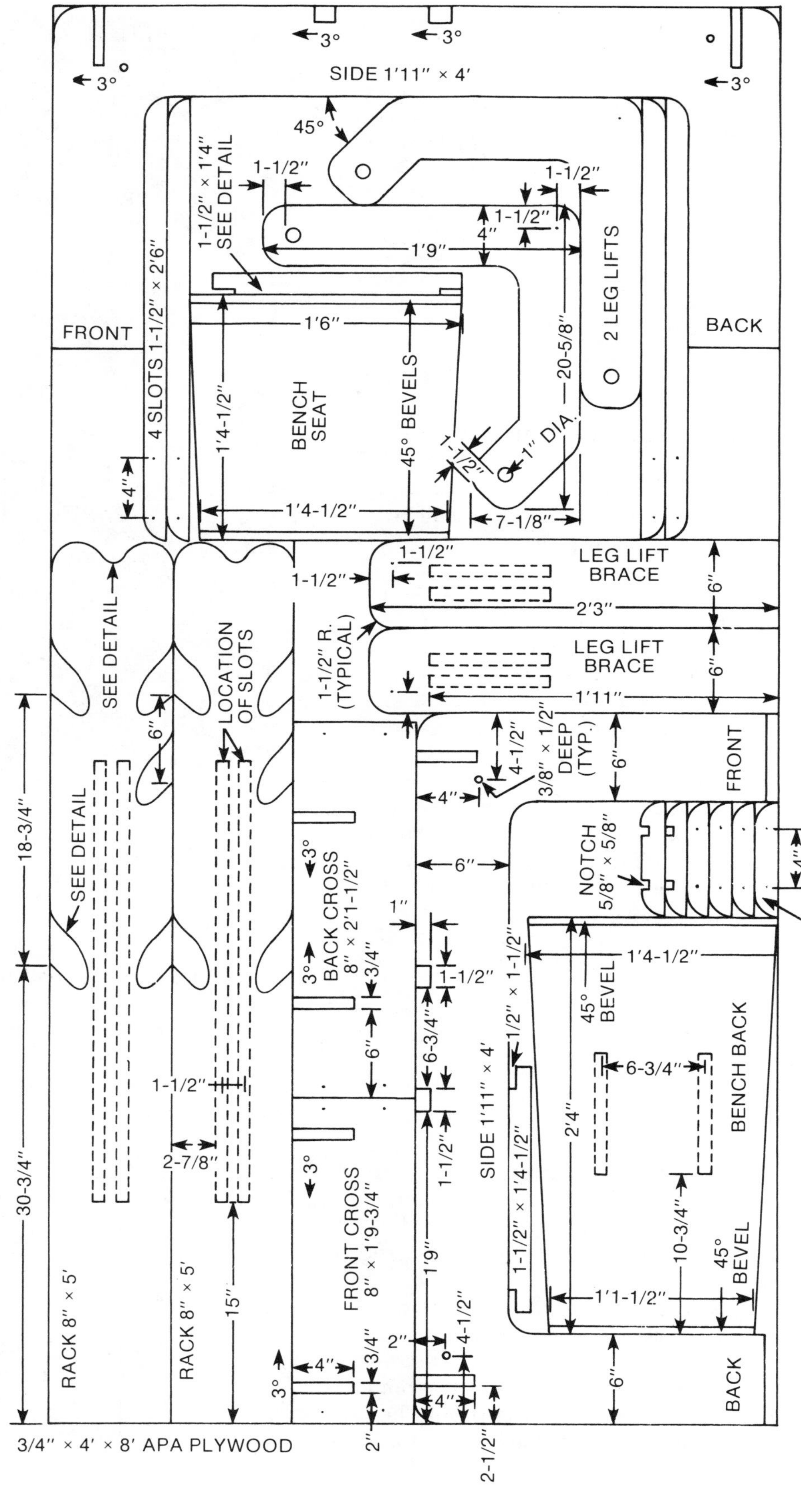

SIDE 1'11" × 4'

45°

1-1/2" × 1'4"
SEE DETAIL

1-1/2"

1-1/2"

1-1/2"

4"

1'9"

4"

FRONT

2 LEG LIFTS

BACK

4 SLOTS 1-1/2" × 2'6"

1-1/2" × 1'4"

1'6"

1'4-1/2"

BENCH SEAT

45° BEVELS

20-5/8"

1-1/2"

1" DIA.

4"

1'4-1/2"

7-1/8"

3°

3°

3°

3°

SEE DETAIL

1-1/2"

1-1/2"

LEG LIFT BRACE

6"

LOCATION OF SLOTS

6"

2'3"

1-1/2" R. (TYPICAL)

LEG LIFT BRACE

6"

1'11"

18-3/4"

SEE DETAIL

4-1/2"

4"

3/8" × 1/2" DEEP (TYP.)

6"

FRONT

NOTCH 5/8" × 5/8"

4"

6"

1"

BACK CROSS 8" × 2'1-1/2"

1-1/2"

1'4-1/2"

45° BEVEL

6-3/4"

30-3/4"

2-7/8"

1-1/2"

3°

6"

6-3/4"

6"

2'4"

BENCH BACK

6 PIECES 1-1/2" × 8'

RACK 8" × 5'

RACK 8" × 5'

15"

3°

FRONT CROSS 8" × 1'9-3/4"

1'9"

1-1/2"

SIDE 1'11" × 1'4-1/2"

1/2"

1-1/2" × 1'4-1/2"

10-3/4"

45° BEVEL

PANEL LAYOUT

3°

4"

3/4"

2"

4-1/2"

4"

1'1-1/2"

6"

BACK

3/4" × 4' × 8' APA PLYWOOD

2"

2-1/2"

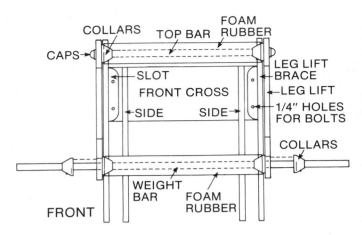

COLLARS TOP BAR FOAM RUBBER
CAPS→
CAPS
SLOT
FRONT CROSS
LEG LIFT BRACE
LEG LIFT
←SIDE SIDE→ 1/4" HOLES FOR BOLTS
COLLARS
WEIGHT BAR FOAM RUBBER
FRONT

MATERIALS LIST FOR WEIGHT LIFTING BENCH

Quantity	Description
1 panel	3/4" × 4' × 8' A-B interior plywood
74-1/2 lin. in.	1" diameter steel pipe
78 lin. in.	3/8" diameter cold-rolled steel rod
2	1" diameter threaded steel pipe caps
1 yd.	60" wide vinyl upholstery material
2 pr.	2-1/2" × 1" butt hinges with screws
8	3" × 1/4" bolts with nuts and washers
2	3" × 5/8" machine bolts (with 1-1/2" shoulders) with 2 locknuts, 6 washers, and 2 finishing caps or acorn nuts
6	1" inside diameter weight lifting bar collars
16	1" right-angle brackets with screws
As required	1" thick foam, 2" thick foam, 1-1/8" diameter cardboard tubing, 1/4" scrap plywood or paneling, upholstery tacks, white or urea resin glue, fine sandpaper, top-quality enamel, and companion primer

Compact Desk

Students and those with a business office at home will find this compact desk a perfect work center. It is just 39" wide, 24" deep, and 30" high, but the desk has a spacious work surface and ample space underneath for office supplies.

Cut all the parts as shown in the panel layout. For hand-sawing, use a 10- to 15-point crosscut. Support the panel firmly with the face up. For power-sawing, a plywood blade gives the best results, but a combination blade may be used. The panel should lie face down for hand power-sawing; the panel should be face up for power sawing on a table or radial saw.

Once the parts are cut, proceed as follows:

(a) Glue-nail each pair of A sections together to form the double-thickness desk sides. Cut the 1-1/2" half round to fit A section dimensions, allowing enough length to cut the 45° mitered half round corners.

(b) Glue-nail 3/4" half round to section B. Cover the entire piece with vinyl.

(c) Glue-nail 3/4" half round to sections C and D.

(d) Assemble the desk with 8d finishing nails. Fill the joints with wood putty as needed, sand as needed, and paint.

MATERIALS LIST FOR COMPACT DESK

Quantity	Description
1 panel	3/4" × 4' × 8' plywood
16 lin. feet	1-1/2" wood half round
14 lin. feet	3/4" wood half round
1 yard	vinyl material
—	8d finishing nails
—	wood dough or putty
—	fine abrasive paper
—	white glue
—	interior semi-gloss enamel paint

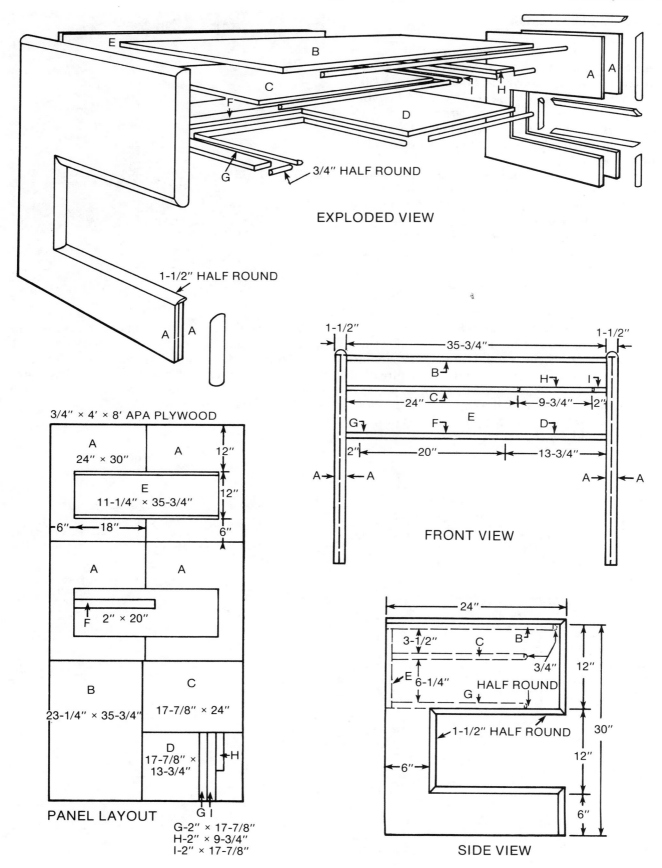

EXPLODED VIEW

1-1/2" HALF ROUND

3/4" HALF ROUND

3/4" × 4' × 8' APA PLYWOOD

A
24" × 30"

A

12"

E
11-1/4" × 35-3/4"

12"

6" — 18" — 6"

A

A

F
2" × 20"

B
23-1/4" × 35-3/4"

C
17-7/8" × 24"

D
17-7/8" ×
13-3/4"

H

G I

PANEL LAYOUT

G-2" × 17-7/8"
H-2" × 9-3/4"
I-2" × 17-7/8"

FRONT VIEW

1-1/2"   1-1/2"

35-3/4"

B

H   I

C

24"   9-3/4"   2"

E

G   F   D

2"   20"   13-3/4"

A → ← A   A → ← A

SIDE VIEW

24"

3-1/2"   C   B

3/4"

E   6-1/4"   HALF ROUND

G

1-1/2" HALF ROUND

12"

30"

12"

6"

6"

Adjustable Sling Chair

Here's a unique means of relaxation that you can make from a half of a sheet of plywood. This adjustable lawn chair has a canvas seat that cradles you like a hammock. A springy rope spindle supports your knees and shoulders so that there are no uncomfortable edges to crease your back and legs. Perfect for the pool, patio, or playroom, this chair slots together for quick assembly.

The basic wood parts of the chair are easily made. First, cut out the parts as shown in the panel layout, and drill the various holes as shown. Notches must be cut in two of the large circles, as illustrated. Then, glue the large and small circles together. Sand all cut edges, and apply finish. Allow the finish to dry completely before continuing.

The rope spindles are constructed by first cutting the 3/8" threaded steel rod to length and attaching the wooden circles so that the outside of the large circles are no more than 24-1/4" apart. This will allow room for the sides of the chair to fit over the ends of the rods. The slotted circles should be paired together. When the circles are spaced properly on the threaded rods, lace the ropes, drawing them as tight as possible before tying them off. Fold the edges of canvas cloth back into a loop and sew. Slide the dowels through these loops and the chair is ready to be assembled.

First, place the dowels, the top crosspiece, and the spindles in place. Tighten the nuts on the spindle rods enough to hold the chair in place while adding the front and bottom crosspieces. After the chair is assembled in this way, insert the screws in the dowel ends and tighten the spindle nuts.

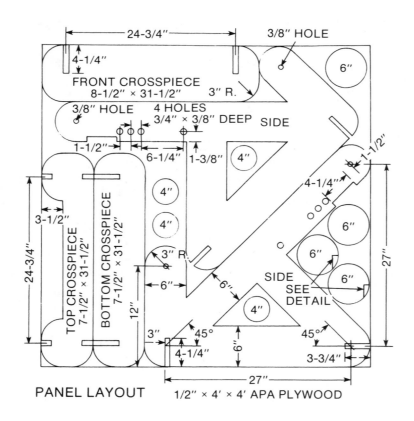

PANEL LAYOUT   1/2" × 4' × 4' APA PLYWOOD

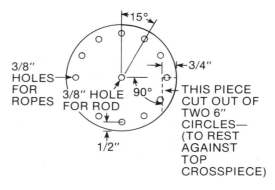

MATERIALS LIST FOR ADJUSTABLE SLING CHAIR

Quantity	Description
1/2 panel	1/2″ × 4′ × 4′ A-C Exterior plywood
53 lin. in.	3/8″ diameter threaded steel rod with 8 nuts and washers
46 lin. in.	3/4″ diameter hardwood dowel
50 lin. in.	1/4″ vinyl-covered twisted wire clothesline, or woven cotton clothesline
4	1-1/4″, #10 flathead wood screws
2 yds.	Canvas cloth
As required	Fine sandpaper, white or urea resin glue, top-quality enamel paint, and companion primer

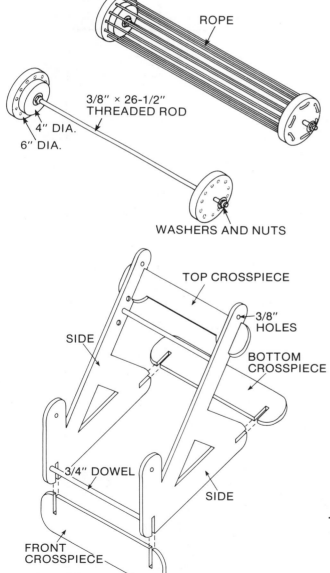

ROPE

3/8″ × 26-1/2″ THREADED ROD

4″ DIA.

6″ DIA.

WASHERS AND NUTS

TOP CROSSPIECE

3/8″ HOLES

SIDE

BOTTOM CROSSPIECE

3/4″ DOWEL

SIDE

FRONT CROSSPIECE

EXPLODED VIEW

Slip Together Bed/Desk

This project is designed for the beginning wood craftsman. It requires no special joining, drilling, or even nailing. The parts just slip together. It's a bed, desk, and playhouse all in one. All you need is three sheets of 1/2″ plywood and a bottle of white glue.

Place the parts as shown in the panel layouts. Very little wood will be left over since the door cutout becomes the desk top and the step-hole cutouts are used to double the width of the ladder steps. Note that the corners of the pieces should be rounded to a radius of 1″. Glue the step doublers to the ladder steps before fitting the parts together. After assembling the bed, fill the gaps left in the slots with wood filler, sand all the rough edges smooth, and apply a good quality finish.

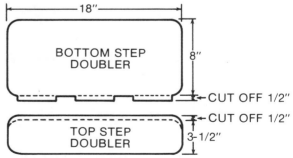

18″

BOTTOM STEP DOUBLER

8″

CUT OFF 1/2″

CUT OFF 1/2″

TOP STEP DOUBLER

3-1/2″

MATERIALS LIST FOR SLIP TOGETHER BED/DESK

Quantity	Description
3 panels	1/2″ × 4′ × 8′ A-B Interior or Exterior plywood
As required	White or urea-resin glue (for gluing step-ladder doublers), wood dough or synthetic filler, fine sandpaper, top quality latex paint

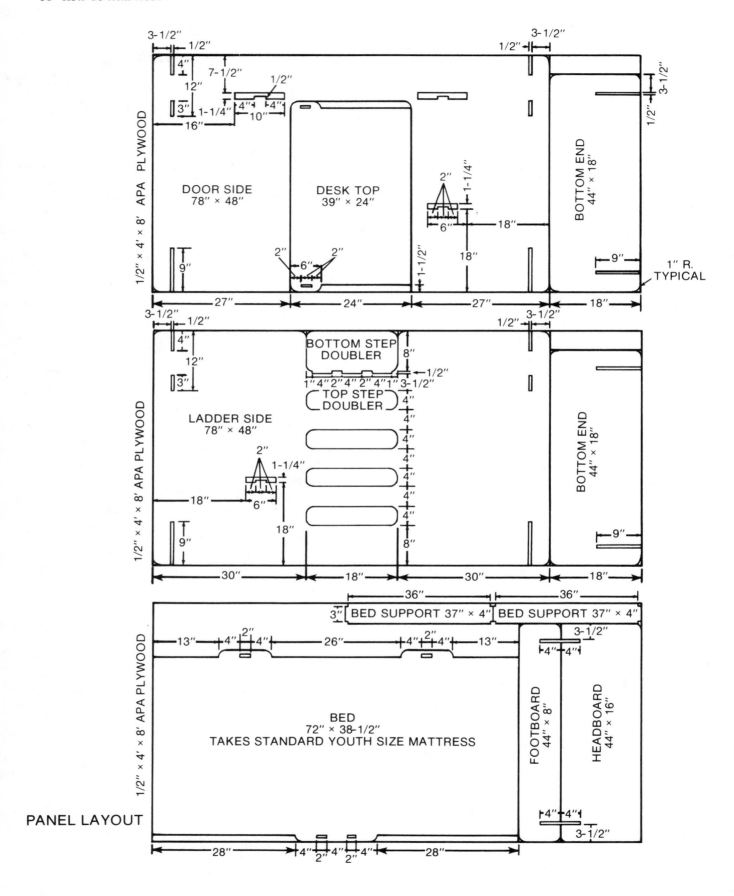

PANEL LAYOUT

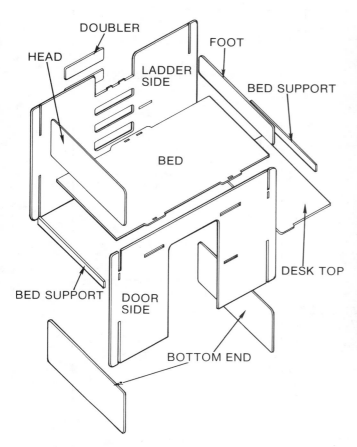

DOUBLER
HEAD
FOOT
LADDER SIDE
BED SUPPORT
BED
BED SUPPORT
DOOR SIDE
DESK TOP
BOTTOM END

Swing-Wing Liquor Cabinet

This handsome party organizer is perfect for entertaining because the sliding glass tray, easy-access pouring shelf, and horizontal bottle storage rack put your favorite beverages at your fingertips. And it's economical because it requires only one sheet of plywood.

First cut out the plywood pieces as shown in the panel layout drawings. Be sure to relieve the inside corners of the door top tabs so that the doors will close. Rout the grooves for rabbet joints in the door tops and front. Make the grooves 3/4" wide and 3/8" deep.

Cut the 1/2" dowel into pegs according to the dimensions shown. File and sand the bottom 1-1/8" of each pin until it is 3/8" in diameter. Drill holes in the front top and in the back cutout according to the details shown. Drill and countersink holes in the door tops.

Assemble the sliding tray and tray fronts with glue and 4d finishing nails. Cut the tray guides and stops to length from 1 × 1 stock. The guides should be 12-3/4" long, and the stops should be 2-1/2" long.

Assemble the cabinet parts with glue and nails. First, attach the sliding tray guides and stops to the front and the divider as shown. Attach the front top to the front. Attach the front, back, and divider to the bottom. Then, attach the shelf edges to the shelf, and install the shelf. Attach the wine rack shelves to the wine rack divider, and install the assembled wine rack. Then, attach the top shelf using metal shelf supports.

Assemble the door and door tops with glue and 4d nails. Attach the piano hinges to the door and install the doors. Install screw eyes in the top shelf 1/2" from the corner edge. The interior of both doors must be relieved to allow room for the screw eyes when the door is closed. Countersink all nails, fill the holes with wood dough, sand the filler smooth, and apply finish.

MATERIALS LIST FOR SWING-WING LIQUOR CABINET

Quantity	Description
1 panel	3/4" × 4' × 8' A-B Interior plywood
30 lin. in.	1 × 1 lumber for sliding tray guides and stops
6-1/2 lin. in.	1/2" diameter hardwood dowel
2	30-5/8" × 3/4" piano hinges with screws
2	2" × 2" right angle metal shelf supports with screws
As required	4d finishing nails, white or urea resin glue, wood dough or synthetic filler, fine sandpaper, top-quality enamel paint with companion primer

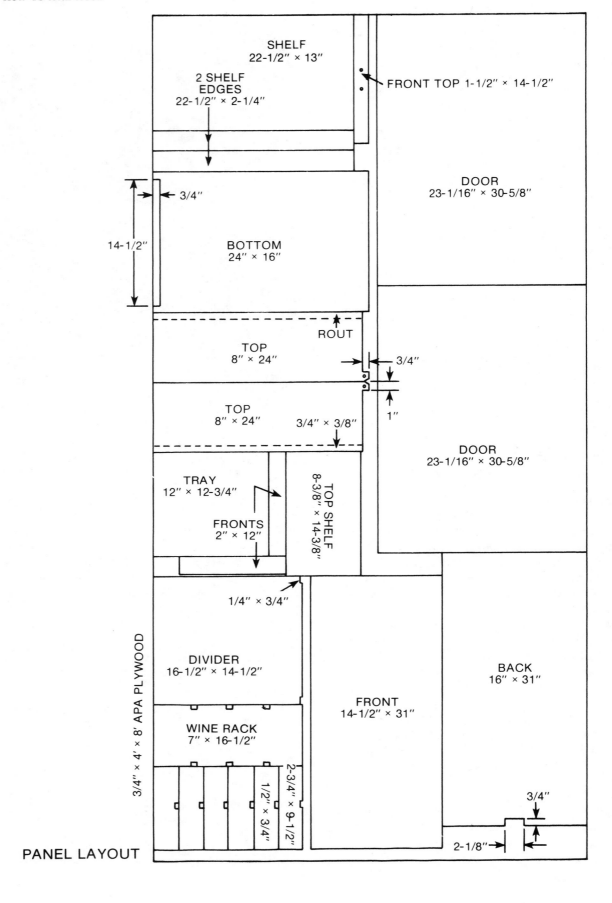

SHELF
22-1/2" × 13"

2 SHELF
EDGES
22-1/2" × 2-1/4"

FRONT TOP 1-1/2" × 14-1/2"

3/4"

14-1/2"

BOTTOM
24" × 16"

DOOR
23-1/16" × 30-5/8"

ROUT

TOP
8" × 24"

3/4"

TOP
8" × 24"

3/4" × 3/8"

1"

DOOR
23-1/16" × 30-5/8"

TRAY
12" × 12-3/4"

TOP SHELF
8-3/8" × 14-3/8"

FRONTS
2" × 12"

1/4" × 3/4"

3/4" × 4' × 8' APA PLYWOOD

DIVIDER
16-1/2" × 14-1/2"

BACK
16" × 31"

FRONT
14-1/2" × 31"

WINE RACK
7" × 16-1/2"

2-3/4" × 9-1/2"

1/2" × 3/4"

3/4"

2-1/8"

PANEL LAYOUT

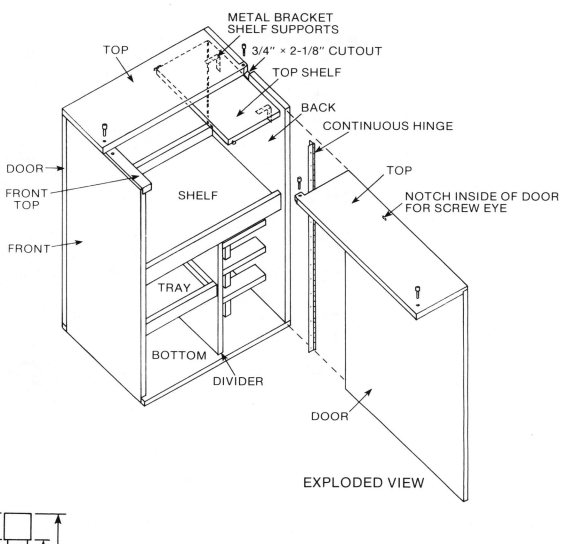

METAL BRACKET
SHELF SUPPORTS

3/4″ × 2-1/8″ CUTOUT

TOP SHELF

TOP

BACK

CONTINUOUS HINGE

DOOR

FRONT TOP

SHELF

TOP

NOTCH INSIDE OF DOOR
FOR SCREW EYE

FRONT

TRAY

BOTTOM

DIVIDER

DOOR

EXPLODED VIEW

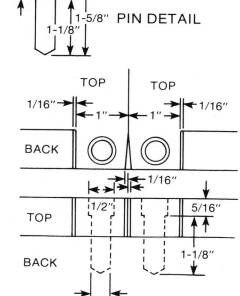

1/2″

1-5/8″

1-1/8″

PIN DETAIL

TOP

TOP

1/16″

1″

1″

1/16″

BACK

1/16″

TOP

1/2″

5/16″

1-1/8″

BACK

3/8″

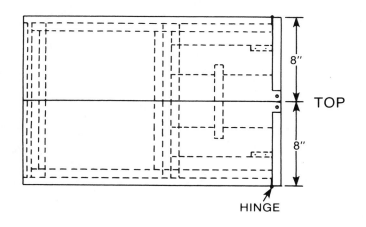

8″

TOP

8″

HINGE

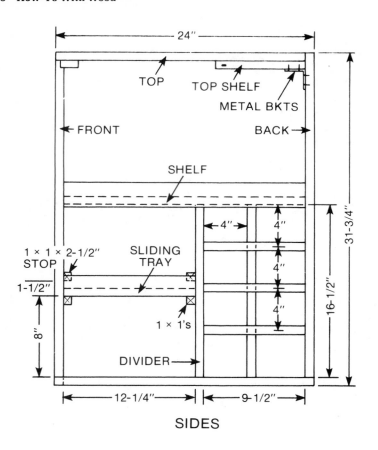

SIDES

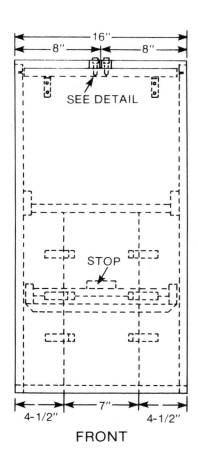

FRONT

CHAPTER
— 6 —

HARDWOOD PLYWOOD

Hardwood plywood is layered just as softwood plywood is, but the outside layers are made of beautiful grained hardwood veneer. Hardwood plywood is made to look good; so, anything you make from it will look good as well. Just imagine building beautiful hardwood cabinets, book shelves, paneling, or furniture. The only difference between the characteristics of these items and those of solid wood (including appearance, strength, and durability) is the cost. Hardwood plywood is less expensive, in most cases, than solid lumber.

To many people, however, hardwood plywood would seem to be of lower quality than solid wood in applications such as furniture making. Actually, the use of solid wood can not only be wasteful, but often may be less attractive than veneered panels. Hardwood plywood takes advantage of the best methods of cutting wood for an attractive surface, yet retains the strength of plywood. This method also makes efficient utilization of rare and valuable species of wood by using lower grade materials for the interior and back, without affecting the appearance of the final product.

MANUFACTURE OF HARDWOOD PLYWOOD

Hardwood plywood is manufactured from veneers which are cut using the following methods: (1) flat sliced, (2) half round, (3) quartered, and (4) rotary. Rotary cutting (Fig. 6-1A) is the most popular method of producing hardwood veneers as well as softwood veneers. As described in Chapter 5, the full log in rotary cutting turns on a lathe against a knife, producing a continuous sheet of veneer. Because the cut is generally parallel to the growth rings, the grain is swirly, broad, and variegated, which is not always desirable with some hardwood.

Flat sliced, half round, and quartered veneers are produced for architectural grade plywood and are not available through the average lumber dealer. Figure 6-1B illustrates the *flat sliced* method of cutting. A half log or *flitch* is mounted so that slicing is started at a tangent to the growth rings of the tree. As the veneer slices are cut, they're kept in sequence, allowing them to be restacked in their original order after they are dried.

Half round cut hardwood (Fig. 6-1C) normally displays a broader and stronger grain pattern than when flat sliced. This is true because the half log or flitch is caused to rotate against the veneer knife in such a way as to cut across the annual growth more gradually.

Unlike flat cut or half round, which are cut from halved logs, *quartered* hardwood veneer is produced from log quarters (Fig. 6-1D). Quarter cut flitches are sliced approximately at right angles to the growth rings

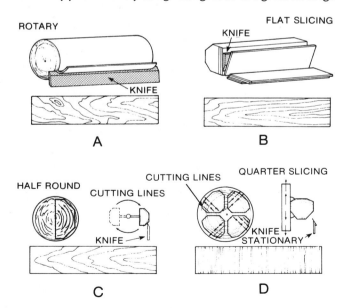

Fig. 6-1: *Plywood veneers are cut in several ways. Four of the most common are: (A) rotary, (B) flat slicing, (C) half round, and (D) quarter slicing.*

to produce a straight or *pencil* stripe grain pattern. A certain amount of quartered hardwood is developed in the process of flat slicing but all true quartered hardwood veneer is produced from logs especially suited to this purpose.

CONSTRUCTION OF HARDWOOD PLYWOOD

The species used in the face plies identify hardwood plywood; that is, black walnut plywood has one or both face plies of black walnut. Some of the more common species used in hardwood plywood include cherry, oak, birch, black walnut, maple, and gum among the native woods; and mahogany, lauan, and teak in the imported category. A major difference in the manufacture of softwood and hardwood plywood is the use of a solid core or extra-thick middle ply in some hardwood panels.

Veneer Core. Veneer core plywood (Fig. 6-2A) is manufactured with layers of wood veneer joined in the same way as softwood plywood. It's intended for uses such as paneling, cabinet and furniture parts, or when the plywood might be bent or curved.

Lumber Core. Lumber core plywood (Fig. 6-2B) contains a thick core made by edge-gluing several narrow strips of solid hardwood (usually basswood, gum, or poplar). This core forms the middle section to which veneer crossbands and face plies are glued. Lumber core plywood is manufactured for specific uses such as tabletops, built-in cabinets, and fixtures and doors where butt hinges are specified.

Particleboard Core. In this plywood (Fig. 6-2C), the core is an aggregate of wood particles bonded together with a resin binder. Face veneers are usually glued directly to the core, although crossbanding is some-

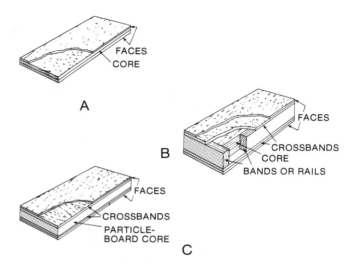

Fig. 6-2: Plywood cores are made of: (A) veneer, (B) lumber, and (C) particleboard.

times used. Particleboard core plywood is used in manufacturing furniture and is particularly adaptable for table, desk, and cabinet tops.

The more plies used in a given thickness, the more nearly equal will be the strength and shrinkage properties along and across the panel, and the greater the resistance to splitting. Warping is controlled by balanced construction. Plies are arranged in pairs about the core, so that for each ply except the core there is an opposite and parallel ply having the same thickness and kind of wood. This construction always uses an odd number of plies. This is to balance out any tendency to warp.

There are other considerations (Table 6-1) besides strength in plywood selection. Plywood with veneers used for all core plies will have the best screw-holding power from the face or the back of the panel, but will have less screw-holding power from the edge than

	TABLE 6-1: CORES FOR HARDWOOD PLYWOOD PANELS		
Core Type	Panel Thickness	Advantages	Disadvantages
Veneer (all inner plies of wood veneers)	1/4″ (3-ply) or less	Inexpensive.	Difficult to machine. Exposed edge shows core voids and imperfections. Most susceptible to warpage (doors).
	5/16″ - 1/2″ (5-ply)	Inexpensive.	
	Over 1/2″ (7-ply)	Best screw-holding power.	
Lumber core (consists of strips of lumber 1-1/2″ to 4″ wide)	5/8″ thru 2″ (usually 5 plies)	Easiest to machine; exposed edges are solid; stable construction.	More expensive.
Particleboard (also called flakeboard)	1/4″ (infrequent) through 2″ (usually 3 plies)	Most stable; least expensive (generally).	Poor edge screw holding; heaviest core.

lumber core plywood. Core imperfections may print through the face veneer to disfigure the surface, particularly when a stain finish is used. Edges are difficult to rout, and exposed edges show core voids and imperfections and are difficult to stain.

Lumber core plywood overcomes many of the disadvantages of veneer construction and has a number of other advantages. While more expensive than the veneer type, lumber core provides an essentially solid wood exposed edge that is easily shaped and finished. Screw-holding through the face and the edge is the same as for solid lumber. This is the plywood to use for anything that will have screws into the edges as for hinges. Lumber core plywood can also be edge-glued as easily as solid lumber. It saws like solid lumber, and you can cut relatively thin slices without it disintegrating.

A particleboard (flake or chip) core has an additional advantage in that it is the most dimensionally stable of any plywood. Because it is less likely to bow, twist, or warp than any other material, it is especially preferred for doors. There is also no core ply print-through. But it does have limitations. Because particleboards are soft, the only screws that will hold are those that are bigger and longer. Particleboards are difficult to edge-glue. You have to fill the edge first, either with adhesive or with special filler. Particleboard core is also the heaviest of all plywood cores. Moulded edges of chipboard are difficult to smooth and finish; edges of flakeboard plywood, while easy to shape (Fig. 6-3), must be covered with an opaque finish instead of stain.

Fig. 6-3: Edges of flakeboard are easy to shape but require an opaque finish.

GRADES AND CLASSIFICATIONS

The Hardwood Plywood Manufacturers Association (HPMA) designates five grades of plywood for the backs and faces of hardwood panels. The grade marking may be stamped on the backs of the panels (Fig. 6-4).

Types. In describing hardwood plywood, the word "type" is used to indicate glue-bond durability—the ability of the plies to stay together under different exposure conditions. The following four types of hardwood plywood are available:

1. *Type I* is manufactured with waterproof adhesives and is used in areas where it would come in contact with water.

2. *Type II* is manufactured with water resistant adhesives and is used in areas where it would not ordinarily be subjected to contact with water. However, it can be used in areas of continued dampness and excessive humidity.

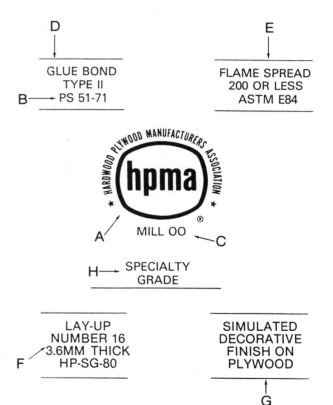

Fig. 6-4: A typical hardwood plywood grade stamp: (A) HPMA trademark; (B) standard governing manufacture; (C) HPMA mill number; (D) plywood glue type (type I, exterior or type II, interior); (E) flame spread rating; (F) structural description; (G) species of wood on face; (H) veneer grade of face (grade of veneer is sometimes shown following grade of face; this is optional).

3. *Type III* is manufactured with moisture resistant adhesives and is intended for use in areas where it will not come in contact with any water. It can be subjected to some dampness and excessive humidity.

4. *Technical* has the same adhesive specifications as Type I but varies in thickness and arrangement of plies.

Grades. The grade of hardwood plywood denotes the appearance of the face and face plies. The grades of the inner plies are important, but the face ply grade in hardwood plywood is exposed, and thus more important. The following are the six basic HPMA grade standards. (These standards are the result of consultations between HPMA and major producers and distributors.)

1. *Specialty Grade* (SP). This is a plywood made to order to meet the specific requirements of a particular buyer, but is seldom available to the individual handyman. Plywood of this grade usually entails special matching of the face veneers.

2. *Premium Grade* (A). The face veneer may be made from more than one piece. With most species, multipiece faces must be book-matched, or slip-matched. The quality of veneer is high—only a few small burls, occasional pin knots, slight color streaks, and inconspicuous small patches are allowed.

3. *Good Grade* (1). The faces are similar to that of Premium Grade faces except that matching is not required. However, sharp contrasts in color and great dissimilarity in grain and figure of two adjacent pieces of veneer in multipiece faces are not allowed. This grade of veneer allows only a few small burls, occasional pin knots, slight color streaks, and inconspicuous small patches.

4. *Sound Grade* (2). This grade provides a smooth surface. The veneer need not be matched for grain or color but must be free of open defects.

5. *Utility Grade* (3). Open defects are allowed—knotholes up to 1" in diameter, worm holes, and splits not exceeding 3/16" wide and not extending half the length of the panel are permitted.

6. *Backing Grade* (4). This grade is similar to Utility Grade except that larger-sized open defects are permitted—knotholes not greater than 3" and splits up to 1" wide, depending on the length of the split.

A grade designation of *A-3* means a panel is Premium Grade on one side and Utility Grade on the other. A grade stamped *1-4* would indicate a panel with Good Grade on the top side and Backing Grade on the back. The grade also indicates the species of the face veneer, the type of construction, and the identification of the manufacturer and inspection testing agency.

BUYING HARDWOOD PLYWOOD

The same basic rules of buying softwood plywood hold true for purchasing hardwood plywood. For instance, hardwood is most commonly sold in panels 4' × 8', although it's usually possible to have plywood made in almost any desired size.

Hardwood plywood is manufactured in 3, 5, 7, and 9 plies with thicknesses ranging from 1/8" to 1". Table 6-2 shows the most common thickness dimensions for the different number of plies.

As you consider what kind of hardwood plywood to use for your particular project, there are certain things to keep in mind. Before trying to purchase the panels, determine the number of pieces you'll need; the width, length, and thickness of each; and the type of core construction best suited to your purpose. Select the grade and species of face veneer you'd like. Also consider the face veneer matching pattern and any special requirements necessary for your project (curved, sanded, or prefinished panels, for instance). Don't forget to select panels suited to the moisture exposure they will have to withstand.

As always, have a number of choices in mind and examine the intended usage to determine the lowest grade panel that will suit your purpose. The purchase of such panels and careful project planning can save you unnecessary expense.

TABLE 6-2:   COMMON THICKNESS DIMENSIONS

Number of Plies	Plywood Thickness (inches)			
3	1/8	3/16	1/4	
5	1/4	3/8	1/2	5/8
7	5/8	3/4		
9	3/4	1		

WORKING WITH HARDWOOD PLYWOOD

Most of the working tips given in Chapter 5 for softwood plywood also apply to the hardwood classification. Here are some working tips that, while they are also good for softwood plywood, apply more to hardwood plywood because of the uses of this classification.

Edge-Gluing

As mentioned earlier in this chapter, lumber core hardwood panels can be edge-glued like solid wood. (Veneer and particleboard core plywoods do not easily edge-glue.) The dowel and spline joint is most commonly used to strengthen an edge joint or to join 3/4" veneer plywood sheets to particleboard cores. The spline, usually about 1/4" thick and 5/8" wide, is continuous and may be made from plywood. The dowels (usually No. 7 or 8 spiral) are on centers anywhere from 4" to 10" (Fig. 6-5A). The tongue and groove (Fig. 6-5B) and tongue and rabbet (Fig. 6-5C) joints are also standard treatments. The tongue is usually 1/4" wide and approximately 5/16" deep. When bowing panels into place, the sides of the tongue are chamfered slightly. The groove is always made a little larger than the tongue. Dowels are also used to provide extra joint security. For thinner plywood, joint treatments recommended for wall paneling can be used. Reinforcement strips must be used behind the thinner materials (it is a good idea for thicker material, too).

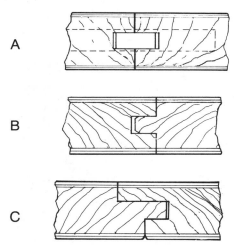

Fig. 6-5: Methods of jointing thicker plywood panels.

Finishing Edges

Plywood edges can be a problem. If care isn't exercised, the finished job will be bonded with raw edges. First, check the design of the piece to be built. Even with plain butt joints, there are an astonishing number of ways to assemble a simple box, and each one makes a difference in the number or position of visible edges. By using rabbets and miters or solid wood mouldings (Fig. 6-6), a little thought at the design stage can reduce the problem. Consider where the piece of furniture will be located, what surface will be exposed, and what finish you'll use.

Frame construction of corner butt joints makes it possible to reduce weight and save money by using thinner hardwood plywood. As shown in Fig. 6-7A, solid hardwood corner posts can be dadoed to receive plywood panel with veneer face of the same species of wood. A tongue and groove joint can also be used with a solid hardwood post to hold a panel (Fig. 6-7B).

Possibly the best treatment for edge grain is shown here in Fig. 6-8A. Two 45° cuts are made from the underside, completely through the wood. The small

piece is removed, and the end is bent. By this method a continuous grain is shown—even on the ends.

A solid piece of material—that is, solid hardwood—in the shape of a T in cross section can be glued to the piece of plywood so that, when the edge is viewed, it will appear as solid lumber (Fig. 6-8B). The procedure shown in Fig. 6-8C is the same, except that the piece of lumber is triangular in cross section. Cutting the edge at an angle, as shown in Fig. 6-8D, is a neat and cheap method; the edge grain may be painted or stained to match the panel.

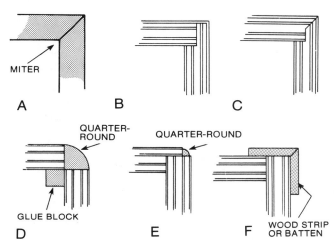

Fig. 6-6: Methods of concealing the plywood edges in corner construction: (A) miter, (B) rabbet, (C) rabbet-miter joint, (D) quarter-round moulding and a glue block, (E) rabbet and quarter-round moulding, and (F) wood strip or batten.

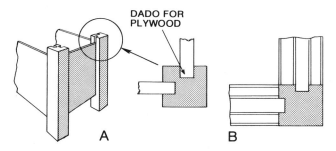

Fig. 6-7: Use of corner posts to conceal plywood edges.

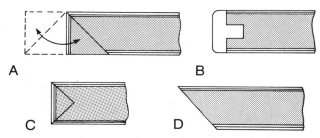

Fig. 6-8: Popular ways of concealing plywood edge grain.

It is also possible to bead the edge with a table saw's moulding head (Fig. 6-9A) or to glue a beading strip or moulding to the edge. A mitered framing strip, secured by glue and by brads that have been set and puttied, is a very effective treatment, especially for table and desk tops. Solid-wood mouldings, either purchased or made with the moulding head attachment, are also good for the exposed top edges of tables and desks (Figs. 6-9B to G). Don't overlook common half- or quarter-round moulding (Fig. 6-9H); its width may be greater than the edge width. Aluminum veneer cap moulding (Fig. 6-9I) may be used to cover edges with good results.

Fig. 6-10: Veneer strip with an adhesive backing is easy to apply.

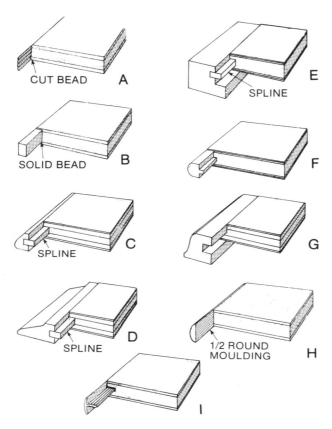

Fig. 6-9: Other methods of concealing plywood edge grain.

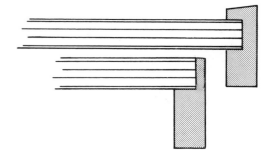

Fig. 6-11: Hardwood strips can be used to conceal plywood edges.

Framed panels will also help to eliminate the problem of plywood edges. The panel can be fitted to the solid wood frame in several ways (Fig. 6-12), and the frame can be treated decoratively with moulding.

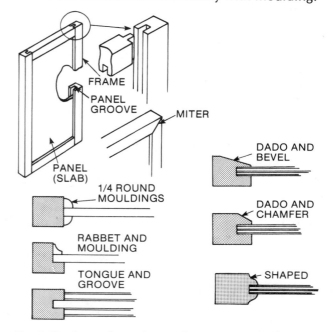

Fig. 6-12: Framed panels can also be used to eliminate the problem of plywood edges.

Thin strips of real wood edge-banding now are available, already coated with pressure-sensitive adhesive (Fig. 6-10). You need only peel off the backing paper and apply it to the edges according to the manufacturer's recommendations. These tapes are sold in several different kinds of hardwood by lumber dealers or home centers. A thicker effect can be secured by nailing or gluing a 1" or 1-1/2" strip all around the under edge. You can also bulk a plywood edge and thus conceal the plies as shown in Fig. 6-11. When bulking the edge, insert the slab in a dado cut in solid material or set the slab in a rabbet cut in solid wood.

Curved and Bent Surfaces

Curved or shaped sections for furniture and cabinets are produced by kerf-sawing or by bending. Plywood of standard construction can be bent to normal radii and held in place with glue, nails, or screws. The radius of the curvature to which a panel can be bent varies with the thickness of the panel and the species of wood or woods of which it is composed (Table 6-3). There are specially constructed bending panels which can be bent to much smaller radii than those obtainable on panels of standard construction; but they are seldom available to the home craftsman.

Exterior grade plywood, steamed or soaked in water until pliable, will have approximately 50% greater flexibility than normal. For example, 1/4" Douglas fir plywood, after soaking or steaming, can be bent to a radius of approximately 12" lengthwise and 4" crosswise. It is essential that only well made plywood, free from gaps in the core, be used; otherwise, when pressure is applied, the outer veneer will split. Also, the plywood should be bent across the grain of the outer veneer.

Thicker plywood (1/2" and up) may be bent by kerf-sawing the back of the board to relieve the resistance of the back veneer and then cross-bending. The kerfing is generally done as described previously. The frequency of the saw cuts will depend upon the thickness of the plywood and the radius desired. For example, to bend 3/4" birch plywood to a radius of 12", saw cuts 1/8" wide spaced 1/4" apart should be ample (Fig. 6-13). When the kerfing has been properly done and the cuts are neither too deep nor too far apart, plywood can be bent to practically any radius without undue risk of splitting or breaking.

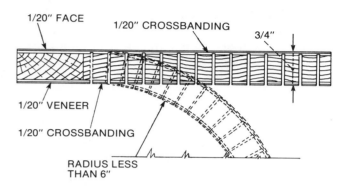

Fig. 6-13: Successive kerfs sawn into the backside of the panel allow the panel to be bent.

TABLE 6-3: BENDING RADII

Type of Panel	Approx. minimum radius parallel to grain	Approx. minimum radius across grain
Softwood plywood		
1/8"	10"	6.5"
1/4"	60"	24"
3/8"	96"	36"
1/2"	12'	6'
5/8"	16'	8'
3/4"	20'	12'
Birch (with poplar core crossband) plywood		
1/16"	7.6"	4.1"
1/8"	13.3"	8.3"
1/4"	28.0"	20.9"
3/8"	39.6"	34.4"
1/2"	55.0"	49.0"
3/4"	79.0"	72.0"
Mahogany (with poplar core crossband) plywood		
1/16"	5.9"	4.1"
1/8"	10.2"	8.3"
1/4"	21.5"	20.9"
3/8"	30.3"	34.4"
1/2"	42.2"	49.5"
3/4"	60.7"	72.5"

Note: This table indicates the normal radii to which panels of standard construction can be bent. These figures are for dry bending.

Door Construction

Doors for furniture pieces and cabinet goods can be swung on hinges or made to slide.

Hinged Doors. There are two basic types of hinged doors, panel and solid. With either type, the edge of the door (Fig. 6-14) may be set in flush with the case edges or butted against the case edges (flush overlay). The door edge may also lip over a portion of the case edges.

While flush doors are the easiest to install, they have a tendency to sag; and when this occurs, the doors will jam against the cabinet form or show an open space along the door edges. Sometimes this problem can be minimized by recessing or attaching the doors so that they project slightly.

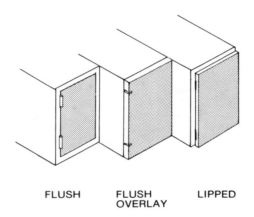

FLUSH   FLUSH   LIPPED
         OVERLAY

Fig. 6-14: Methods of setting doors.

Lipped doors minimize sagging problems and therefore give a better appearance. The lip is nothing more than a 3/8" or 1/2" rabbet cut around the edge of the door. This lipped edge will completely cover the door opening at all times, and minor sags won't be noticed.

Panel hinged doors are constructed in the same manner as the frame and panel construction shown in Fig. 6-12. The solid, hinged door consists of a simple slab of suitable material—solid lumber, plywood, or particleboard.

Hinges and Their Installation. The edge of the door, lipped or flush, will determine the type of hinge to use. In fact, there are many different styles and designs of hinges from which to select when you mount swinging doors on a cabinet. Usually, the better hinges come with mounting instructions, some even with templates or patterns, to make attaching the doors a simple job. Some of the more popular methods of hinging doors are shown in Fig. 6-15.

How to Add a Doorstop. The basic use of single or double doorstops is to seal a furniture compartment and so protect its contents from dust and other injury.

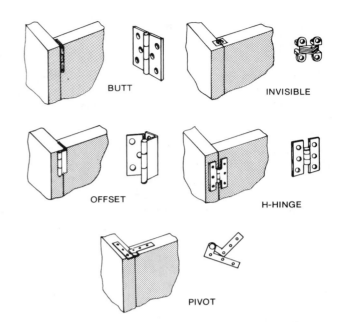

BUTT   INVISIBLE

OFFSET   H-HINGE

PIVOT

Fig. 6-15: The more popular methods of hinging doors.

Doorstops also help to mask the gaps that appear when the wood shrinks. Some ways of accomplishing doorstops are as follows:

1. *Butt Stop.* The easiest method is to have the side opposite the hinge act as the stop. The door fits over the side (Fig. 6-16A). When closed, it can't go any farther.

2. *Door Rabbet Stop.* By cutting a rabbet along the inside edge of one side of the door, it can overlap the side and thus it can be stopped when it is closed (Fig. 6-16B). When cutting the rabbet, its width should be the thickness of the door if the remaining extending part of the door is thicker than 1/4".

3. *Side Rabbet Stop.* This is merely a modification of the door rabbet. In this instance, the rabbet is cut into the side rather than the door (Fig. 6-16C).

4. *Miter Stop.* This type of stop is generally used in fine work (Fig. 6-16D).

For double doorstops, using the rabbet is considered to be the best method (Fig. 6-16E). The scoreline shown in Fig. 6-16F helps to hide any movement or shrinking of the doors.

Sliding Doors. Here are several ways in which you can install sliding doors in cabinets or built-ins.

Double Dado. Two dadoes cut into the bottom surface of the cabinet top and two dadoes in the top surface of the cabinet base provide the grooves in which the doors will slide (Fig. 6-17A). To make the sliding doors removable, follow this formula: W equals X minus the sum of Y and Z; Y equals 2Z.

Rabbet Dado. A modified method of the double dado, this is used when a faceplate trim is to be added

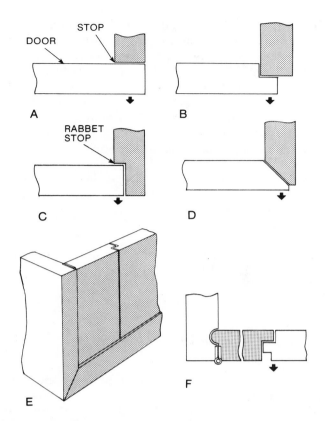

Fig. 6-16: Several doorstop arrangements.

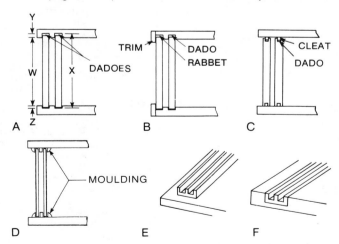

Fig. 6-17: Four methods of installing sliding doors.

1/4″ quarter-round moulding. The strip between is 1/4″ square. Use glue and brads or finish nails to fasten strips securely. Sliding door cabinet track also may be used.

Plastic track that may be surface mounted (Fig. 6-17E) is available at most hardware stores and home centers. For better appearance, the plastic track can be sunk into channels routed in the top and bottom of the cabinet (Fig. 6-17F). If channels are routed, the cabinet material must be at least 3/8″ thicker than the deeper track. In either case, the track is installed as follows:

1. Cut the plastic track to the proper length, using a fine hacksaw.

2. Place the track in the desired position. (Both top and bottom pieces should be located inside the front edge of the cabinet.) Then mark the position of the track.

3. Fasten the track with brads or glue. The top and bottom channels should be parallel to each other.

With all plywood doors, seal all edges and give the backs the same finish treatment as the front to prevent warping.

Drawers and Drawer Guides

Drawers come in handy for hundreds of everyday uses. They are pulled out and pushed back many times a day in the office, shop, and home. Often they are treated carelessly. And yet if drawers are carefully built, they'll last for years without even sticking.

There are many forms of drawer construction that can be made if the proper equipment is available. There are a variety of designs for a multitude of purposes and different kinds of furniture (Fig. 6-18). It's practically essential that all woodworkers have an understanding of basic drawer construction as applied both to cabinetmaking and house carpentry.

Any drawer is made to fit a definite opening of fixed dimensions (Fig. 6-19), making due allowance for clearance to provide a sliding fit. The minimum amount of clearance through the body part of the drawer is about 1/16″ at the sides and top. The actual closing part of the drawer—the front—can be worked to a closer fit if desired, but the body of the drawer should have ample clearance to prevent binding.

Average drawer stock will run to 3/4″ for the front, 1/2″ for the sides and back, and 1/4″ or 3/16″ plywood or hardboard for the bottom. (Hardwood should only be used on the front; softwood plywood can be used on sides and back.) Given these fixed wood sizes and a definite type of construction (Fig. 6-20), the net width and length of each piece can be expressed in terms of

to the outside of the unit (Fig. 6-17B). In this way only one dado is cut, while a rabbet is cut along the edge.

Dado and Cleat. A single dado is cut into the top and bottom of the door itself rather than into the top and bottom of the unit (Fig. 6-17C). This groove in the door rides on a 1/2″ by 1/2″ cleat that is nailed and glued into the cabinet's top and bottom.

Quarter-Round Moulding. This is easy for providing sliding doors and is ideal if you have only hand tools (Fig. 6-17D). The front and back strips are stock

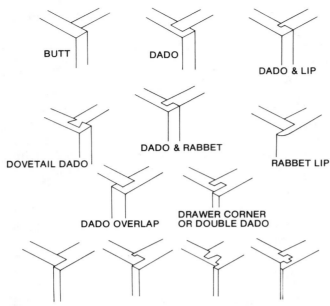

Fig. 6-18: Joints used in drawer construction.

the size of the opening, minus a certain amount for clearance and construction.

Drawer Guides. Commercial drawer guides (also known as slides) are available. These can be either

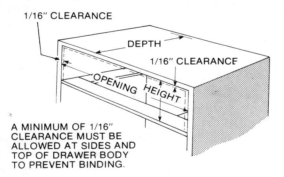

Fig. 6-19: Dimensions that determine a drawer's size.

bottom or side mounted guides. Side mounted guides come as a matching pair that fits against the inside of the case and along the outside of the drawer sides (Fig. 6-21). The amount of clearance needed between the drawer sides and case varies with the size and kind of guides. Therefore, it is important to buy the guides before building the drawers. Drawer guides, of course, can be made on your table saw. The two most popular designs are side and center guides.

Fig. 6-21: Side mounted drawer guides.

Center guides (Fig. 6-22) extend between the front rail and back of the cabinet. Butt and dowel the ends, or notch the fronts over and into the rails. A toenailed butt is generally used in built-in cabinets. The front end acts as a drawer stop, while the lower edge is flush with the underside of the rail and serves as a hold-down for the drawer below it, keeping its front from dropping when the drawer is open. Top drawers, of course, need a separate hold-down.

Square each guide from the front rail and be sure it is parallel to the guides above and below. Insert a drawer and, using the sides of the guide as a gauge, scribe lines on the bottom for placing the strips. Little sliding clearance is needed. Construction is improved if channels are installed at the sides of the cabinet to relieve the guides of most of the weight of the drawer.

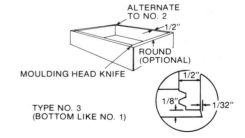

PIECE	THICK	WIDTH	LENGTH
FRONT	3/4	H LESS 1/16	O-1/8
SIDE	1/2	H LESS 1/16	D-1/4
BACK	1/2	H LESS 5/8	O-1-1/8
BOT	1/4 PLY	D LESS 9/16	O-11/16

TYPE NO. 1

PIECE	THICK	WIDTH	LENGTH
FRONT	3/4	H-1/16	O-1/16
SIDE	1/2	H-1/16	D-1/4
BACK	1/2	H-5/8	O-11/16
BOT	1/4 PLY	D-9/16	O-11/16

TYPE NO. 2 (BOTTOM LIKE NO. 1)

PIECE	THICK	WIDTH	LENGTH
FRONT	3/4	H-1/16	O-1/16
SIDE	1/2	H-1/16	D-1/8
BACK	1/2	H-5/8	O-11/16
BOT	1/4 PLY	D-9/16	O-11/16

TYPE NO. 3 (BOTTOM LIKE NO. 1)

Fig. 6-20: Three standard types of drawer construction.

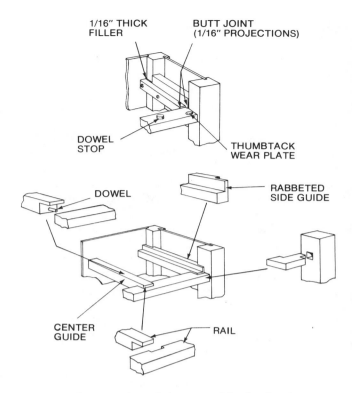

A

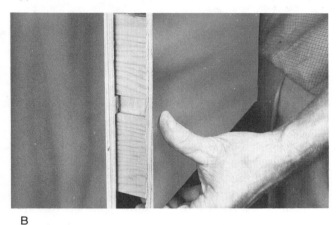

B

C

Fig. 6-22: Construction of drawer guides for furniture.

Methods of installing side guides are also shown in Fig. 6-22. If these guides are allowed to project 1/16" beyond the rails and stiles where this is possible, much wear will be prevented. Heavy drawers require a greater projection.

Figure 6-23 shows several dado cut drawer guides. In Fig. 6-23A, the extended bottom is set in a dado groove cut in the side panels. You can also cut a dado in the side of the drawer and add a cleat to each side of the cabinet (Fig. 6-23B). This keeps the drawer bottom off of the shelf and puts all of the weight on the trim. When the added strips are made of hardwood, you should encounter little difficulty in opening and closing the drawer. Incidentally, the dado needn't be cut into the drawer front if the cleat doesn't extend all the way to the front of the unit. Even heavy drawers slide easily on guides like these if they have been waxed or lubricated with paraffin after finishing.

In Fig. 6-23C, the procedure is reversed, and the cabinet side is dadoed before assembly. A matching strip is glued and screwed to the drawer side. You can also design drawers like this without cutting the dadoes. A 3/8" or 1/2" plywood bottom extends 3/8" beyond the sides of the drawer, forming a lip along each side (Fig. 6-24). This lip fits into slots formed with 3/8" plywood pieces glued to the inner surface of each side of the cabinet. A gap just wide enough to take the lip is left between the pieces.

Fig. 6-23: Dado cut drawer guides: (A) extended bottom, (B) cleat on cabinet side, and (C) cleat on drawer side.

Fitting Drawer Fronts. After the guides have been installed and the drawer otherwise completed, insert it in its opening and dress the ends and top until the front will enter. Pull the drawer out again and bevel inward slightly, continuing the fitting until a uniform joint of about 1/16" is obtained. This provides space for several coats of paint or varnish.

Labels in Fig. 6-22:
- 1/16" THICK FILLER
- BUTT JOINT (1/16" PROJECTIONS)
- DOWEL STOP
- THUMBTACK WEAR PLATE
- DOWEL
- RABBETED SIDE GUIDE
- CENTER GUIDE
- RAIL

Fig. 6-24: A guide for an extended bottom may be made with strips of plywood spaced just far enough apart to receive the lip.

Fitting such as this requires the use of closing stops. Dowels inserted in the lower rail and filed or chiseled in front to allow the front to be pushed back into place are excellent for drawers having side guides. Hardwood strips tacked until adjusted and then nailed or screwed permanently are also good. If drawers are set back behind the edges of the rails, the stops must be set back correspondingly.

Lip drawers, having fronts with rabbeted top and side edges that lap over rail and stiles to conceal the joints, require little fitting. Side clearance is also less critical than with flush fronts. Close the drawers and lay a straightedge across the fronts to mark the ends for cutting to length. The lips customarily act as stops, but for drawers subjected to abuse, stops may be placed behind the drawers to take the shock of closing off the fronts.

If you wish to have dust panels for your drawers, groove the rails and slides to take the edges of the dust shelves, or rabbet them to hold the shelves flush with the lower edges (Fig. 6-25). Flush shelves leave no projections to catch on contents of drawers beneath them.

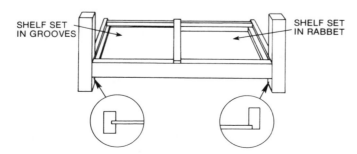

Fig. 6-25: Fitting dust panels in drawer compartments.

Shelves

In fitting shelves in furniture projects, you have a choice of several methods of construction. The simplest of all is the plain butted joint, either nailed or screwed. The most popular is the housed joint. Running the groove right through, as in Fig. 6-26A, presents the simplest method of working, but exposes the joint. Half-round moulding is often used to face the edges, as in Fig. 6-26D, to cover the joint. The best housed joint is stopped a little short of the edges, as in Fig. 6-26B. Vee jointing (Fig. 6-26C) makes an attractive joint. The vee must be very blunt, since any angle of 45° or over would cut the work in two. A method of housing the shelf in a square-cut groove with only the exposed edge vee jointed is shown in Fig. 6-26E.

Housed dovetail joints make excellent construction, as shown in Fig. 6-27, but they take longer to construct than the other shelf fittings. In addition to being dovetailed, the joint must also be tapered so that it can be driven in from the back.

Where adjustable shelves are needed, it is best to use one of the metal adjustable shelving systems available from your local hardware store or home center dealer.

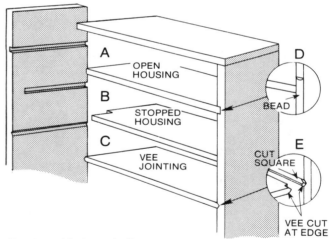

Fig. 6-26: Various shelf joints.

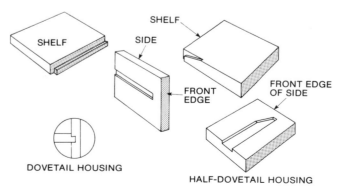

Fig. 6-27: Two types of housed dovetail joints.

Cabinet Backs and Dividers

The standard method of applying backs to cabinets and other storage units calls for rabbeting the sides. For movable furniture units, the rabbet may be just deep enough to take the plywood or hardboard back (Fig. 6-28A). For large units that must fit against walls that may not be perfectly smooth, the rabbet can be made 1/2" or even 3/4" deep. The lip that remains after the back has been inserted can be trimmed to make the plywood unit fit the wall perfectly. In either case, nail the cabinet back into the rabbet by driving nails at a slight angle. Use 1" brads or 4d finish nails. Where the back won't be seen, 1" blue lath nails may be used.

Another method of installing a back is to set it in a groove cut about 1/2" to 3/4" from the back edges of the unit (Fig. 6-28B). This arrangement requires that the back is assembled with the sides.

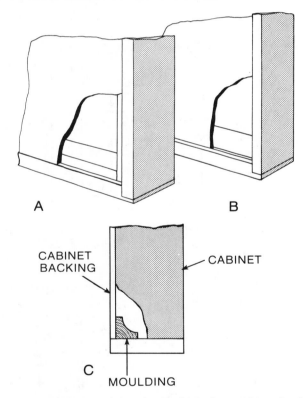

CABINET BACKING

CABINET

C

MOULDING

Fig. 6-28: Three simple methods of attaching cabinet backs.

If you don't have power tools, attach strips of 1/4" quarter-round moulding for the back to rest against (Fig. 6-28C). Glue and nail the back to the moulding.

Cabinet backs can also be applied without rabbets or mouldings. Nail the back flush with outside edge; beveling the edge slightly with a block plane will make it less conspicuous. Or you can set the back 1/2" to 7/8" away from the edges. The back will not be noticeable when the cabinet is against the wall.

HARDWOOD PLYWOOD PROJECTS

Here are a few projects you can build with hardwood plywood. Be sure you understand the material in "Working with Hardwood Plywood" before beginning actual construction of the projects.

Folding Dining Table

For unexpected company, this folding table will serve up to ten people and can be folded away to a compact size of 16" × 32". The versatile design of the table will readily lend itself to most dining areas.

The tabletop sections are cut on a table saw from 3/4" plywood for the various sizes needed.

Lay out the legs, using the square method, on a piece of brown wrapping paper. Nail two pieces of 3/4" × 6-1/2" × 28-1/4" plywood together, tack the pattern onto the top piece, and proceed to cut the outline. Drill a hole 1/2" deep and with a 1" diameter on the inside of all four legs. These holes are for dowel stretchers.

To assemble the leg, cut two 4-7/8" × 25-1/2" workpieces from 3/4" plywood. From solid stock, cut four 3/4" × 3/4" × 4-7/8" cleats. The cleats and workpiece are predrilled.

Assemble the leg to the workpiece with glue and 6d finishing nails; then, strengthen the leg with a cleat. Attach the top to the workpiece with six No. 8 × 1-1/4" wood screws.

Make four gatelegs following the layout and dimensions shown. Notches—both dadoes and rabbets—for the gatelegs can be cut on a table saw with two passes of a dado head.

One leg of each gateleg assembly is 1/4" shorter, allowing the top rail to clear the continuous hinge barrel. Assemble with glue and 6d finishing nails. Attach the gatelegs to the leg assemblies with 1-1/2" brass butt hinges. Two hinges for each gateleg are required.

To assemble the table, turn the tabletop panels and the leg assemblies bottom side up. Place one panel on each side of the leg assembly and join them together with continuous hinges. The continuous hinge is screw fastened at the gateleg assembly end of the leg assembly to within 1-3/4" of the leg, opposite the hinged side of the gatelegs. Gateleg stop blocks are mounted 3-1/2" from the end of each table panel.

Fold both leg assemblies with the attached panels and join together the two center panels with a continuous hinge. Note that the continuous hinge is the full width of the panels. Also, install furniture glides on all 16 table leg bottoms.

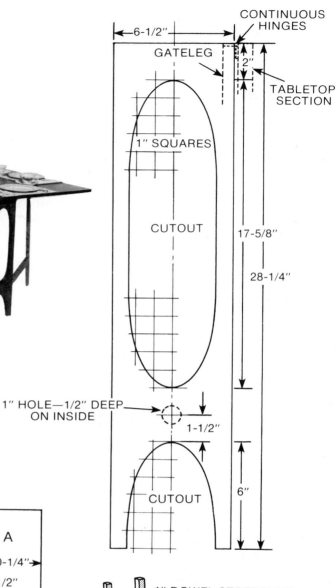

CONTINUOUS HINGES

6-1/2"

GATELEG

2"

TABLETOP SECTION

1" SQUARES

CUTOUT

17-5/8"

28-1/4"

1" HOLE—1/2" DEEP ON INSIDE

1-1/2"

CUTOUT

6"

Turn the table right side up and attach the flat brass hooks to the panel. The panel is only used to fill space when the table is closed. Use flexible wood trim to cover the exposed edges of the plywood. This type of veneer should be applied with contact cement and tapped with a rubber-headed mallet to achieve a good bond. Use a penetrating oil resin finish per manufacturer's instructions to complete the project.

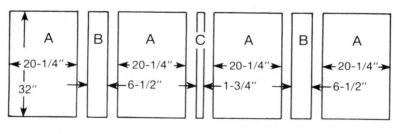

A   B   A   C   A   B   A

20-1/4"   20-1/4"   20-1/4"   20-1/4"

32"   6-1/2"   1-3/4"   6-1/2"

LAYOUT OF THE TABLETOP BOARDS

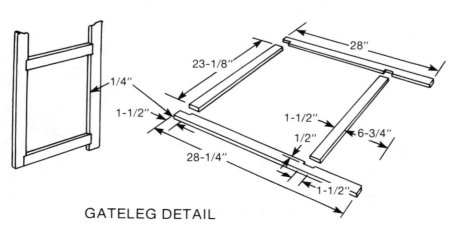

1/4"

23-1/8"

28"

1-1/2"

1-1/2"

6-3/4"

1/2"

28-1/4"

1-1/2"

GATELEG DETAIL

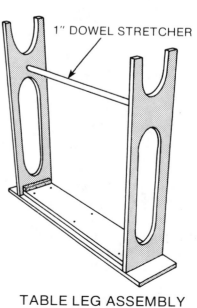

1" DOWEL STRETCHER

TABLE LEG ASSEMBLY

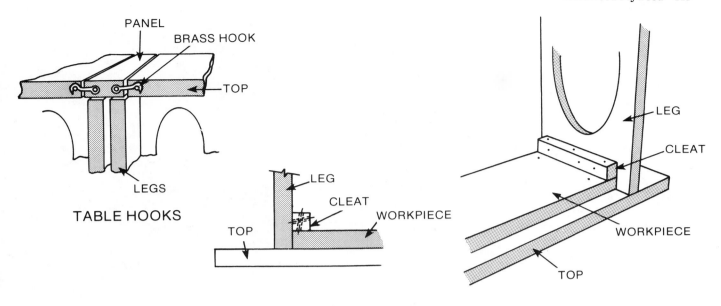

PANEL
BRASS HOOK
TOP
LEGS

TABLE HOOKS

LEG
CLEAT
WORKPIECE
TOP

LEG
CLEAT
WORKPIECE
TOP

LEG ASSEMBLY

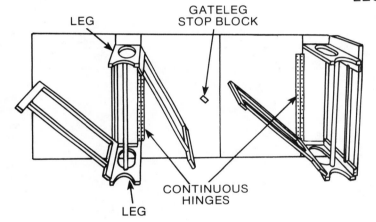

LEG
GATELEG STOP BLOCK
CONTINUOUS HINGES
LEG

BOTTOM VIEW (OPEN)

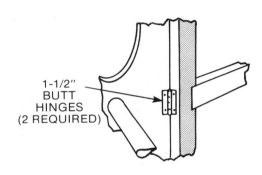

1-1/2″ BUTT HINGES (2 REQUIRED)

GATELEG/TABLE LEG HINGE

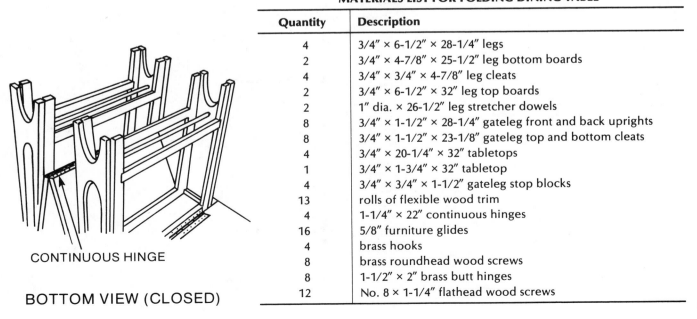

CONTINUOUS HINGE

BOTTOM VIEW (CLOSED)

MATERIALS LIST FOR FOLDING DINING TABLE

Quantity	Description
4	3/4″ × 6-1/2″ × 28-1/4″ legs
2	3/4″ × 4-7/8″ × 25-1/2″ leg bottom boards
4	3/4″ × 3/4″ × 4-7/8″ leg cleats
2	3/4″ × 6-1/2″ × 32″ leg top boards
2	1″ dia. × 26-1/2″ leg stretcher dowels
8	3/4″ × 1-1/2″ × 28-1/4″ gateleg front and back uprights
8	3/4″ × 1-1/2″ × 23-1/8″ gateleg top and bottom cleats
4	3/4″ × 20-1/4″ × 32″ tabletops
1	3/4″ × 1-3/4″ × 32″ tabletop
4	3/4″ × 3/4″ × 1-1/2″ gateleg stop blocks
13	rolls of flexible wood trim
4	1-1/4″ × 22″ continuous hinges
16	5/8″ furniture glides
4	brass hooks
8	brass roundhead wood screws
8	1-1/2″ × 2″ brass butt hinges
12	No. 8 × 1-1/4″ flathead wood screws

Child's Rocker

The sturdy little rocker pictured here is a perfect gift for children on their birthday or on any occasion. The miniature chair is something a young son or daughter can call their very own. Not only will the rocker be a joy to present as a gift, but it will also be easy to build.

The entire rocker is constructed from 3/4" birch plywood or any other veneer plywood desired. One piece, measuring 48" square, is all that is needed.

Use the squares method to transfer the shape of the side of the rocker to the plywood. The sides can be cut out on a band saw or scroll saw. Note that both sides are cut at one time by tacking the two pieces of plywood together.

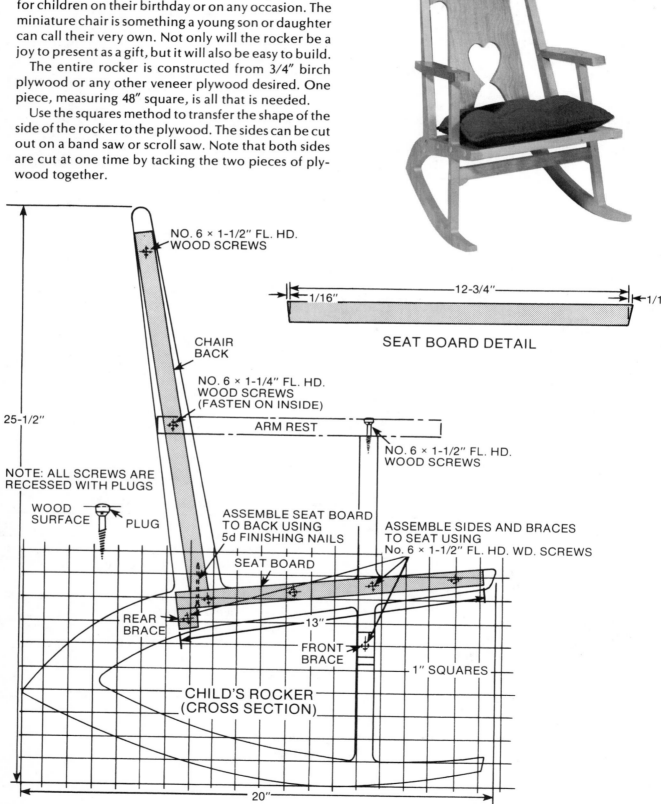

NO. 6 × 1-1/2" FL. HD. WOOD SCREWS

CHAIR BACK

NO. 6 × 1-1/4" FL. HD. WOOD SCREWS (FASTEN ON INSIDE)

25-1/2"

NOTE: ALL SCREWS ARE RECESSED WITH PLUGS

WOOD SURFACE   PLUG

1/16"   12-3/4"   1/16"

SEAT BOARD DETAIL

ARM REST

NO. 6 × 1-1/2" FL. HD. WOOD SCREWS

ASSEMBLE SEAT BOARD TO BACK USING 5d FINISHING NAILS

SEAT BOARD

ASSEMBLE SIDES AND BRACES TO SEAT USING No. 6 × 1-1/2" FL. HD. WD. SCREWS

REAR BRACE

13"

FRONT BRACE

1" SQUARES

CHILD'S ROCKER (CROSS SECTION)

20"

A table saw or radial saw is used to cut the rocker back, the seat board, and the arm rests to shape. A 4° angle is required on the sides of the seat board, as well as on the ends of the front and rear braces. These are also cut on a table or radial saw. A taper cutting jig is needed to cut the sides of the back panel. Note the 4° angle on the bottom edge of the back. The design on the back is cut out with a scroll saw or band saw. Cut the arm rest notches on the table saw or radial saw. If a table saw is used, set the miter gauge at 11-1/2° to the right for the right arm rest and 11-1/2° to the left for the left arm rest. Use a stop clamp to ensure uniformity in the cuts on both arm rests. If a radial saw is used, the arm is rotated 11-1/2° to the right and left to make the angle cuts.

Predrill all holes in the sides and arm rests for the screws and screw hole plugs before assembly. Glue, sixteen No. 6 × 1-1/2″ flathead wood screws, two No. 6 × 1-1/4″ flathead wood screws, and 5d nails are needed to assemble the rocker. When screw fastening into the end grain, hardwood dowels may be added for additional strength.

An adjustable screw setter greatly simplifies the assembly of the rocker. In one operation, it predrills, countersinks, and counterbores for the flathead wood screws and wood plugs used in the assembly.

Flexible wood veneer makes it easy to cover the exposed plywood edges. The veneer, also called edging tape, is fastened with contact cement. Apply it with hand pressure, then tap it down with a rubber-headed mallet to achieve a good bond. Make sure all of the corners are rounded and any sharp edges are sanded smooth. Complete the project with a clear semi-gloss wood finish, sanding lightly between coats.

A 12″ × 12″ knife edge or box style cushion will add comfort and enhance the beauty of the project.

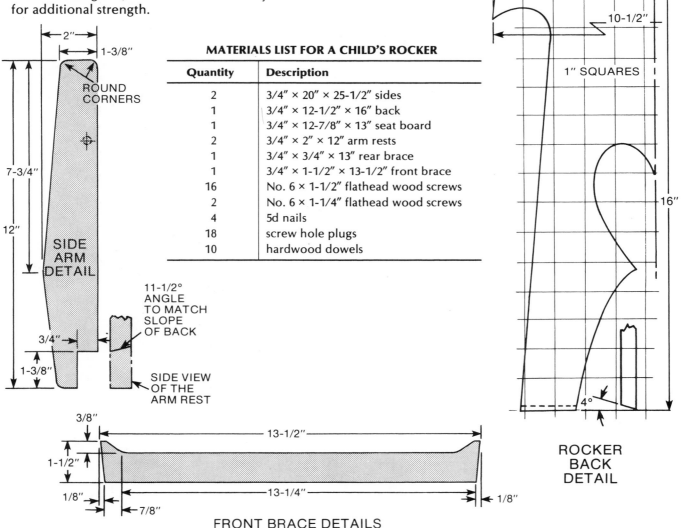

MATERIALS LIST FOR A CHILD'S ROCKER

Quantity	Description
2	3/4″ × 20″ × 25-1/2″ sides
1	3/4″ × 12-1/2″ × 16″ back
1	3/4″ × 12-7/8″ × 13″ seat board
2	3/4″ × 2″ × 12″ arm rests
1	3/4″ × 3/4″ × 13″ rear brace
1	3/4″ × 1-1/2″ × 13-1/2″ front brace
16	No. 6 × 1-1/2″ flathead wood screws
2	No. 6 × 1-1/4″ flathead wood screws
4	5d nails
18	screw hole plugs
10	hardwood dowels

ROUND CORNERS

2″
1-3/8″
7-3/4″
12″
SIDE ARM DETAIL
3/4″
1-3/8″

11-1/2° ANGLE TO MATCH SLOPE OF BACK

SIDE VIEW OF THE ARM REST

10-1/2″
1″ SQUARES
16″
4°

ROCKER BACK DETAIL

3/8″
13-1/2″
1-1/2″
1/8″
13-1/4″
1/8″
7/8″

FRONT BRACE DETAILS

School Desk and Chair

Children will get plenty of use out of this sturdy, easy-to-make desk and chair set. The overall dimensions are appropriate for youngsters in the 5- to 10-year-old group; however, the dimensions can be changed to suit younger or older children as desired. Also, the cutout designs on the desk sides and the chair back can be changed to meet individual preferences. For instance, initials might be used for the cutouts. The desk and chair can be made entirely of 3/4" birch or maple plywood.

First, trace the outline of the sides of the desk on a piece of brown wrapping paper. Before cutting the outline, make a 3/4" dado in each side piece for the school supply shelf. Next, cut the top taper, setting the miter gauge at 4°. A 1/4" rabbet to accommodate the desk top is made on a table saw with one pass of the two 1/8" outside blades of the dado head or with two passes of a regular saw blade. The two outside dado blades are then used to make 1/4" blind dadoes in the side pieces for the dado and rabbet joint. Decorative holes in the sides of the desk and the back of the chair can be bored on a drill press.

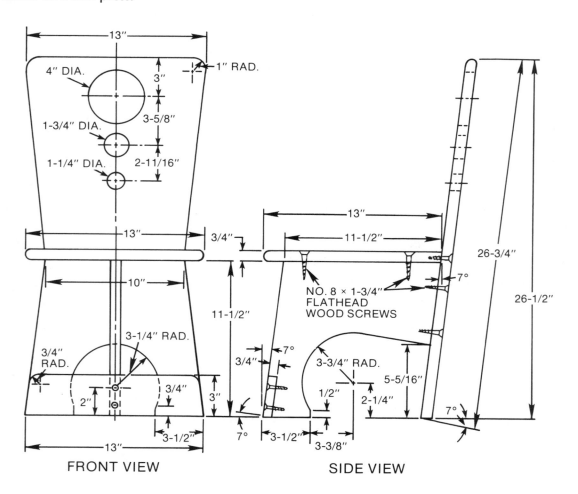

FRONT VIEW

SIDE VIEW

On the underside of the desk top, three 1/4″ × 1/4″ blind grooves are made; two are for the desk sides and one for the 1/4″ back panel. A 1/2″ × 1/2″ round-edge stop strip is glued to the desk top, 1/2″ from the edge. The pencil groove is made on the table saw with a moulding cutterhead and 1/2″ flute cutter knives. The desk pieces are glued and screw-fastened together with No. 8 × 1-3/4″ flathead wood screws. No screws are needed for the top and the back panel.

The chair parts are cut to the dimensions shown. The back of the chair has a bevel cut of 7° at the bottom. The front leg brace is also bevel cut 7° on the bottom edge only. The entire chair is butt jointed and held together with glue and No. 8 × 1-3/4″ flathead wood screws. Sand all edges and apply matching edge-banding. Finish as desired.

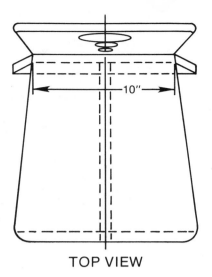

TOP VIEW

MATERIALS LIST FOR DESK AND CHAIR

Quantity	Description
2	3/4″ × 12-1/2″ × 23″ sides
1	3/4″ × 13″ × 21″ top
1	3/4″ × 8-1/2″ × 18-3/4″ shelf
1	1/2″ × 1/2″ × 21″ top stop strip
1	1/4″ × 5-1/4″ × 18-3/4″ back panel
13	No. 8 × 1-3/4″ flathead wood screws
1	3/4″ × 13″ × 26-3/4″ chair back
1	3/4″ × 13″ × 13″ chair seat
1	3/4″ × 13″ × 11-1/2″ chair center support
1	3/4″ × 3″ × 13″ chair front leg brace

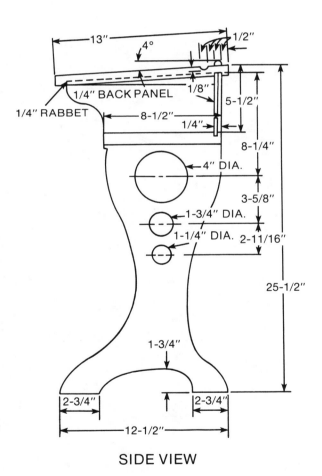

SIDE VIEW

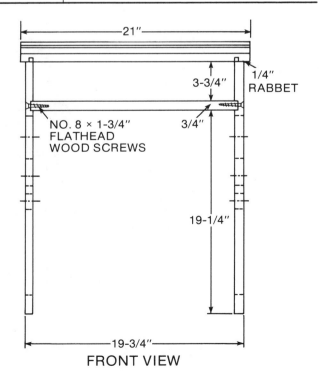

FRONT VIEW

Interlocking Plywood Desk/Workbench

A single 3/4" × 4' × 8' A-2 birch plywood panel provides an easy to assemble, yet sturdy, desk or hobby workbench. No nails, screws, or glue are needed, which allows easy disassembly for storage or moving. The secret is in the interlocking slots. Paint it, stain it, or coat it with a clean natural finish for a child's room or recreation area.

Lay out all measurements as indicated on the diagram. If you are cutting with a hand saw, lay out dimensions with the good side up. But if using a circular or saber saw, lay out dimensions on the back surface.

Cut off the 33" section and then divide into the two leg units (A); then, rip the remaining panel for leg brace (B), back brace (C), and desk top (D). Round all major corners to a 2-1/2" radius with a coping or saber saw.

Cut the 3/4" slots; saw to the inside line of the 3/4" slot for a snug fit. With a scrap piece of plywood, check width of each slot as you progress. Slots must fit together easily by hand. A wood rasp or sandpaper will help enlarge slightly undersized slots.

Assemble by dropping the side legs onto the leg brace slots, installing back brace and, finally, slipping the desk top section into place. If you want a natural finish or stained finish, band plywood edges with matching 3/4" birch wood tape. For a painted project, use either wood tape or fill plywood edges with putty; sand smooth and then paint.

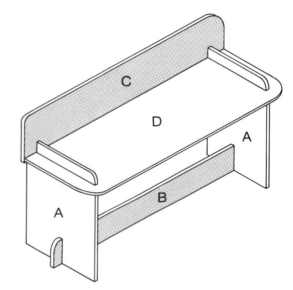

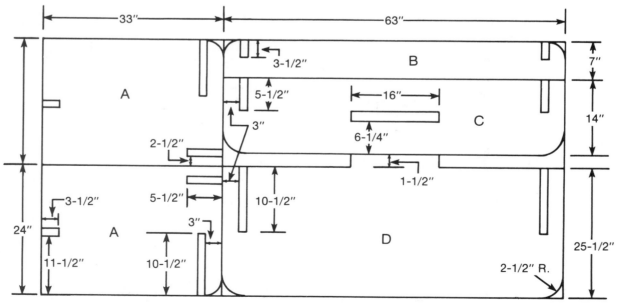

CHAPTER

—— 7 ——

HARDBOARD

In the previous chapters of this book, we've primarily concerned ourselves with wood products that have not been altered significantly from when they were part of a tree. Plywood is in one sense a remanufactured product in that the thin veneers, when glued together, become a panel with a completely new set of physical properties. The wood, however, is still recognizable as wood, and this is one of plywood's most appealing attributes.

Another group of manufactured wood products is made by reducing wood to small fractions, then putting it back together again to make something else. These "engineered" wood products are manufactured in panel form and bear no resemblance at all to the tree from which they came. Hardboard, particleboard, and Waferwood are the most popular of these wood products (Fig. 7-1). This chapter will deal with hardboard.

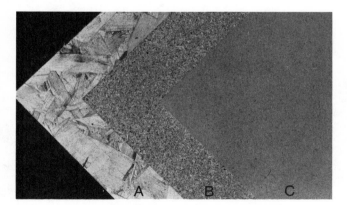

Fig. 7-1: Hardboard is one of three widely used "engineered" wood products: (A) waferboard, (B) particleboard, and (C) hardboard.

PROPERTIES OF HARDBOARD

Hardboard is more dense than many woods, resulting in panels which are stronger, more durable, and better able to resist dents, abrasion, scuffing, and general hard use. Because hardboard has no grain, it is equally strong in all directions and is as strong and sometimes stronger than natural wood across the grain. However, hardboard is generally not as strong as wood along the grain.

Hardboard has natural water resistance which is increased by tempering or other special processing. However, like natural wood, hardboard tends to shrink and swell with changes in moisture content. Since it is commonly produced in thicknesses of 1/8" to 1/4", uneven moisture exchange between the two surfaces may result in bulging or warping. Hardboard is also a natural insulator.

You'll find hardboard easy to work with using standard tools. You can saw, shape, route, drill, bend, and die-cut hardboard. Because of its smooth, hard surface, it's free of slivers and splinters. This surface is also an ideal base for opaque finishes or wallpaper because it has no grain to raise or check the finish. You should seal hardboard with a coat of shellac, enamel undercoater, or primer sealer before applying a final finish.

Another important characteristic of hardboard is its excellent racking resistance when nailed 4" on center along all edges and 8" on center on intermediate supports. If you glue hardboard to framing before nailing as described, its racking resistance even exceeds that of plywood.

MANUFACTURE OF HARDBOARD

Hardboard is considered to be a fiber product (a category which also includes softboard, pasteboard, and other low density wood product boards). Its name serves as an excellent description of its properties—it is very hard and is truly a board. Figure 7-2 illustrates the steps in the manufacture of hardboard, which are:

1. Wood residues of shavings and chips are reduced to individual wood fibers by either the steam or the mechanical defibering processes.

Fig. 7-2: Production of hardboard: (A) A control panel is used in the hardboard mill. The highly automated production uses sophisticated equipment to monitor weight, density, and fiber mix. (B) Refined fibers mix with resin and are deposited on a continuously moving belt at the forming stations. Trim saws (right) edge the panel prior to being fed into the large rotary drum presses (left). (C) Side view of continuous drum hardboard presses. (D) Finished continuous panels 8' wide exit presses and approach trim saws. (E) Multiple head trim saws give accurate right angle trim cuts. (F) A variety of hardboard thicknesses and grades are loaded for shipment to customer.

2. Fibers are put through certain mechanical processes varying with the method of manufacture, and small amounts of chemicals may be added to enhance the resulting board properties.

3. The fibers are interlocked in the felter into a continuous mat and compressed by heavy rollers.

4. Lengths of mat, or "wetlap," are fed into a continuous rotating press or into multiple presses where heat and pressure produce the thin, hard, dry board sheets.

5. As it leaves the press, moisture may be added to the board in a humidifier to stabilize it to surrounding atmospheric conditions.

6. The board is trimmed to standard specified dimensions, wrapped in convenient packages, and readied for shipment.

TYPES OF HARDBOARD

There are many types and classifications of hardboard. While some are available from retail lumber dealers, others go into industrial markets only. Table 7-1 describes four classifications available to the do-it-yourselfer.

TABLE 7-1: CLASSIFICATION OF HARDBOARD BY SURFACE FINISH, THICKNESS, AND PHYSICAL PROPERTIES

Class	Surface	Nominal Thickness	Water Resistance (max avg. per panel)				Modulus of Rupture (min avg. per panel)	Tensile Strength (min avg. per panel)	
			Water Absorption Based on Weight		Thickness Swelling			Parallel to Surface	Perpendicular to Surface
			S1S	S2S	S1S	S2S			
	S1S	inch 1/12	percent 30	percent —	percent 25	percent —	psi	psi	psi
1 Tempered	S1S and S2S	1/10	20	25	16	20	7000	3500	150
		1/8	15	20	11	16			
		3/16	12	18	10	15			
		1/4	10	12	8	11			
		5/16	8	11	8	10			
		3/8	8	10	8	9			
2 Standard	S1S and S2S	1/12	40	40	30	30	5000	2500	100
		1/10	25	30	22	25			
		1/8	20	25	16	18			
		3/16	18	25	14	18			
		1/4	16	20	12	14			
		5/16	14	15	10	12			
		3/8	12	12	10	10			
3 Service-tempered	S1S and S2S	1/8	20	25	15	22	4500	2000	100
		3/16	18	20	13	18			
		1/4	15	20	13	14			
		3/8	14	18	11	14			
4 Service	S1S and S2S	1/8	30	30	25	25	3000	1500	75
		3/16	25	27	15	22			
		1/4	25	27	15	22			
		3/8	25	27	15	22			
		7/16	25	27	15	22			
		1/2	25	18	15	14			

Standard hardboard can be found around your home in drawer bottoms (Fig. 7-3), cabinet backing, vertical dividers, etc. Tempered hardboard has a higher density than standard hardboard and is treated with oils, resins, and heat curing to improve water resistance, hardness, and strength. The tempered panels are often employed in exterior applications, such as soffits on the underside of eaves and porches, carport and breezeway ceilings, fences, storage sheds, etc. Also, tempered hardboard should be used for interior applications where abrasion resistance, strength, and moisture resistance are required.

Fig. 7-3: Standard hardboard is commonly used for drawer bottoms and for other hidden furniture parts.

Hardboard Siding and Paneling. Hardboard is also manufactured into siding and paneling. Siding (Fig. 7-4) is available in sheets 4' wide and up to 16' long or in lap siding 9", 12", 16", or 24" wide and 8', 12', or 16' long. Hardboard paneling offers a wide variety of decorative and wood grain finishes (Fig. 7-5). This material is specifically treated for resistance to stains and moisture; it's highly resistant to dents, mars, and scuffs. The thickness is usually 3/8" or 7/16", and the most common size is 4' wide and up to 10' long.

Perforated and Filigree Hardboard. Two other hardboard products are perforated hardboard and filigree hardboard. Perforated hardboard (Fig. 7-6) has been punched to receive hooks and hanging hardware. Available in 4' × 8' sheets, perforated hardboard can provide extra storage space for tools, kitchen utensils, sports equipment, and many other items. Filigree hardboard, although similar to perforated hardboard, is decorative rather than functional. It has been die-cut into a grillwork that can be used as room dividers, free standing screens, and imaginative decorations (Fig. 7-7).

Embossed Hardboard. This tempered hardboard panel has a patterned surface that is produced by embossing the finished side. While travertine marble and

Fig. 7-4: Hardboard is available as exterior siding.

fine-grain leather patterns are the most commonly used, new patterns are occasionally introduced. Embossed finished hardboard is used primarily in furniture making and for wall paneling, but offers the do-it-yourselfer an excellent opportunity to achieve various decorative effects. The 4' wide panels are 1/8" or 1/4" thick and usually come in lengths of 4', 6', and 8'.

Fig. 7-5: Hardboard paneling is available in decorative and wood grain finishes.

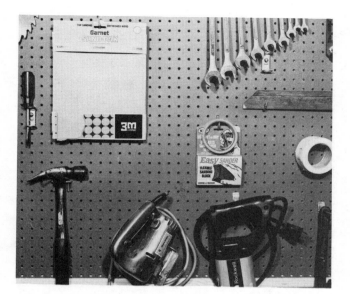

Fig. 7-6: *Using perforated hardboard is a good way to put a wall to work for you.*

Fig. 7-7: *Filigree hardboard is die-cut to form a decorative grillwork, as in this picture frame.*

Two other popular hardboards used by do-it-your-selfers in construction and remodeling work are *hardboard underlayment* and *concrete-form hardboard*. The former is a material especially developed for use over old wood floors or subfloors to provide an extremely smooth, flat surface upon which to lay vinyl, tile, or carpeting. Hardboard underlayment is sanded to a uniform thickness of .215″ and comes in handy 3′ × 4′ and 4′ × 4′ sizes.

As its name implies, concrete-form hardboard is a special tempered material that can be employed for building concrete forms. Because it can bend to form smooth curves, it is most useful in creating unusual, irregular, or free-form shapes. It imparts a smooth finish to the concrete.

PURCHASING HARDBOARD

When purchasing hardboard, determine and designate thicknesses, widths, and lengths of pieces; the number of pieces needed; S1S or S2S surfaces; the density required; the type of surface pattern desired; and whether or not the panels must be tempered. When selecting prefinished hardboard, you must also choose the design you prefer.

In transport and storage, protect the panels from moisture or general mistreatment and keep the pieces flat. If you must stack the panels outside, be sure to cover them with plastic and place them on supports so they don't touch the ground.

WORKING WITH HARDBOARD

As stated earlier in this chapter, ordinary shop tools are used to work hardboard (although cutting tools are dulled rapidly). To best cut hardboard, use fine-tooth standard combination or plywood blades. When extensive cutting is to be done, use a carbide-tipped blade, especially when using tempered hardboard. The 10- or 15-tooth saber saw blade should be employed when saber sawing (Fig. 7-8). Hardboard can be cut by hand with a fine-toothed crosscut saw. Keyhole, compass, and coping saws can also be used. When sawing, always follow the same rules as when cutting plywood; that is, always saw with the finished surface toward you when using a hand saw, table saw, or radial arm saw. When a circular saw is used, the good side should be down.

Fig. 7-8: *Because hardboard is just that—a hard board—use a 10- or 15-tooth saber saw blade when cutting with a saber saw.*

For drilling operations in hardboard, twist drills and spade bits work easier than auger bits. All drilling should be done from the finished surface (Fig. 7-9A) not the rough (screened) side. Solid back-up material will reduce the tear-out problem where the bit breaks through the back side of the hardboard (Fig. 7-9B).

A

B

Fig. 7-9: *Drill from the good side to avoid splintering and chipping the finished surface.*

Nails, screws, or staples combined with glue or contact cement can be used to fasten hardboard. Always drive nails at right angles to the panel surface; don't attempt to toenail hardboard. Except when bending panels, always begin nailing at the center of the panel and work out toward the edges so that the panel will lie flat. Never drive nails closer than 1/4" from the edge, or more than 4" apart.

When making hardboard joints, be sure that they are solidly supported from behind. Also remember that since hardboard has a tendency to expand and contract with changes in moisture conditions, panels should not be *tightly* butted against each other. If the panels absorb moisture and swell, something will have to give—and usually a buckle appears at the joint. It is best to leave a *slight* space at the joint to avoid this problem.

Hardboard panels can be bent to simple, one-directional curves. When in a "cold dry" state, the material can be wrapped around a curved frame (Fig. 7-10) if the radius isn't too sharp (Table 7-2). When

forming a curve, fasten one end of the hardboard to the frame and then carefully bend the panel, nailing every few inches to hold the curve.

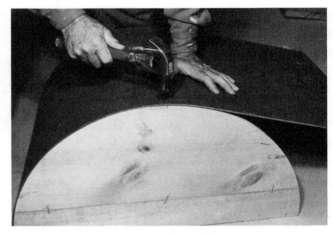

Fig. 7-10: *Hardboard can be bent into circular shapes. First, nail one edge to the frame; then, bend the board, nailing every few inches until the board is fastened in place.*

TABLE 7-2:   MINIMUM BENDING RADII*

Thickness of Stock	Cold Dry Bends		Cold Moist Bends	
	Smooth Side out	Smooth Side in	Smooth Side out	Smooth Side in
Standard Hardboard (S1S)				
1/8	12	10	7	5
3/16	18	16	10	8
1/4	27	24	15	12
5/16	35	30	22	18
Both Faces Smooth (S2S)				
1/8	10		7	
3/16	16		12	
Tempered Hardboard (S1S)				
1/8	9	7	6	4
3/16	16	14	9	6
1/4	25	22	14	10
5/16	35	30	20	16
Tempered, Both Faces Smooth (S2S)				
1/8	10		7	
3/16	16		12	

*All dimensions in inches.

When sharper bends are required, the panels should be soaked in cold water for a minimum of one hour or scrubbed with water on the screened side and stacked for 24 hours or more, to allow the hardboard time to absorb moisture. If only one panel is to be bent, apply wet newspaper or cloths to the screened side for the same period.

HARDBOARD PROJECTS

Although you will probably find fewer uses for hardboard than you will for other lumber products, hardboard is especially useful for construction that will not be seen, for hard, smooth surfaces, and for curved surfaces. The following projects will give you experience in working with hardboard as well as provide additions to your home and workshop.

Workbench

You won't spend much time working with wood before realizing the value of a workbench. The one shown here provides plenty of work space, a large shelf, and a perforated pegboard backing for hanging your tools close at hand. The tabletop is made of a half sheet of 3/4" Waferwood covered with a half sheet of 1/4" hardboard. The hardboard may be permanently glued to the Waferwood or attached with screws so that it can be replaced once it becomes scarred. Although this bench is 8' long, you can make it to any length that best suits your work space.

Begin this project by cutting the Waferwood, hardboard, and lumber to size. Make dadoes in the front and back legs, and slots in the bottom shelf. If you intend to glue together the Waferwood and hardboard sheets that form the tabletop, do so now by spreading glue along the edge of the Waferwood, placing the hardboard over this, and tacking the two sheets together. Clamp and set aside to dry.

Assemble the 2 × 4 framing pieces together with 10d common nails and glue. Use your framing square to be sure the frames are square.

Next, fasten the front legs to the frames with 2-1/2" screws and glue. Then turn the table face down and attach the back legs with 2-1/2" screws and glue. Frames should fit into dadoes.

Set the table upright and place the Waferwood and hardboard top shelf in position against the back legs. There should be approximately 1-1/2" overhang on each end that can be used to clamp material to your workbench. Drill and countersink screw holes through the top to the framework below. Space holes approximately 12" apart on edges and center supports.

Before inserting the screws, remove the top and spread glue on the framework. Reposition the top and screw into place with 1-1/2" screws, driving them approximately 1/16" below the bench top surface to protect edged tools.

Place the bottom shelf in position by first placing the 1/8" grooves around the back legs and then lowering the front edge into place. Nail and glue the shelf to the frame. Stand the 48" × 96" perforated hardboard sheet on its side and attach it to the back leg uprights and 2 × 2 crossbar with 1" screws 12" on center.

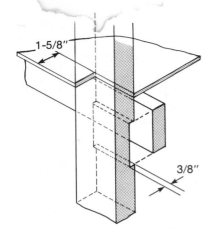

1-5/8"

3/8"

DETAIL OF LEG

MATERIALS LIST FOR WORKBENCH

Quantity	Description
1 panel	3/4" × 48" × 96" Waferwood
1/2 panel	1/4" × 24" × 96" hardboard
1 panel	1/4" × 48" × 96" perforated hardboard
3	2" × 4" × 36" front legs
3	2" × 4" × 83-1/2" back legs
4	2" × 4" × 93" top and shelf frame
9	2" × 4" × 19-1/2" top and shelf frame crosspieces
1	2" × 2" × 93" top tool support
1/2 lb	10d common nails
1/2 lb	4d finish nails
24	2-1/2" #8 flathead wood screws
24	1-1/2" #8 flathead wood screws
14	1" #8 flathead wood screws
—	glue

For permanent stability, use 1-1/2" or 2" angle irons to screw legs and bench to floor and wall. Install a vise at either end of the bench and arrange your tools on standard perforated hardboard tool holders.

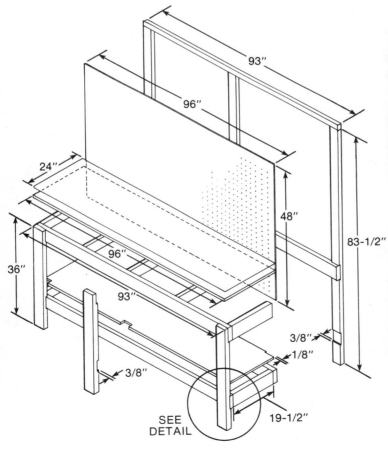

EXPLODED VIEW

Corner Umbrella Rack

The umbrella rack is made of particleboard and hardboard. The 1/8" hardboard is used because it is easy to bend. Waferwood or plywood can be used in place of particleboard.

Start by cutting the particleboard top, bottom, and sides to the dimensions shown. Rout a dado 1/8" wide and 1/4" deep, 1/2" from the edge of the top and bottom panel. Drill nine holes 2-1/2" in diameter spaced as shown. Cut the hardboard front panel to size.

Assemble the umbrella rack by first gluing and nailing the bottom and sides together. Use 6d finishing nails. Then, run a bead of glue inside the bottom dado. Set the front panel in the groove, and fasten the edges to the side panels with 4d finishing nails and screen mouldings. Fasten the top with glue and 6d finishing nails.

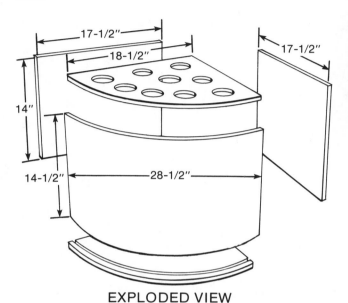

EXPLODED VIEW

MATERIALS LIST FOR CORNER UMBRELLA RACK

Quantity	Description
1	1/2" × 48" × 48" particleboard
1	1/8" × 14" × 28" hardboard
—	28" screen moulding
—	6d finishing nails
—	4d finishing nails
—	glue

Child's Easel

This easel is lightweight, collapsible, and made from 1/4" hardboard for a dent-free, smooth surface.

Begin by cutting the legs and crosspieces to size. Cut a dado half the thickness of the stock and 2-1/2" wide, 12-1/2" from the bottom of each leg. Rabbet the ends of each crosspiece and the top ends of each leg to the same dimensions as the dado cuts. With these cuts made, glue and clamp the legs and crosspieces together.

While these are drying, cut the hardboard and tray pieces to size. The sides of the trays are 5" long with a

10° angle on one end and a 45° miter on the other. The front of the trays can be any length you desire. In our example, the tray front is 22" long and mitered 45° on each end. Next, cut a dado in each tray piece 3/8" deep, 1/4" wide, and 3/8" from the bottom edge of each piece. Cut the hardboard tray 21-1/4" long. With the hardboard bottoms in place, glue and nail the trays together with 1-1/4" brads. With glue and brads, attach the four 2" glue blocks in place with a slight setback so that they will pull the trays snugly when screwed to the easel frame.

When the glue is dry, connect the two halves of the easel with a piano hinge and folding leg braces. Position the leg braces to allow the easel to open wide enough to prevent the easel from tipping. Next, glue and screw the hardboard to both sides with #8 flathead screws. Drill three evenly spaced 1/4" holes through the hardboard and into the top brace on each

MATERIALS LIST FOR CHILD'S EASEL

Quantity	Description
4	1" × 3" × 60" pine legs
4	1" × 3" × 30" pine crosspieces
2	1" × 3" × 22" pine tray fronts
4	1" × 3" × 5" pine tray sides
4	1" × 1" × 2" pine glue blocks
2	1/4" × 47-1/2" × 30" easel faces
2	1/4" × 4-1/2" × 21-1/4" tray bottoms
1	30" piano hinge
2	1-1/2" × #10 flathead screws
26	3/4" × #8 flathead screws
4	large spring clips
—	1-1/4" brads
—	glue

side. In each hole, glue a 1/4" dowel that has been tapered to a dull point. Then, glue and screw the trays to the easel through the glue blocks with #10 flathead screws. The bottom of the trays should be level with the bottom of the crosspieces. Always drill holes before screwing, and counterset each screw.

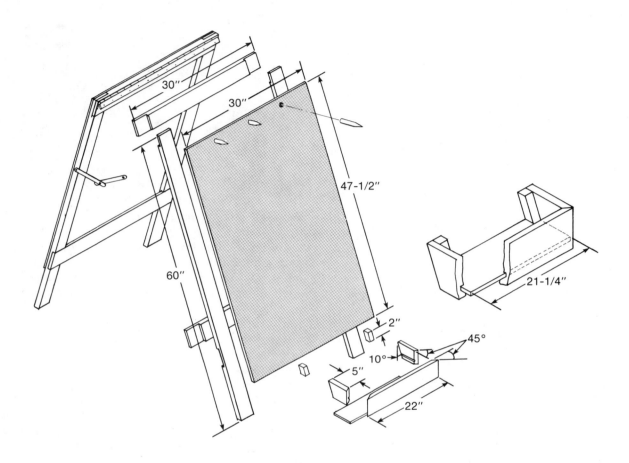

EXPLODED VIEW

CHAPTER
— 8 —

PARTICLEBOARD AND WAFERWOOD™

Newest of the "engineered" woods are the solid-wood composite particleboard and Waferwood. In the making of these products, wood particles, wafers, or fibers are rebonded with resin adhesives. To some people, this implies that these materials are of poor quality. However, when used for suitable purposes and when particular characteristics are taken into account, particleboard and Waferwood produced today can be superior to both solid lumber and plywood in certain applications.

Although particleboard and Waferwood are produced in much the same manner and may be used for the same projects, they are two different materials. Let's first look at particleboard—the more common and older of the two.

PARTICLEBOARD

Wood particles, chips, flakes, splinters, fragments, and/or sawdust are used to make particleboard. Most of the wood used is residue planer shavings, plywood mill waste, slabs, edgings, trimmings, and so on. Trees that are bent or broken or those cut during thinning operations also add to the supply.

Figure 8-1 shows the steps in the production of particleboard. Flakers, hammermills, or chipping machines reduce the various forms of wood into the desired type of tiny particles, and screens sort the particles into proper mixtures of particle sizes. Dryers then remove excess moisture from the particles and bring the moisture content to a desired, uniform level. Resin binders and other treatment chemicals are blended in with the wood as they are sprayed onto the particles at a controlled rate.

Particle mats are then formed to roughly the size of the finished panels and sent to heated hydraulic presses to be consolidated. The binders are cured at temperatures of up to 400°F and pressures of up to 1000 pounds per square inch. Finally, the particle-board is trimmed to desired lengths and widths and is sanded to final dimensions. The resulting panels are heavy, dense, and grainless composition board. The surface is typically smooth, with the wood particles showing.

Particle products are now being made for very specific properties and applications. For instance, the board may have controlled layering, with coarse particles placed in the center and flakes or finer particles at the surface to produce a panel with both strength and a uniform, smooth surface.

Properties of Particleboard

Particleboard is a panel product, but possesses characteristics all its own. To use particleboard for appropriate applications and to take advantage of its strengths, you should become familiar with its properties and characteristics.

Because of the random distribution of wood particles, properties are uniform across the board faces. Particles are mutually stabilized, resulting in a panel with stability and warp resistance. Particleboard is least stable perpendicular to the surface; therefore, the edges of particleboard have poor holding power since it is usually less dense at the center than near the surface. Fasteners driven perpendicular to the surface, on the other hand, hold well, especially when pilot holes are drilled first. When it is necessary to fasten into panel edges, edge-banding with solid wood or the use of special fasteners is recommended. Various types of particleboard may be prone to horizontal shear failure, due to their low internal bond strength. When used as shelving, the supports should be more closely spaced than for shelf boards of equal thickness.

Particleboard is not waterproof (even when waterproof resins are used). Although a highly moisture resistant board is manufactured, it will not withstand exterior weathering conditions without protection. If

Fig. 8-1: *Steps in the manufacture of particleboard: (A) Dry pine planer shavings and chips are stored. (B) At the forming line, overhead boxes meter the face and core particles onto a moving belt. Scales record and maintain particle densities as material moves down the line. (C) Close-up of multi-layer particles on moving caul sheet prior to being moved into the press. (D) Inventory of finished particleboard is ready for shipment.*

it is to be used outdoors, be certain that it's well protected with proper painting. (The effective shrinkage percentage of particleboard is generally in the same range as plywood, averaging around 0.5%.)

Particleboard accepts most paints readily. The uniformly smooth surface also takes plastic laminates well. Particleboard is therefore ideal as a single core for laminates or veneers, as in the construction of hardwood plywood.

Grades and Classifications

The National Particleboard Association (NPA) regulates the manufacture of all types of particleboard. The new standard for particleboard is ANSI A 208.1. The NPA performs extensive tests on particleboard, documenting properties and qualities of various par-

ticleboards. Particleboard is classified on the basis of a number of factors: particle type, adhesive type, density, and strength class.

Type I particleboard is intended for interior, moisture-free applications. Type I uses urea-formaldehyde resin, which has low resistance to water and moisture. *Type II* can be used in applications where greater heat and moisture resistance are required. This type is made with phenolic resin, which is moisture and heat resistant. It is *not waterproof* however. It may be used for limited exterior applications if protected by paint or for interior applications where moisture is prevalent. Table 8-1 shows where to use these two types of particleboard.

Particleboard is manufactured in density ranges from 25 to 70 pounds per cubic foot, depending on the percentage of resin and the compaction of the particle mat. Within each density grouping—*low,*

TABLE 8-1: WHERE TO USE PARTICLEBOARD

	Interior Type	Exterior Type
Room Dividers	x	
Doors	x	x
Partitions	x	
Shelving	x	
Counter Tops	x	
Drawers	x	
Paneling	x	
Siding		x
Valances	x	
Soffits		x
Mantels	x	
Radiator Enclosures	x	x
Speaker Enclosures	x	
Work Benches	x	
Tabletops	x	
Pool Tables	x	
Ping Pong Tables	x	
Game Boards	x	
Portable Displays	x	x
Built-ins	x	
Cabinets	x	
Store Fixtures	x	
Signs	x	x

medium, and *high*—boards are produced in two strength classes, *Class 2* being stronger than *Class 1.*

As mentioned earlier, particleboard can be manufactured for specific purposes. Some materials with directional particles have been developed to give oriented strength properties, as preferred in structural uses. Some particleboards equal solid wood of low density species in strength. Particleboards are also being developed for use as structural materials, such as "Com-Ply," which substitutes for solid-wood structural members. To make Com-Ply, particle beams are faced with double thicknesses of high-quality veneer.

Some panels are made from large particles or oriented strands in specific layering patterns. Such boards have properties equivalent to plywood for use as sheathing.

Special grades of particleboard are also manufactured specifically for painting. The surfaces are formed from very fine particles and are filled and sealed. Generally, higher density and the use of finer particles achieve a smooth surface, while lower density and larger particles yield greater overall dimensional stability.

Purchasing Particleboard

Before purchasing particleboard, you must realize that it is available in a wide variety of densities, is manufactured with different particles and resins, and comes with a number of surfaces. After considering the end-use of the particleboard, decide on the type, density, strength class, and surface necessary for your purpose. Also designate the number of pieces you need and the dimensions you desire. Particleboard panels commonly measure 4' × 8', but are available in dimensions ranging to 5' wide by 14' long. Thicknesses range from 3/16" to 1-7/8". Special pieces are also produced for step treads, shelving, door cores, and so on. Most dealers will also cut panels to size if you need smaller pieces than those in stock.

Applications of Particleboard

In the wood-products industry, the manufacture of particleboard is the youngest and fastest growing major segment. As the quality of particleboard has increased, so has knowledge of its strengths and weaknesses. Today, builders and home woodworkers alike are learning to use particleboard to the greatest advantage.

The largest single use for particleboard is as core material in furniture, counter tops, sliding doors, sink tops, paneling, case goods, and built-ins. Particleboard is usually the core of good hardwood plywood in such applications, since it's well suited to facing with veneer (see Chapter 6). Particleboard is often too heavy, however, for such applications as swinging doors. Table 8-1 serves as reference for particleboard applications. Some particleboard applications are shown in Fig. 8-2.

WAFERWOOD

Waferwood or waferboard consists of multilayers of wood wafers that are bonded by waterproof resin under heat and pressure. What makes Waferwood different from typical particleboard is the use of wafers of various widths and carefully controlled lengths and thicknesses, rather than small particles. The engineered wafers are arranged in multilayers and bonded together under extreme heat and pressure with waterproof phenolic resin glue. The result is a flat, solid panel which resists splitting or puncture. The exterior glue permits use either in the home or a variety of outdoor projects. From the side, you can see the thin interlocked wafers, like small sections of plywood veneer, that give Waferwood its strength and stability characteristics.

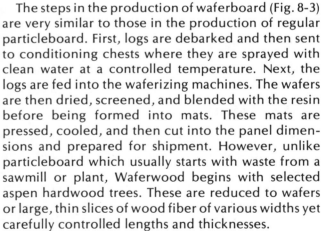

Fig. 8-2: Some typical particleboard applications.

The steps in the production of waferboard (Fig. 8-3) are very similar to those in the production of regular particleboard. First, logs are debarked and then sent to conditioning chests where they are sprayed with clean water at a controlled temperature. Next, the logs are fed into the waferizing machines. The wafers are then dried, screened, and blended with the resin before being formed into mats. These mats are pressed, cooled, and then cut into the panel dimensions and prepared for shipment. However, unlike particleboard which usually starts with waste from a sawmill or plant, Waferwood begins with selected aspen hardwood trees. These are reduced to wafers or large, thin slices of wood fiber of various widths yet carefully controlled lengths and thicknesses.

Waferwood is lightweight in comparison to most composite boards (especially particleboard), making it easier to use for home projects. The use of wafers instead of small particles gives Waferwood a more interesting and attractive surface. The panel is relatively smooth on both sides and is free of knots, core voids, patches, splits, and checks. Since it is a basic wood

panel, it saws cleanly, drills, shapes, and sands with standard woodworking tools. Waferwood panels are easily assembled with conventional nailing, screwing, stapling, and gluing techniques. Waferwood panels may be treated with a variety of finishes—clear, stain, or paint. Finishes are easily applied with brush, roller, or spray techniques.

The linear stability of waferboard is very good so that if the moisture content of the board changes, it will not swell much. It also has good bending strength. So if you need a panel with high bending strength, good stiffness, and good stability, you might want to look at waferboard.

Waferwood is produced in thicknesses which range from 1/4" to 3/4". Where a decorative surface is needed, 1/4", 5/16", or 3/8" thicknesses will do the job. The 7/16" and 1/2" panels are a good choice for economical decorative/structural projects. Where strength is the most important factor, 5/8" and 3/4" panels will handle most tougher requirements. The point is—there is a Waferwood panel thickness for almost every do-it-yourself project.

Fig. 8-3: The production process of waferboard: (A) The raw material for waferboard production is aspen logs. (B) One-hundred-inch bolts are run through a debarker. (C) Clean, debarked aspen logs are fed into a waferizer. (D) Aspen wafers are dried to uniform moisture content and sorted. (E) Material for waferboard panel is mixed with phenolic exterior resin and felted down onto large 8' × 16' caul plates contained within the moving boxes. (F) Before entering the press, the boxes are removed and the caul plate with wafer mat is fed into the press opening. A mat 5"-6" in depth will be compressed to a finished 3/4" thick panel. (G) The opening press receives the 8' × 16' mat, then under heat and pressure bonds the panel into a solid, void-free product. (H) Leaving the press, rough panels are weighed to maintain uniform density and quality control, and then proceed to trim saws. (I) The final step is banding the trimmed panels into uniform bundle sizes with identifying side cards giving piece count, thickness, and type of product.

WORKING WITH PARTICLEBOARD AND WAFERWOOD

Although particleboard and Waferwood are wood panel products, they, as we've seen, contain certain built-in properties and characteristics that make them quite unique from natural wood or lumber. For instance, particleboard and Waferwood are "grainless" materials; therefore, unlike wood, they can neither be ripped nor crosscut when sawn, regardless of direction. That is, these two panel materials must be sawn by a combination of the two cutting methods.

Sawing

When cutting particleboard and Waferwood, use a fine-tooth blade to obtain the cleanest cut. As with any wood material, the point where the saw breaks through the back will be rougher than where the teeth enter the surface. Although particleboard and waferboard are smooth on both sides, one surface of your project will usually be to the outside or more visible than the other. When working with most saws, keep the "good side" up and facing you (Fig. 8-4A). The only exception is when using a saber saw or circular saw. Here the teeth move upward toward the sole plate of the tool as they cut through the material. With a saber saw or circular saw, place the good side of the panel down, away from you (Fig. 8-4B).

Drilling

Holes less than 1/4" in diameter are usually drilled with a twist bit (Fig. 8-5). Slightly larger holes use an auger bit and a brace or flat spade bits in a hand drill. A hole saw or fly cutter can produce holes from 1-1/2" to 4". Anything larger should be cut with a saber saw or compass saw for best results.

As with any wood material, it's important to clamp a scrap piece of wood behind the panel to reduce break-out and grain tearing where the drill bit exits on the back side of the material. This way, the drill goes through the Waferwood and into the back-up scrap, minimizing damage.

Check the hole size when using a variable speed hand drill or drill press to determine the correct speed. The larger the hole diameter, the slower the drill speed. Consult the tool manufacturer's directions or test drill a few holes in a scrap piece to determine the correct speed for the cleanest cut.

When cutting openings for sink rims, electrical outlets, etc., it is often quicker to drill two 3/8" holes in diagonally opposite corners just inside the cut-out

A

B

Fig. 8-4: Particleboard should be cut (A) with the good side facing up when using hand tools and (B) with good side facing down when using a circular saw or saber saw.

Fig. 8-5: Different kinds of bits are useful in drilling different sizes of holes.

lines. Insert a compass or saber saw blade into the hole and make your cut down both legs.

A quicker method is to make a pocket or plunge cut with a saber saw. Tilt the saw on the front edge of the base with the blade over the cut-out area. Turn the saw on, hold it firmly, and slowly lower the blade into and through the material.

Fastening Particleboard and Waferwood

Particleboard and Waferwood can be joined together by using any of the following conventional fasteners.

Nails. When face nailing, apply the thinner material to the thicker. Use a nail 2-1/2 to 3 times longer than the thickness of the material it holds—a 3/4" nail for 1/4" particleboard or Waferwood; a 2" nail for 3/4" material. Stainless steel, aluminum alloy, or top quality hot-dipped galvanized nails are all recommended for exterior applications. Cement or resin coated nails will rust as quickly as uncoated nails and shouldn't be used. Remember that those made of noncorrosive materials may cost a little more, but are well worth the extra cost in lower maintenance and improved appearance.

Large head common nails should be used where strength is important; thinner finish nails for appearance. The interlocking wafers allow you to nail to within 3/8" of the panel edge without the risk of splitting. When finish nail heads are countersunk below the surface with a nail set, the Waferwood texture tends to hide the nail hole.

Screws. Drill a hole the exact diameter of the screw shank through the piece to be fastened. Drill a pilot hole in the back-up support piece 2/3 the shank diameter and 1/2 the depth of the screw length. This allows the screw threads to bite solidly into the wood. Nailing or screwing into the *edge* of particleboard or Waferwood presents the same problem found in plywood. Unless short, thin nails or screws in a predrilled pilot hole are used, there is a real danger of splitting the material.

Staples. Thin particleboard or waferboard—1/4", 5/16", and 3/8"—may be stapled, but most staples are too short to provide a strong joint. However, staples used with glue quickly hold the material in place until the glue sets.

Glue. All standard wood glues do an excellent job with particleboard or Waferwood. Follow the manufacturer's recommended application procedure, tack or staple material in place, and weight or clamp until the glue sets completely. Exterior grade glue must be used on all outdoor projects.

Joint Construction

When fastening particleboard or waferboard, the following methods of forming the joints can be used.

Butt Joint. Where two sections meet at right angles is the simplest and weakest joint (Fig. 8-6A). With small nails or screws plus glue, it may be adequate for non-stress joints.

Mitered Joint. Two pieces beveled at 45° to form a right angle provide more gluing surface and hide any edge grain from view (Fig. 8-6B).

Rabbet Joint. An "L" shaped notch cut 2/3 into one edge supplies a square shoulder for the second piece, maximizes the gluing area, and minimizes edge grain showing (Fig. 8-6C).

Internal Joints. For example, shelving or dividers in a bookcase or cabinet can be built with a dado joint—a square edged channel plowed to receive one member—or dowel joints either all the way through the material or stopped 2/3 into the Waferwood for a blind dowel joint.

Metal Angle Irons. Metal angle irons or corner braces screwed in place with glue on the joint provide a solid right angle construction (Fig. 8-7).

Wood Corner Glue Blocks. These are the easiest and strongest construction for most household projects. Nail and glue square, triangular, or quarter-round moulding in place to provide support along the entire length of the joint (Fig. 8-8). Nails and screws plus glue are recommended for tight, permanent joint construction.

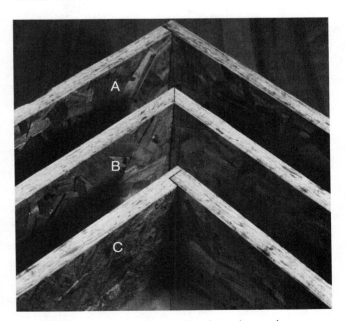

Fig. 8-6: Several end joints utilized in plywood construction are (A) the butt joint, (B) the mitered joint, and (C) the rabbet joint.

Fig. 8-7: Metal angle irons or corner braces add strength to the joint.

Fig. 8-8: Square, triangular, or quarter-round moulding can be used as corner glue blocks.

Shaping, Smoothing, and Sanding

The relatively smooth panel surface of particleboard or waferboard needs no further sanding for most home projects.

Plane. The larger standard jack plane will do an acceptable job, but the smaller block plane with its blade at a sharper 12° angle will give the smoothest cut. A sharp blade adjusted for light cuts gives best results. Angle the plane slightly to the material surface so it cuts cleanly with a shearing action.

Rasp, Surform Tools. These are used similar to the plane, but since the multiple cutting edges are somewhat coarse, hand sanding may be needed for a final finish. To minimize edge splintering, use light pressure and work from the panel surface toward the core.

Routing. Sharp bits may be used to form a bevel or rounded edge or to V-groove the particleboard and Waferwood surface with good results that require only a minimal final sanding. However, straight flute cuts on the surface or rabbeted edges are less satisfactory. Shear cuts are acceptable, but where the router bit cuts a right angle to the layered wafers, a crosscutting leaves a more ragged edge. A saw or dado blade is a better method to use.

Sanding. All conventional sanding techniques work well on Waferwood. Either a block hand sander or power sander can be used. Standard 80 grit sandpaper will provide a good surface for most projects, but a finer, 120 grit paper should be used where extra smoothness is desired.

Edge Treatments

As stated, particleboard and Waferwood sand to a clean edge with fine grades of paper; but where an ultrasmooth edge is desired, apply paste wood filler, sand lightly, prime, and paint. Alternate treatments include standard wood mouldings nailed and glued in place (Fig. 8-9). Corner guard moulding wraps around the edge. Quarter-round or half-round mouldings give a softer or more modern look. Thinner screen moulding, either flat or beaded, is equally effective.

Fig. 8-9: Wood mouldings can be used to hide unattractive edge surfaces.

PARTICLEBOARD AND WAFERWOOD PROJECTS

To get the most out of each panel, a little preplanning is required. Laying out your project on graph paper first can save you time and assure the maximum use of each panel. Use a 1/4" graph paper and let 1" equal 1'. This way, a 4" by 8" area on the paper represents the full size panel and each 1/4" square equals 3".

If your project has a number of angled cuts and odd shapes, it may be helpful to scale and cut out the paper parts, then lay them on the scaled panel outline, and try several different arrangements until you determine the most efficient pattern. The "grainless" surface allows you to run parts in any direction.

When you translate your dimensions from the graph paper to the full size panel, be sure to allow space between various parts for the width of the saw kerf. Run your hand or power saw through a scrap piece of wood and measure the width of the cut made by the saw blade. In almost all cases, you will want to cut just outside of your pencil line and the saw kerf may range from less than 1/16" for a fine-toothed saber saw blade to almost 1/4" wide for carbide tipped blades.

Use the smooth factory panel edges and square corners to position key pieces. Lay out your dimensions carefully with tape measure, straightedge or chalk line, and square. Where possible, plan for several initial crosscuts to reduce the large 4 × 8 Waferwood panel into more manageable sections.

The following projects can be made from either particleboard or Waferwood.

Storage Shed

You can bring some order to your outdoor equipment with this handsome storage shed. The shed is an attractive and functional addition to any home. Built-in prefabricated panel sections can be taken apart and moved easily. The 8'-square module is sided with inexpensive Waferwood and trimmed with either durable redwood lumber for a natural finish or with pine lumber for paint finish. It provides ample storage for lawn tools, furniture, bicycles, and sports gear. If you wish, add shelves or benches to create a potting shed or outdoor workshop. The basic plan can be expanded easily to a 12' or 16' wide shed.

Build the entire unit—walls and roof—in panel sections on a flat surface like a floor, driveway, or shed floor before final assembly. Then fasten sections together with 16d duplex (double headed) nails for quick disassembly.

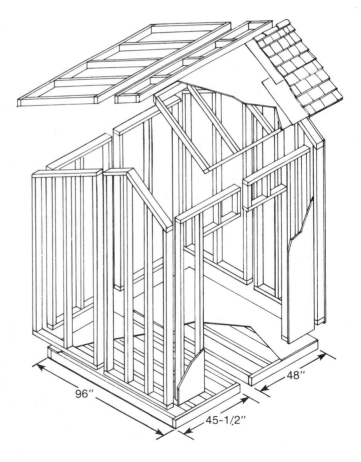

EXPLODED VIEW

Construct the Base.   Prepare a foundation for the shed—either a concrete slab, pier blocks, level gravel pad, or treated 4 × 4 timbers. Construct the base frame from 2 × 4 heart redwood or pressure treated lumber, making one frame 48" × 96", the other 45-1/2" × 96". Apply floor panels of Waferwood with 6d galvanized nails, then tie the two floor panel sections together with several 16d duplex nails.

Back Wall.   From 2 × 4 lumber, cut four top and bottom plates measuring 43-1/4" long. Cut six studs 67" long (this provides a total back wall frame height of 71" and allows a 6' panel to overlap the floor system by 1"). Assemble the back wall frame panels in two sections with 10d common nails, spacing studs approximately 24" on center. There will be a double stud where the two panel sections join. Cut two sheets of Waferwood to measure 46-3/4" wide × 72" high and apply to the frame with 4d galvanized siding nails. (Set the two 24" × 48" scrap panels aside for use on the roof section.) Note that there is a 1" overhang on the bottom and a 3-1/2" overhang on each outside back corner. This allows front and back wall siding to overlap side wall panels.

Front Wall.   From your 2 × 4 lumber, cut two top plates 43-1/4" long and two bottom plates 13-1/4" long. Cut four wall studs 80" long. Cut door headers 30-1/4" long and four 8" header cripples.

Assemble the front wall frame panels, checking to make sure that there is a net door opening 72" high and 60" wide. Apply two sheets of Waferwood siding 46-3/4" wide × 84" high allowing 3-1/2" overhang at outside edges and 1" at bottom.

Doors.   Cut out the door panels now. To determine the outline of the panels, measure 16-1/2" in from each side and 11" down from the top edge. If your shed will be trimmed as illustrated, cut out the door panels and apply hinges to the trim boards until after the shed is erected and trimmed. If, however, you decide against trim boards, cut and install hinges at this stage.

Side Walls.   To accurately duplicate roof angles, place two 48" × 96" Waferwood panels side by side on a flat surface. For the left hand wall, measure up 1" from panel bottom and draw a horizontal line across both panels. This is the 1" overlap for the base. On the left hand panel, measure from the line up 83" and

BACK WALL

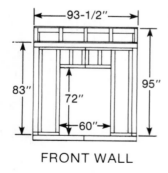

FRONT WALL

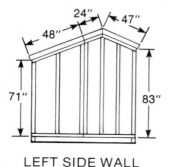

LEFT SIDE WALL

MATERIALS LIST FOR STORAGE SHED

Quantity	Description
12	7/16" × 4' × 8' Waferwood (3/8" or 1/2" is also suitable)
10	2" × 4" × 8' redwood heart or treated lumber—floor system
3	2" × 4" × 8' sill plate
1	2" × 4" × 3' sill plate
14	2" × 4" × 8' wall studs
8	2" × 4" × 6' wall studs
4	2" × 4" × 8' top plates
2	2" × 4" × 6' door header
8	2" × 4" × 8' roof sections
4	2" × 4" × 4' roof sections
2	2" × 4" × 2' roof sections
2	1" × 4" × 6' roof trim
1	1" × 4" × 8' roof trim
2	1" × 3" × 6' corner trim
2	1" × 3" × 7' corner trim
2	1" × 4" × 6' corner trim
2	1" × 4" × 7' corner trim
11	1" × 2" × 6' door trim
4	1" × 4" × 8' base trim
5 lbs.	10d common nails (general construction)
2 lbs.	6d flathead galvanized (floor construction)
2 lbs.	4d flathead galvanized siding nails (siding, corner trim, etc.)
1 lb.	16d duplex head nails
1 lb.	2d flathead galvanized nails (door trim)
3 pair	4" butt hinges and screws (weather resistant)
2	door handles or 1 hasp
1 roll, 15 lb.	roofing felt
1 square, 235 lb.	asphalt shingles or wood shingles
1 lb.	flathead roofing nails or wood shingle nails

mark the top of the front edge. Measure 36″ in from the left panel edge and 95″ from the bottom line to determine the ridge location. From the outside edge of the right panel, measure up 71″ to locate the top of the back wall. With a straight 2 × 4, connect front and back top wall locations to the ridge point. Cut two bottom plates 48″ long from 2 × 4 lumber and position them above the bottom line. Place studs vertically on top of the plate, spacing approximately 24″ on center. There is a double stud where panels join in the center. Check that each stud is perfectly square and true. Position the top plate 2 × 4 just beneath drawn roof line, then mark the studs and the top plate ridge angles. Cut studs and top plate angles, then assemble frame with 10d nails and apply siding panels to frames. Repeat the process reversing the layout to build the opposite side wall.

Roof.   The roof, like the walls, is made up in panel sections—one section for the front and two for the back. The front panel frame is 47″ long (allowing for 1″ roof overhang); rafters are 91-1/2″ long for a net frame size of 47″ × 94-1/2″ (leaves 3/4″ overhang on each roof side edge). Back panels are 24″ and 48″ long and the same width as the front panel. Frame edges are beveled to meet at the ridge line.

After the shed is assembled, apply roofing felt and either asphalt or wood shingles to the roof sections, overlapping 2″ where panels meet. Run a bead of caulking under the overlap joint to give a weather-tight seal after panels are in place on the roof.

Assembling the Shed.   Lift the back wall into place and nail through the sole plate into the floor. Check for plumb and temporarily brace in place. Then, apply the side walls, nailing through the sole plate and into the floor and stud corners.

The same procedure is followed for the front wall. For a permanent installation, nail sections in place. For a shed that can be easily disassembled and moved, use 16d duplex nails.

Position the roof panels and nail in place, fastening up through the wall top plates. Tie the roof panels together with nails as you go. From scrap 2 × 4 lumber, insert small blocks 24″ on center where the roof panels meet the front and back top plates.

Trim.   For a professional look, finish your shed project with redwood lumber or pine trim. Nail 1 × 3 or 1 × 4 boards at each corner. Use 1 × 4′s for roof and fascia trim on the front sides. Trim door edges with 1 × 2 lumber nailed from the inside, using 1″ galvanized flathead nails. If desired, 1 × 2 or 1 × 3 strips can be applied to sides and back walls for a board and batten effect to cover panel joints.

Finishing Touches.   Your storage shed is now ready for the finish of your choice. Waferwood can be finished with latex or enamel paint, stain, or clear finish.

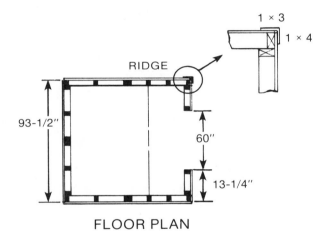

FLOOR PLAN

Doghouse

The typical doghouse resembles a square box with a peaked roof design and a large open doorway. This Waferwood doghouse is different. The L-shaped floor plan provides both security and warmth for your pet. The entrance and interior doors have raised thresholds to reduce drafts. Another practical design feature is the slanted roof, which can be quickly removed by pulling out four corner pins. This allows easy cleaning and changing of the dog's bedding.

The Waferwood doghouse design is inexpensive and easy to build with ordinary hand tools and basic construction skills. The plan illustrated here is proportioned for a medium sized dog, but you'll also find instructions on how to adapt the plan to any size breed from a beagle to a Saint Bernard. Optional construction suggestions for cold climate doghouses are also provided. The materials you will need for the project are given in the materials list.

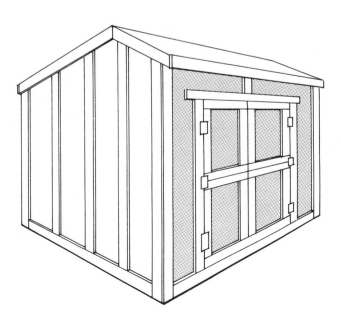

Determining the Sizes. Measure your dog's shoulder height, then find the corresponding column on the size chart to determine correct part dimensions. In the example here, sizes are taken from column II. Lay out the parts on each sheet, allowing space between parts for the saw kerf.

Base. The doghouse rests on a base frame of 2 × 4 lumber laid flat on its side. This raises the structure slightly off the ground, reducing the chilling effect of ground moisture.

Construct the base of redwood heartwood or pressure treated lumber. Cut the 2 × 4's, lay them flat, and assemble with corrugated fasteners. Then apply floor panel to frame with exterior glue and nails.

Framing the Doghouse. From the bottom edge of the side panel, measure up 1-1/4" and apply the corner post flush with the outside edge using nails and glue. This spacing allows the side panel to overlap the base frame by 3/4". Repeat procedure for opposite side wall. Position front and back walls allowing the same 3/4" base overlap and fasten to corner posts with nails and glue. The final step is to trim the top of the corner posts to conform to the side wall angles.

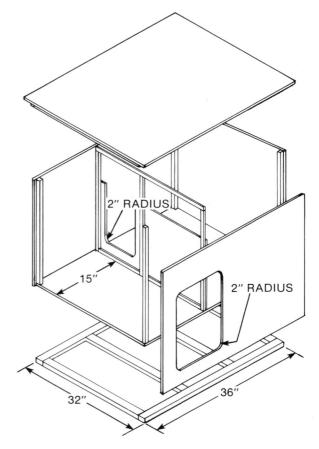

EXPLODED VIEW

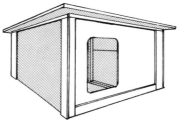

TRIM DETAIL

DOGHOUSE SIZE CHART

Dog's Shoulder Height	I	II	III	IV
	20″ to 24″	15″ to 19″	10″ to 14″	6″ to 9″
Floor	40″ × 44″	32″ × 36″	24″ × 27″	16″ × 20″
Roof	48″ × 51-1/2″	38-1/2″ × 41″	27″ × 30-1/2″	19″ × 21″
Front	45″ × 37″	37″ × 30″	28″ × 22″	21″ × 14″
Sides	40″ × 37″-33″	32″ × 30″-26″	24″ × 22″-19″	16″ × 14″-12″
Back	45″ × 33″	37″ × 26″	28″ × 19″	21″ × 12″
Divider (from side)	18″	15″	12″	9″
Doorways	14″ × 26″	12″ × 21″	9″ × 16″	6″ × 11″

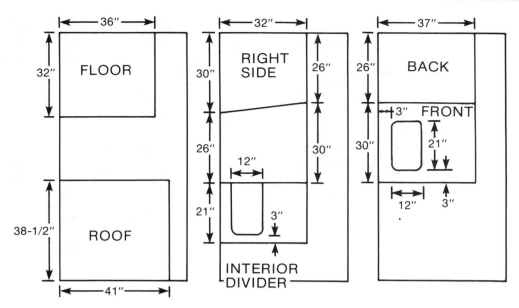

Interior Divider. Measure the height of the back wall and width of the floor inside dimensions. The interior door cutout should be the same size as the entrance door. Apply Waferwood wall panel to the frame with nails and glue, then drop into position approximately 3″ to the right of the front door opening. Nail and glue frame into place.

Roof. Position the roof panel on the doghouse with a uniform overhang on all four sides. Hold firmly in position and run a pencil around the underside of the roof panel where it meets the wall sections. Build a vertical 1 × 2 lumber frame slightly outside these panel lines—about 1/8″ larger—and glue and nail to the roof panel.

INSULATED PANEL

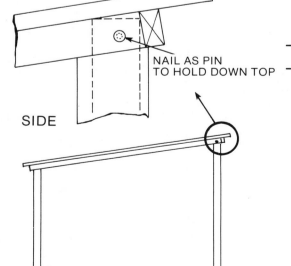

NAIL AS PIN TO HOLD DOWN TOP

SIDE

MATERIALS LIST FOR DOGHOUSE

Quantity	Description
3 panels	7/16″ or 1/2″ × 4′ × 8′ Waferwood
1	2″ × 4″ × 8′ redwood heart or treated wood—base
2	2″ × 4″ × 6′ redwood heart or treated wood—base
4	2″ × 2″ × 3′ corner posts
1	1″ × 2″ × 16′ interior divider frame
1	1″ × 2″ × 7′ roof trim
1	1″ × 2″ × 8′ roof trim
4	1″ × 2″ × 3′ side corner trim
4	1″ × 3″ × 3′ front and back corner trim
1	1″ × 3″ × 4′ front base trim
2 lbs.	2d galvanized flathead common nails
1 box	corrugated fasteners
4	16d duplex nails

Place the roof on the house and drill 3/16" holes through the roof frame into each of the four corner posts. Use 16d duplex (double headed) nails through the holes to lock roof into position.

Adding Trim.   Trim the base of the doghouse in 1 × 3 lumber. Then apply 1 × 2 vertical strips to the side corners and 1 × 3 front and back corner trim overlapping the side trim. The doghouse can now be finished with stain or with latex or enamel paint.

Colder Climates.   In colder climates, you may wish to use a layer of insulation material in the roof, floor, and side walls. As shown, the easiest method is to sandwich 3/4" foam insulation between layers of 1/4" Waferwood panels. Frame the insulated panels in 1 × 2 lumber, allowing outside panel to overlap base frame by 3/4". Adjust the doghouse dimensions to allow for these thicker panels.

Toy Barn

A barn made of Waferwood, authentic in design and detail, can provide many hours of playtime fun for most youngsters. The easy-to-form and assemble pieces are scaled in the traditional 1" to 1', so that standard construction materials and furnishings will be correctly proportioned.

Layout and Cutting.   All barn pieces can be cut from a single 1/4" thick 48" × 96" sheet of Waferwood. Carefully lay out the pieces as shown, allowing for saw kerfs between each piece. Mark each piece clearly to avoid confusion and double check for accuracy. Miter cuts are used on the barn's front, back, and upper partition pieces. The roof ridge panels are bevel cut at 30° and 15° on their lower edges. The center panels are cut at 15° on their top edge and 7-1/2° on their bottom edge. The bottom panels are bevel cut 7-1/2° on the upper edges and square on the bottom edges.

Window and door openings should be cut before assembly. See the following table for the dimensions of window and door openings. A saber saw will make this job easier. It is also best to test fit all miniature windows and doors prior to assembly.

WIDTH AND HEIGHT OF WINDOW AND DOOR OPENINGS

10-1/2" wide × 9" high back door

5" wide × 7-1/2" high hayloft doors

9" wide × 8-1/2" high front double doors

3-1/2" wide × 7" high front door and second floor partition door

5" wide × 7-1/2" high first floor partition opening

2-1/2" wide × 2-1/2" high side windows (Seven Openings)

2" wide × 4" long access to hayloft

Assembly.   Fasten the side wall to the bottom base with a quality wood glue and 5/8" brads or staples. Then, attach the front panel to the side wall and base. Next, attach the back panel.

The middle, lower partition is sized to create an aisle on the window side of the barn. Place it exactly 14-3/4" back from the front wall. Its edges should be flush with the barn's open side. Secure with glue and brads driven from the underside of the floor. Lay the second floor panel in place; then, glue and nail it to the middle, lower partition and the front and back walls. Notice the small cutout of this panel. A small ladder can be made and positioned here to provide access to the hayloft. Side pieces can then be fastened to the barn in the same manner.

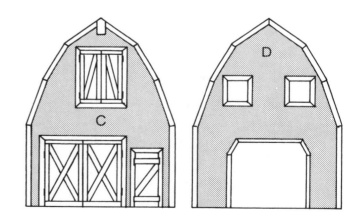

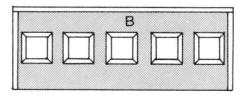

TRIM DETAIL

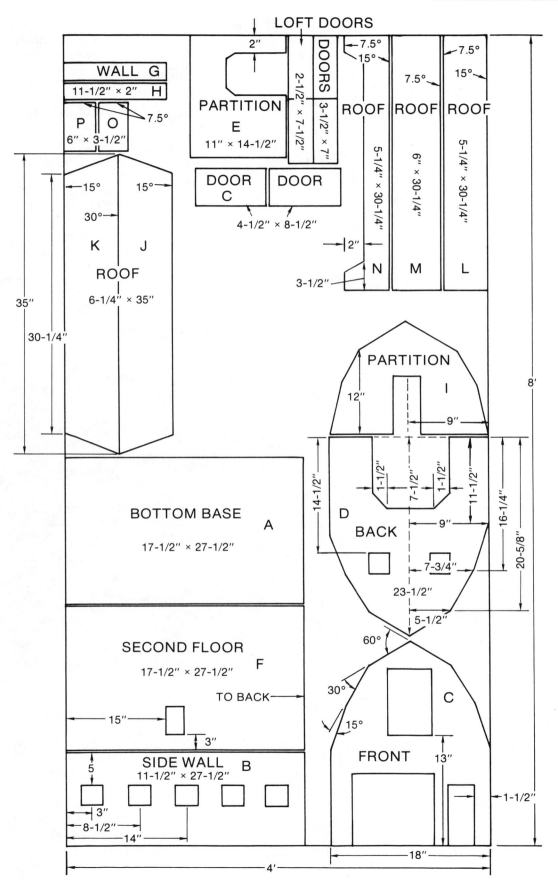

LOFT DOORS

WALL G

11-1/2" × 2" H

P   O

6" × 3-1/2"

7.5°

2"

PARTITION

E

11" × 14-1/2"

DOORS

2-1/2" × 7-1/2"

3-1/2" × 7"

7.5°

15°

7.5°

7.5°

15°

ROOF ROOF ROOF

5-1/4" × 30-1/4"

6" × 30-1/4"

5-1/4" × 30-1/4"

2"

3-1/2"

N M L

DOOR DOOR

C

4-1/2" × 8-1/2"

15°   15°

30°

K   J

ROOF

6-1/4" × 35"

35"

30-1/4"

PARTITION

I

12"

9"

14-1/2"

1-1/2"

7-1/2"

1-1/2"

11-1/2"

7-1/2"

D

BACK

9"

16-1/4"

20-5/8"

7-3/4"

23-1/2"

5-1/2"

BOTTOM BASE

A

17-1/2" × 27-1/2"

SECOND FLOOR

17-1/2" × 27-1/2" F

TO BACK

15"

3"

60°

30°

15°

C

FRONT

13"

1-1/2"

5

SIDE WALL B

11-1/2" × 27-1/2"

3"

8-1/2"

14"

18"

4'

8'

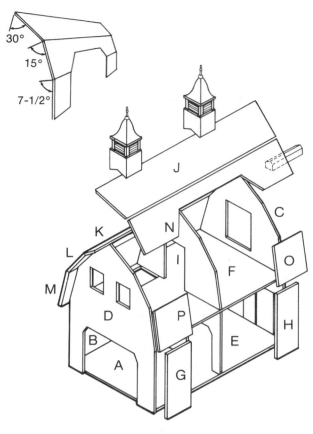

EXPLODED VIEW

Position the upper, middle partition directly above the lower, middle partition and glue it to the second floor (this piece cannot be nailed from the underside). The upper roof pieces can then be glued and nailed. Make sure the beveled edges provide tight fits around the mitered cut. Then, fasten the lower roof pieces.

Finishing. Countersink all nails and lightly sand all edges smooth with fine 120 grit abrasive paper. The barn can be left with the natural Waferwood finish or it can be painted with latex or enamel paints. If you paint the barn, do it before you install the windows, doors, and trim.

Glue all scale windows into the appropriate window openings, holding them in place with strips of masking tape until the glue is completely dry. Frame all door openings and decorate all doors with thin strips of balsa wood glued in position.

The front, side, and loft doors should all be fastened with small hinges and screws. If you use small hinges, make the barn door 1/8" smaller than the plan calls for to allow for the thickness of the hinges.

As an alternate method, pieces of heavy tape can be used. When positioned correctly, the tape acts as a hinge so the doors can be swung open and closed. After securing the doors, glue the two cupolas in place on the ridge of the barn roof.

You'll notice that you have just enough Waferwood remaining to fashion some barnyard animals scaled 1" to 1'. Some creative cutting with a saber, coping, or band saw will do the job.

MATERIALS LIST FOR TOY BARN

Quantity	Description
1 sheet	48" × 96" Waferwood
1 box	5/8" brads
1 bottle	wood glue
7	2-1/2 × 2-1/2 miniature windows
2	miniature cupolas
5 pair	miniature hinges and screws
42"	1/16" × 1/2" balsa wood stripping
—	fine 120 grit abrasive paper

Entertainment Center

This easy plan for a freestanding entertainment and storage center combines two basic box shapes—square and rectangular—to create a variety of storage options, from drop front desk to wine rack. The units can be arranged in dozens of combinations and are ideal for a family room, child's room, or apartment.

To build, you will need a saber saw, circular saw, or table saw, plus hammer and drill. If using a hand saw, a router may be needed for some of the modules. Build the entire project with economical Waferwood, then paint or stain to complement your room decor.

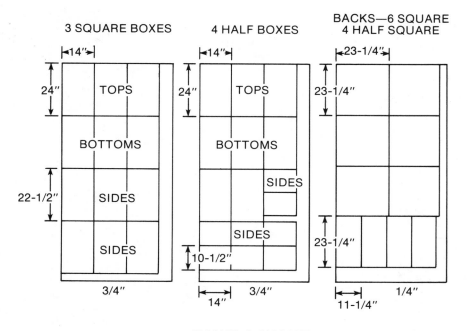

3 SQUARE BOXES 4 HALF BOXES BACKS—6 SQUARE 4 HALF SQUARE

PANEL LAYOUT

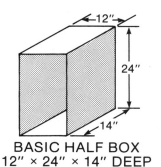

BASIC SQUARE BOX
24" × 24" × 14" DEEP

BASIC HALF BOX
12" × 24" × 14" DEEP

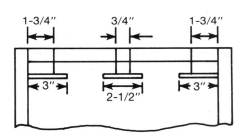

GLASS STORAGE UNIT

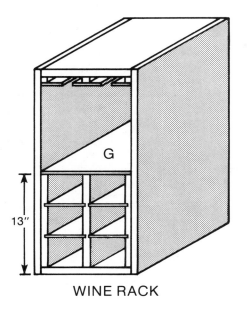

WINE RACK

Custom Design your Project. This plan illustrates a variety of square and rectangular boxes with various shelf and door combinations. Using the basic material and assembly instructions, you can customize your entertainment center design to match your space limitations and storage/display needs. Use graph paper to determine your space size. Then, try a number of square and rectangular arrangements until you find the best design to satisfy your requirements.

Basic Boxes. Determine the number of square boxes and half boxes to be built, then make a cutting layout on graph paper to get the best use of full Waferwood panels. The diagrams yield three square boxes and four half boxes from two 3/4" thick panels and one 1/4" panel. Additional material will be required for shelves, drawers, doors, and other designs.

Cut sides, top, and bottom pieces from 3/4" Waferwood. Cut backs from 1/4" Waferwood. If using a table saw, cut backs 23-1/4" × 23-1/4" (square box) or 11-1/4" × 23-1/4" (half box) and rabbet box back 1/4" deep and 3/8" wide to accept rear panel. If using a hand saw, cut backs approximately 24" × 24" or 12" × 24" in size. All shelf and drawer dimensions on plans are for rabbet jointed boxes. Adjust dimensions if backs are nailed flush to side.

Glue and nail pieces together to form boxes using 4d (1-1/4") finish nails. Measure from corner to corner diagonally when assembling to be sure boxes are square. Then, apply backs with glue and 3/4" brads. For a satisfactory storage/entertainment center project, it is important that all boxes are square and uniform in size.

Base. A solid lumber base will provide stability on uneven floors as well as a finished appearance to the project. The plan illustrates a basic 8′ wide base, but the same system can be used for a 6′, 10′, 12′, etc. wide unit. The storage boxes will overhang the base by 1/2″ on the front and sides. Cut the front, back, and divider pieces of 2 × 4 lumber as shown on the plan. Glue and nail in place.

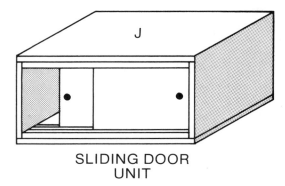

SLIDING DOOR UNIT

TOP TRACK

SLIDING DOOR

BOTTOM TRACK

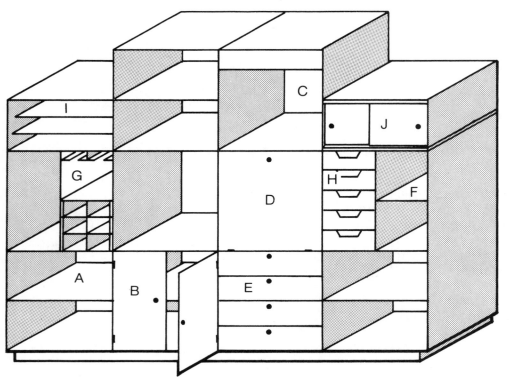

ENTERTAINMENT CENTER

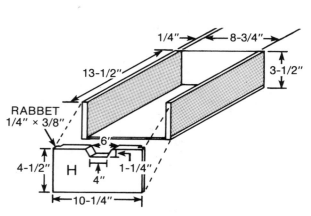

5 SMALL DRAWER UNIT

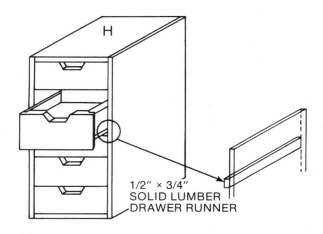

5 DRAWER UNIT

Storage Box Units Built from Square Boxes.   After constructing the basic square box, follow the instructions to complete your choice of storage units.

Single Shelf.   To construct a square box with a single shelf:

(a) Cut shelf 22-1/2" wide × 13-3/4" deep.

(b) Glue and nail in place from sides and back, approximately 12" from bottom box.

Box with Shelf and Two Doors.   To add a shelf and two doors to a square box:

(a) Cut shelf 22-1/2" wide × 13" deep to allow room for doors.

(b) Cut two doors 11" × 22-1/4" each.

(c) Glue and nail shelf to box. Attach doors with 1-1/2" hinges. Add a magnetic latch and knobs, or drill finger holes.

Lighted Display Box.   To make a lighted display box:

(a) Attach a 4" × 22-1/2" wide piece of 3/4" Waferwood to front of box at top.

(b) Install 18" fluorescent light stick behind valance piece.

(c) Drill 1" hole in back of box for light cord plug.

Drop Front Desk. To construct the drop front desk:

(a) Cut three shelves 22-1/2" wide × 11-1/4" deep.

(b) Dado two lower shelves for nine letter slot dividers. Space dado approximately 2" apart, 1/4" × 1/4" deep.

(c) Cut nine letter slot dividers 6" high × 11-1/4" deep from 1/4" Waferwood. Glue and nail in place as shown.

(d) Cut drawer pieces and assemble, joining back with rabbet joint dado in drawer bottoms. Finish dimensions of drawer: 7" wide × 5-1/2" high × 11-1/4" deep. Drill 1" finger holes.

(e) Cut three 1/4" shelves for paper dividers, 9-1/2" wide × 11-1/4" deep.

(f) Cut vertical divider 9-1/4" high × 11-1/4" deep. Dado slots for 1/4" shelves.

(g) Glue and nail all pieces in place.

(h) Cut drop desk front 22-1/4" × 22-1/4".

(i) Screw front to box with three hinges, attach two 22" chains and add magnet latch, then drill 1" finger holes.

Four Drawer Units.   To build a square box with four drawers:

(a) Add three 3/4" shelves 22-1/2" wide × 13-1/4" deep to square box. Space shelves 5" apart.

(b) From 3/4" material, cut drawer fronts 5" high and 22-1/4" wide. Then rabbet on inside back edges 1/2" × 3/4" to receive drawer sides.

(c) Drawer sides are 4" high × 12-3/4" long. The back is 4" high by 20-3/4" wide, of 3/4" material. Drawer bottom is 1/4" × 13" × 22".

(d) Assemble drawer sides and back, then add bottom and drawer front flush with bottom edges. Nail and glue parts.

(e) Drill 1" finger holes or attach knobs to drawer fronts.

Storage Units Built from Half-Boxes.   To add a single shelf:

(a) Cut shelf 10-1/2" wide × 13-1/4" deep.

(b) Glue and nail to box, 12" from bottom.

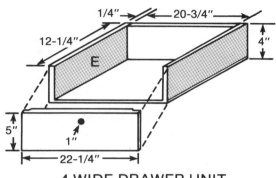

4 WIDE DRAWER UNIT

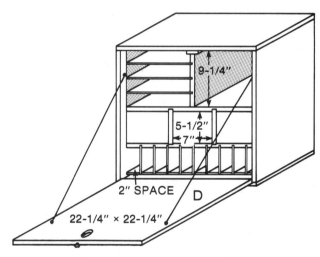

DROP FRONT DESK

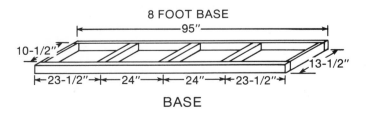

BASE

Wine Rack and Glass Storage Unit. To construct a wine rack and glass storage unit in a half-box:

(a) Cut three 3/4" vertical dividers for bottle storage 13" high × 13-3/4" deep. Then cut 1/4" × 1/4" dadoes spaced 4-1/4" apart on sides and double dado center support.

(b) From 1/4" material, cut four pieces 4-1/2" wide × 13-3/4" long and a top piece 10-1/2" × 13-3/4". Assemble bottle storage unit with brads and glue.

(c) For wine glass holders, cut two pieces 3/4" × 1-3/4" × 13-3/4" and apply to the top outside corners of the box. Cut one 3/4" × 3/4" × 13-3/4" and fasten in center. Then, from 1/4" material, cut two pieces 3" × 13-3/4" and one piece 2-1/2" × 13-3/4", then nail and glue to 3/4" strips above.

Five Drawer Unit. To create a five drawer unit from a half-box:

(a) For drawer runners, cut ten pieces of solid wood 1/2" × 3/4" × 13.

(b) From 3/4" material, cut five drawer fronts 4-1/2" high × 10-1/4" wide. Rabbet outside back edges 1/2" × 3/4" to receive drawer sides. Cut 4" wide at bottom and 1-1/4" deep.

(c) From 3/4" material, cut 10 drawer sides 3-1/2" high × 13-1/2" long; five drawer backs 3-1/2" high × 8-3/4"; and five drawer bottoms from 1/4" material, 10" × 13". Assemble drawers with brads/glue construction, mounting drawer front flush with top of drawer sides.

(d) Fasten two solid wood strips on outside bottom corners of box and place bottom drawer on top. Use top of drawer sides to mark position for next set of drawer runner strips. Sand all parts carefully for tight fitting, smooth sliding drawers.

Stepped Magazine Rack. To construct a stepped magazine rack:

(a) From 3/4" material, cut shelves 10-1/2" wide × 10" deep and 10-1/2" × 12" deep.

(b) Glue and nail to box 3" apart with 10" deep shelf on top.

Sliding Door Unit. To make a sliding door unit:

(a) Install plastic guides for 1/4" sliding doors on inside top and bottom edge of box.

(b) Measure height between top and bottom track channels and cut two doors of 1/4" material approximately 9-1/4" high × 11-1/2" wide.

(c) Attach knobs or cut finger holes in doors and slide in place on tracks.

Finishing the Boxes. When your storage/entertainment center is fully assembled, thoroughly sand all of the rough edges with medium sandpaper. Countersink all nails slightly below the surface. Putty them and sand smooth. The project can be finished with any standard latex or enamel paint, various stains, or a clear finish. To give the wall storage center a unified appearance, stain or paint all boxes the same color, such as walnut or flat white. Use accent colors for drawers or door fronts, if desired. Stain or paint the base to match, or paint it dark brown or black to anchor the unit visually.

CHAPTER
— 9 —

WOOD MOULDINGS

More than 350 standard wood moulding profiles, plus many special shapes and sizes, are produced throughout the United States. Some are sold only in certain areas due to the architectural history of that area. Because of this, you may not be able to find every type of moulding shown in this chapter in your vicinity. Many mouldings can be combined to simulate larger, more detailed patterns (Fig. 9-1). With a little imagination and some suggestions from your wood moulding salesperson, you'll be able to substitute available moulding patterns for those that cannot be found in your area. The common names of the standard mouldings are given in Fig. 9-2 as a reference for purchasing the types you need.

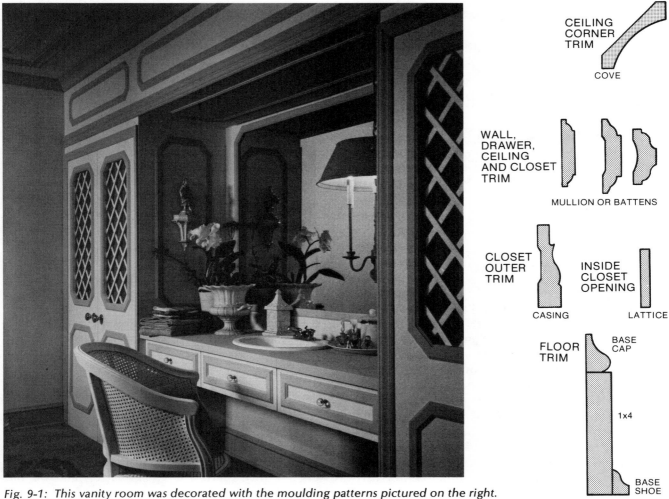

Fig. 9-1: This vanity room was decorated with the moulding patterns pictured on the right.

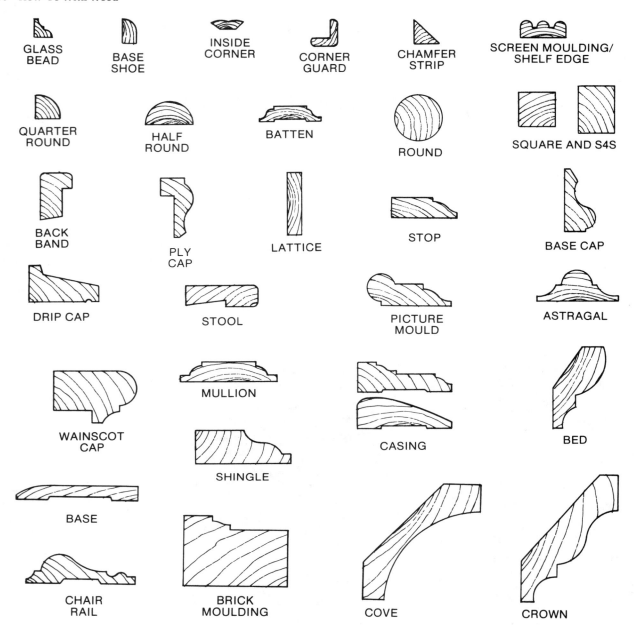

GLASS BEAD

BASE SHOE

INSIDE CORNER

CORNER GUARD

CHAMFER STRIP

SCREEN MOULDING/ SHELF EDGE

QUARTER ROUND

HALF ROUND

BATTEN

ROUND

SQUARE AND S4S

BACK BAND

PLY CAP

LATTICE

STOP

BASE CAP

DRIP CAP

STOOL

PICTURE MOULD

ASTRAGAL

WAINSCOT CAP

MULLION

CASING

BED

SHINGLE

BASE

CHAIR RAIL

BRICK MOULDING

COVE

CROWN

Fig. 9-2: Common names and shapes of standard mouldings.

Generally, ready-made moulding can be classified as functional (architectural) or decorative. The terms relate more to how the mouldings are used than to individual designs. A moulding might be functional when used in house constructions to cover the gap that exists between a door frame and the adjacent walls, but the same moulding can be used to decorate the side of a cabinet or the front of a drawer.

There may be a limited number of wood species that functional mouldings are available in, especially in a local lumberyard. Typically, these would be available in pine, hemlock, or fir. Some home centers carry a line of hardwood or composition-type mouldings

that fall in the decorative category. Craftsperson mail-order supply houses will often list functional and decorative mouldings made of walnut, cherry, birch, or oak. Sometimes they are pointed out as being mouldings for clock cases and fine furniture.

PRODUCTION OF MOULDING

Lumber thicknesses used in the manufacture of wood mouldings and jambs include 4/4" (four quarter), 5/4" (five quarter), 6/4" (six quarter), and to some extent 8/4" (eight quarter), with 5/4 and 6/4 accounting for the largest volume. These thicknesses allow resawing in the moulding and millwork plant so that two, three, or more mouldings can be produced from one lumber thickness. The lumber used for mouldings is dried to 8-12% moisture content, ensuring size stability and providing smooth surface when milled.

Most of the lumber employed for solid wood mouldings comes from the outer portion of the log that develops clear lumber. The grade of lumber used to manufacture mouldings is referred to as Moulding and Better and includes the grades of Moulding, D Select, and C and Better Select. Finger-jointed mouldings are most often taken from the shop or cutting types of lumber that require crosscutting to eliminate undesirable characteristics. The clear pieces that develop are finger-jointed and joined by adhesives to produce long clear lengths suitable for paint finishes.

To manufacture a given wood moulding profile, lumber of preselected thickness is sawn or ripped lengthwise into strips of various widths for maximum utilization of the board. The rips are then sorted by width. Appropriate widths are sent through a band saw or "resaw" where they are converted into "blanks," shapes ideally suited for moulding specific patterns with minimum waste. These blanks are sent through a moulder which has four or more cutterheads to shape the profile. The cutterheads hold a series of identical knives, each shaped to conform to the exact moulding pattern profile. As blanks are fed into the moulder, the cutterheads and knives rotate at high speed, carving or planing the blanks into finished moulding shapes. At the outfeed end of the moulder, mouldings are inspected to ensure conformance with industry quality standards.

In finger-jointing, two additional steps take place between the ripping and the resawing operations. First, unacceptable characteristics or defects are trimmed out of the lumber rips by crosscutting at the cut-off line. Then, after sorting, the remaining strips of clear wood pass through a finger-jointer which cuts small "fingers" in the ends of each piece (Fig. 9-3).

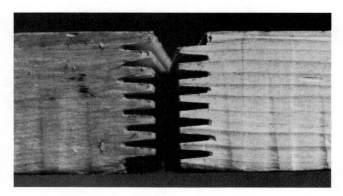

Fig. 9-3: Finger-jointed moulding.

These fingers are glued and joined (the fingers interlock for a strong tight joint) into long lengths of clear finger jointed lumber, ready to be resawn and moulded. Finger-jointed mouldings are intended for paint or opaque finishes (paint-grade).

Aside from the basic manufacturing process, a number of specialty services and processes may be performed on wood mouldings. These include priming, water preservative treating, cutting-to-length, carton packaging, film shrink wrapping, premitering, and prefinishing. Prefinished wood mouldings may be grain printed, prepainted in solid colors, vinyl wrapped, or toned (prestained and varnished). Most grain printed and vinyl wrapped wood mouldings are finger-jointed. The wood profile beneath the finish is called substrate. Toned mouldings are always solid lineal stock.

GRADES AND CLASSIFICATIONS

Wood mouldings are manufactured in two grades: *N-Grade* and *P-Grade*. Both grades may have a few minor defects, but a serious combination is not permitted in a single piece. The number and extent of defects permitted varies with the area of the piece.

N-Grade mouldings are suitable for any type of finish, having the exposed face of a single piece. On the basis of a net face 2″ by 12′, specific defects are permitted, such as a small spot of torn grain, one or two small pin knots, a light skip in the dressing on the back, or medium stain in occasional pieces.

P-Grade is intended for opaque paint finishes or overlays. The moulding may be finger-jointed or edge glued to form tight joints. Patching, filling, and plugging are permitted. P-Grade is otherwise in conformance with the regulation of defects in N-Grade, except that stains are not considered to be defects since P-Grade is intended for opaque finishes. If you don't intend to put an opaque finish on your moulding, then be sure you buy N-Grade moulding.

PURCHASING MOULDINGS

Mouldings are available in a wide variety of styles and sizes. You can purchase the pattern of your choice in lengths of 3′ to 20′. Most moulding is ordered by the linear foot. Always measure for the length you'll need, then round off to the next highest foot. It's much better to have a few inches of excess than to come out short. If you plan to make mitered joints, the width of the moulding should be added to the measurement for *each* joint (Fig. 9-4). If your moulding is 3″ wide, and you'll be making two miters, 6″ should be added

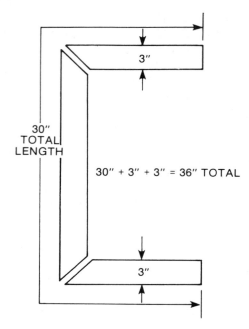

Fig. 9-4: In mitering, allow for the width of the cut by adding the width of the mitered pieces to give you an outside dimension.

in length. Then round off to the next highest foot. *Note:* At times, you'll be able to use shorter pieces than standard. Over half of a home's interior trim requirements are for lengths under 8', so ask your dealer about random pieces which may save you money.

When designating moulding sizes, quote the thickness first, the width second, and the length last. Remember that thickness and width are measured at the widest dimension (Fig. 9-5).

If you select a specific moulding profile from a catalog rather than from a moulding display, you may find

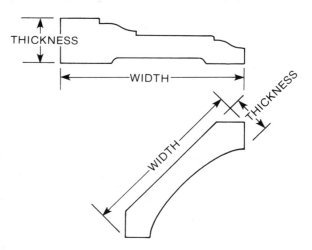

Fig. 9-5: Moulding dimensions are taken from their widest point.

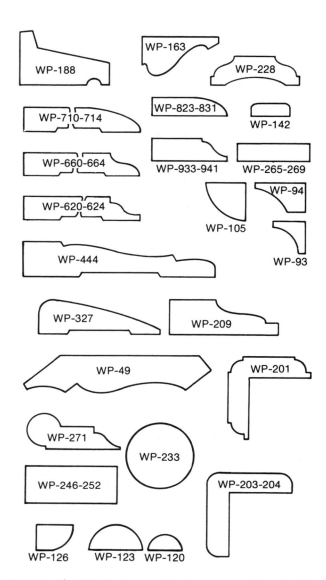

Fig. 9-6: The WP/Series numbering system helps in identifying and ordering moulding patterns. (Refer also to the adjacent key.)

each specific pattern indicated by "WP" followed by some numbers. This numbering system is known as the *WP/Series* and is the industry standard for identifying wood moulding patterns (Fig. 9-6). To identify the shape and size of each pattern, "WP" is followed by a two- to four-digit number and appropriate measurements (thickness, width, length).

TYPICAL MOULDING APPLICATIONS

The use of wood mouldings is truly limited *only* by your imagination. With the wide variety of sizes, styles, and finishes available, you can create nearly any effect you want, for any type of decor.

KEY	
NUMBER	**NAME**
188	Drip cap
163	Cap & brick
142	Screen
823-831	Stop
933-941	
228	Batten
265-269	Lattice
710-714	
660-664	Casing
620-624	&
444	base
327	
209	Shingle
49	Crown
271	Picture
233	Rounds
201	Corner guard
203-204	
246-252	Screen stock
123	Half round
120	
126	Base shoe
105	Quarter round
94	Cove
93	

Fig. 9-7: Base mouldings protect as well as decorate a wall.

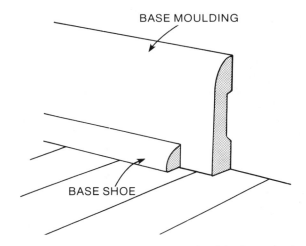

Fig. 9-8: The base shoe adds a finished look to the base moulding.

Functional Uses

Most of us are familiar with the functional uses of moulding. The rooms of our homes usually have base mouldings, door and window casings, ceiling mouldings, and frequently chair rails. Let's take a look at each of these mouldings.

Base Moulding. Base moulding is a decorative trim used to cover the joining of the wall to the floor. It also protects the wall when vacuuming or sweeping, and adds a finished look to the room (Fig. 9-7).

The base shoe is used at the intersection of the base moulding and the floor (Fig. 9-8). It gives the base moulding a finished appearance and helps cover any possible uneven places in the floor. Base moulding variations are shown in Fig. 9-9.

Door and Window Casing. Casing is the trim that goes around most windows and doors and is used to seal gaps between the window and door jambs and the walls. It also gives the opening a decorative finished look (Fig. 9-10).

When applying the casing, a 1/4" reveal should be left between the face of the jamb and the edge of the casing. Miter the corners and attach the top casing first (Fig. 9-11A), then do the sides, using small finishing nails. Countersink the nails (Fig. 9-11B) and fill with putty when finished. Figure 9-12 illustrates several casing variations.

Ceiling Moulding. Ceiling moulding is used at the junction of the wall and the ceiling. It gives the room a finished look, besides adding a pleasant transition

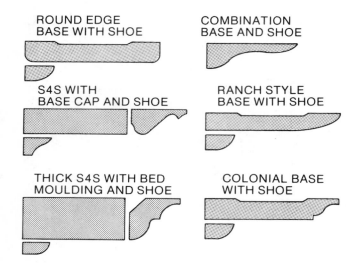

ROUND EDGE
BASE WITH SHOE

COMBINATION
BASE AND SHOE

S4S WITH
BASE CAP AND SHOE

RANCH STYLE
BASE WITH SHOE

THICK S4S WITH BED
MOULDING AND SHOE

COLONIAL BASE
WITH SHOE

Fig. 9-9: Variations and combinations of base, shoe, and cap mouldings.

Fig. 9-10: Door and window casing.

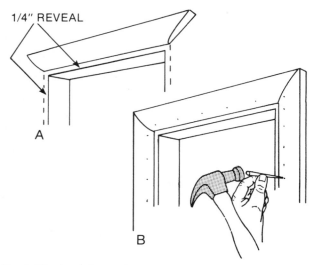

1/4" REVEAL

A

B

Fig. 9-11: Applying casing.

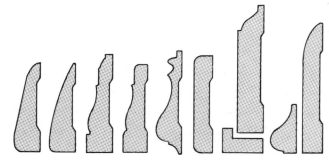

Fig. 9-12: Casing variations.

from one surface to the other (Fig. 9-13). Patterns can be used alone or in combination with others, as shown in Fig. 9-14. When joining ceiling moulding at the corner, either a mitered or a coped joint should be used.

Chair Rail. Chair rail is the most common of the wall mouldings and adds both interest and protection (Fig. 9-15). It prevents chairs from marring the walls and can be used to separate two types of materials, such as wallcovering and paint. It's usually placed at chair height, between 33" and 35" from the floor. Chair rail variations are illustrated in Fig. 9-16.

Keep the following tips in mind when installing moulding:

1. Start at a door or window (*after* door or window trim has been applied) or at some other point where the moulding is interrupted.

2. Place the moulding in position and test the fit *before* nailing it permanently. If there is a problem with the fit, check for one of the following: inaccurate cuts, debris behind the trim, unlevel floor or wall, corners not exactly 90°, or insufficient undercut in the trim.

Fig. 9-13: Ceiling mouldings.

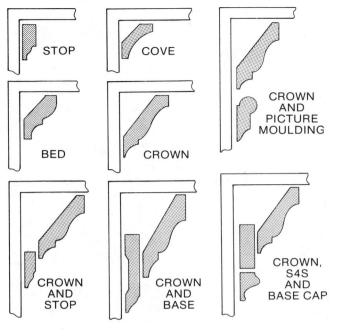

Fig. 9-14: *Various combinations used as ceiling mouldings.*

3. Do mitering or splicing *before* installing the two pieces involved. Coping can be done after one of the pieces is fastened.

4. When applying moulding through the middle of a wall, ceiling, or door, use a chalk line as a placement guide.

5. When applying long pieces of moulding as, for example, on walls, try to plan the sequence of installation so that the last wall to receive moulding is either a short wall (to make the fitting of a single length easier) or one of the longest walls (so that you can splice the moulding to make fitting the corners easier).

6. Position the joint of pieced moulding over a stud for solid fastening.

Fig. 9-15: *Chair rails offer protection from chairs.*

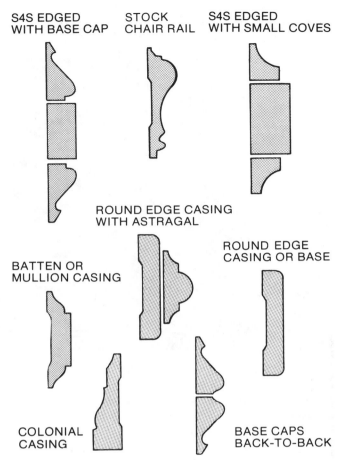

Fig. 9-16: *Various combinations used to create a chair rail.*

Decorative Uses

There are many decorative uses for wood moulding, including the following:

Walls. The many types of mouldings that can be applied to walls provide unique decorating opportunities with the effects limited only by one's imagination. They can add richness, depth, accent, and color. Shown in Fig. 9-17 are a few suggested wall treatments.

Ceiling. If your ceiling is a little dull, you can enhance it with wood mouldings. There's a variety of patterns available which can be used alone or in combinations (Fig. 9-18). Since you'll be viewing it from many directions, it's usually best to choose a symmetrical moulding pattern. The layout of the overall design, however, depends on the shape of the room, the lighting arrangements, and your own interest. Color and ceiling material can also add uniqueness.

Door and Cabinet Trim. If your front door does not have the appearance that you would like it to, you can give it a new look by adding a little wood moulding (Fig. 9-19). Use one pattern or a combination of patterns. Remember, when mitering, good accurate

Fig. 9-17: Mouldings can be used to create decorative patterns on walls.

measurements are important. It's best to cut all the pieces to size before attaching them to the door. It's also a good idea to take the door off its hinges and lay it on saw horses to do the work. When all the pieces are cut and positioned, glue and tack them in place. Since most outside doors swing in, do not position any moulding clear to the edge of the door or it will not close properly. Now paint or stain your door to complete its new appearance.

The possibilities for customizing your kitchen or bathroom cabinet doors are almost endless (Fig. 9-20). The variety of moulding patterns available, multiplied by the many ways they can be placed on the cabinets,

Fig. 9-18: A dull ceiling can be enlivened with mouldings.

Fig. 9-19: Doors take on a character of their own when decorated with mouldings.

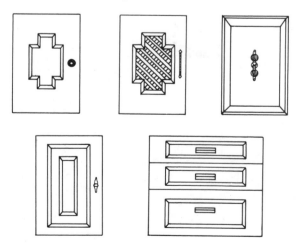

Fig. 9-20: Give your kitchen a new look by applying decorative mouldings to cabinet doors.

plus stains and paint choices, and the use of vinyl wall-covering, all add up to an unlimited assortment of designs. Wood mouldings can also be used as a framework to hold tile or stained glass.

Furniture Trim. Wood mouldings can be added to an old chest of drawers or a new unfinished chest of drawers. Figure 9-21 shows a basic chest which be-

comes a more exciting project because of the added moulding details. The mouldings on the drawer front can be preassembled as a frame which is then added to the project, or they can be attached one piece at a time. The best bet for the base is to do the front piece first, mitering the ends so the inside of the cut is exactly in line with the corner of the chest. Cut the side mouldings a bit longer than necessary so you can trim them to exact length after you have cut the miter and are sure it is right.

Figure 9-22 shows a similar chest which takes on a Spanish motif simply because of the different types of moulding which are used. The mouldings on the drawer fronts can be attached as described for the first chest. The base treatment is different because of the crown moulding that is called for. Because of the slope at which the moulding sits, the corner joint becomes a compound angle. The easiest way to cut it is

A

B

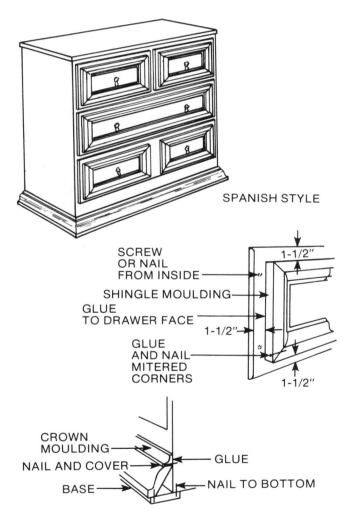

SPANISH STYLE

SCREW OR NAIL FROM INSIDE

1-1/2"

SHINGLE MOULDING

GLUE TO DRAWER FACE

1-1/2"

GLUE AND NAIL MITERED CORNERS

1-1/2"

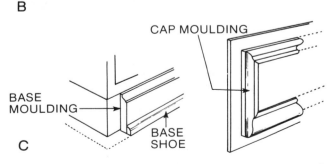

CAP MOULDING

BASE MOULDING

BASE SHOE

C

CROWN MOULDING

NAIL AND COVER

BASE

GLUE

NAIL TO BOTTOM

Fig. 9-21: A basic chest (A) can be transformed into a much fancier piece (B) by adding mouldings (C).

Fig. 9-22: Shingle mouldings and crown mouldings were used on this project. Ready-made mouldings are good to use, especially when you don't have the equipment to form your own designs.

to place the moulding in a miter box at the same slope it will have on the project and then to do a simple 45° miter cut. Cut the front piece first. Do the two sides by starting with stock that is longer than you need. Trim to length after you are sure the miter joint is exact.

A stronger way to do the base is shown in Fig. 9-23. Since it's not possible to add the glue blocks *after* assembly, the base structure must be completely pre-assembled and then added to the chest. Careful work is required to be sure the fit will be perfect, but the actual joint cutting procedure doesn't differ from what was described previously.

Figure 9-24 shows how mouldings can be functional as well as decorative. If you use this idea, glue the two pieces of cove moulding together first so they can be attached to the drawer fronts as a unit. The base moulding requires simple miter cuts, but follow the usual procedure. Do the front piece first, then add the sides.

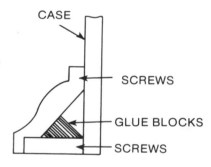

Fig. 9-23: Another way to use cornice or crown mouldings at the base of a chest.

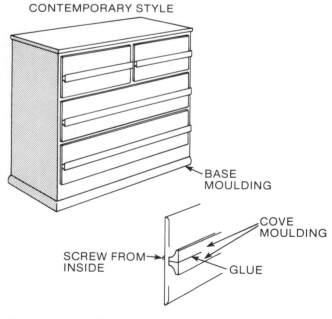

Fig. 9-24: Moulding can be functional as well as decorative. Here, cove moulding is used to form drawer pulls.

WORKING WITH MOULDING

Few wood products are as easy to work with as mouldings. With a few easy-to-learn skills, you can totally change the character of a room without damaging your walls or furniture. The basic skills necessary to work with moulding include mitering, coping, splicing, and finishing. It's wise to try out these techniques on scrap pieces before trying to construct your particular project.

Mitering

Mitering is done when moulding must form an outside corner. To miter a moulding, trim the two mitering members at opposite angles (Fig. 9-25). Since most moulding miter joints form 90° corners, you'll normally set your miter box at 45°. (To make corners of *less* than 90°, your miter box cuts must be at angles wider than 45°. For corners of *more* than 90°, the miter angle must be less than 45°.)

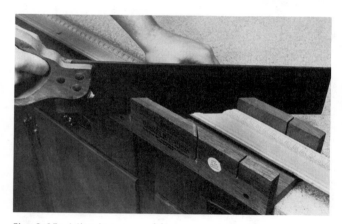

Fig. 9-25: Mitering a moulding.

When mitering or coping ceiling moulding, the moulding must be inserted in the miter box upside down (Fig. 9-26). The edge of the moulding that will be in contact with the ceiling (A) must be set on the *bottom* of the miter box. The edge of the moulding that will be in contact with the wall (B) must be set against the *back* side of the miter box. The length of the piece must be marked on the bottom edge of the moulding as it will be installed.

Use both glue and nails to fasten the adjoining edges, as shown in Fig. 9-27. The nails should always be countersunk below the surface.

If you come across a project that requires absolutely accurate mitered frames, use a jig (Fig. 9-28). A jig is used to help make frames more rapidly and uniformly. The inside dimensions of the jig are equal to the out-

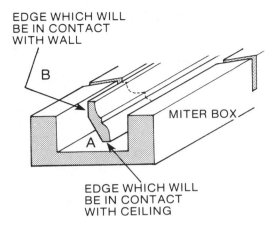

Fig. 9-26: *Place the moulding upside down when mitering a ceiling moulding.*

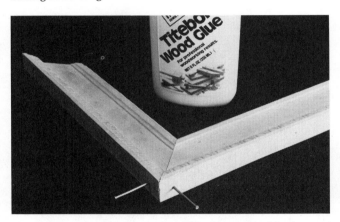

Fig. 9-27: *Moulding joints should be fastened with glue and nails.*

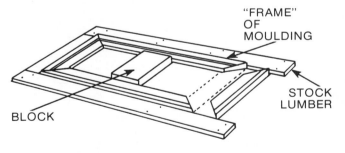

Fig. 9-28: *A jig aids in producing accurate mitered frames.*

side dimensions of the frame. You can easily make a jig by nailing stock lumber pieces to any flat surface. Blocks can be used to straighten the moulding pieces against the sides of the jig.

Coping

When one piece of moulding must butt up against the face of another moulding at an inside corner, you must shape the edge of one piece to fit the profile of the other. The first step is to trim the end of the moulding to a 45° angle (Fig. 9-29A). Set the moulding in the miter box upright against the back plate and in the position it is to be installed. Angle the cut so that a slanted raw edge will show from the front.

The resulting cut will expose the profile of the moulding. Use the profile as a guide, and at a 90° angle to the face of the moulding, use the coping saw vertically to cut away the waste (Fig. 9-29B). Cut straight back across the moulding so that all of the slanted raw wood is removed. Be sure to follow the profile. (The teeth of the blade should point downward, whether the handle is up or down.) To undercut and form a beveled edge, simply tilt the saw blade slightly. The finished edge should then fit tightly against the face of the adjoining moulding (Fig. 9-29C). *Note:* For regular trim, the edge need only be undercut 2° or 3°. On cove, crown, or bed moulding, however, the edge should be undercut as much as possible, up to 45° where the moulding is to be used on ceiling borders.

A

B

C

Fig. 9-29: *To cope a moulding: (A) cut the ends at a 45° angle, (B) cut along the profile to remove the excess, and (C) fit snugly against the adjoining moulding.*

Splicing

Splicing, or piecing mouldings, is done by cutting a scarfed, or diagonal, joint (Fig. 9-30A). To make the cuts, place the pieces in the miter box as if the back of the miter box were the wall, and make 45° cuts. One piece will overlap to form the joint (Fig. 9-30B). To make a tight joint, glue the ends of the two pieces, locate the joint over a solid piece of lumber (stud, top, or bottom plate), and nail both members securely (Fig. 9-30C).

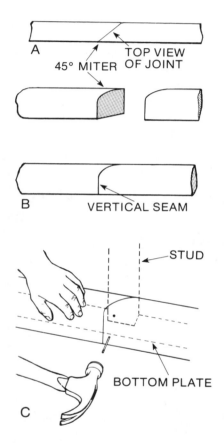

Fig. 9-30: To splice two pieces of moulding: (A) cut both ends 45° in the same direction, (B) fit the two mitered pieces together, and (C) nail through the mitered cuts of both pieces.

MOULDING PROJECTS

Here are several other projects that can be made with wood mouldings. You can build these or choose another style of moulding to create your own. Available mouldings vary from one locality to another; any similar shape may be substituted for the mouldings used in these projects.

Wooden Spoon Rack and Holder

Like most utensils used in the kitchen, large spoons have a habit of getting lost in a drawer or misplaced. This can be avoided by building a special holder for them.

The wooden spoon wall racks illustrated are constructed of one piece of S4S connected to another with appropriately sized holes drilled for the spoons. The racks are dressed up by attaching various mouldings to the front, top, and bottom edges. Any number of mouldings can be used to accent the basic rack design. Of course, your spoon supply and kitchen wall space will determine the length of the rack.

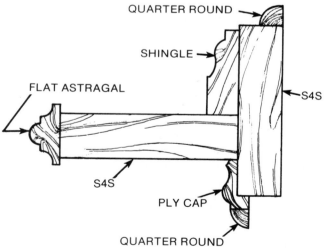

A second type of spoon rack design.

Picture Frames

Picture frames have two purposes: to present and to protect the picture. The presentation is achieved by the size, shape, and color of the frame. The protection is given by the cover and security the frame gives the picture, along with the mat and glass, if any. When making your own frames, remember the design of the moulding you choose should relate to the picture, whether it's traditional or contemporary. The variety of moulding pattern combinations shown are but a few of the many possibilities. One of these or one of your design will be just right for your picture.

The first step in making the frame is to combine the different mouldings so the finished profile is completely put together. Do this before any cutting is

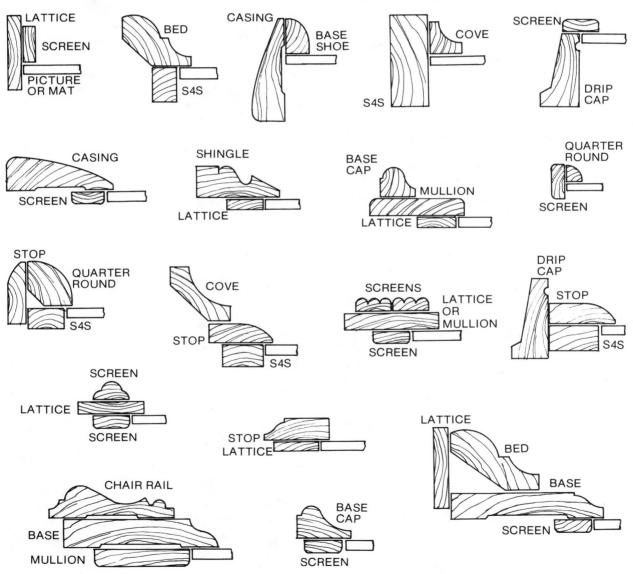

done. Start by adding the smaller pieces to the larger ones. Use glue and brads. Careful nailing is required here to prevent cracking. Clamp or tape together overnight. Next, saw off the end of the moulding at a 45° angle. Carefully measure the longest side of the picture; add 1/8" to this measurement to allow your picture to fit into the frame easily. The long side of the frame should be cut first. By doing this, if a mistake is made on the long piece, it could be used for a short piece. Transfer this measurement to the moulding, starting from the edge of the miter at a point where the picture inserts into the frame (the rabbet), and mark and cut a 45° miter at the opposite end of the piece just cut. You will need another piece exactly like this one for the opposite side. Measure the second piece from the first so that the length will be identical. When cutting the 45° miter on the ends of the pieces, it is wise to try to clamp the pieces to the miter box so a nice cut can be made. Now measure the short sides of the picture and cut two pieces in the same way as before. You're now ready to assemble your frame. Take one side piece and the bottom piece, coat the ends to be joined with glue, and place carefully in your corner clamp. When the corner is aligned just right, tighten the clamp so as to exert sufficient pressure to hold the pieces rigidly enough so that you can nail the corner together. Now drive two or more brads through the corner from each side, allowing the heads of the brads to protrude slightly. At this time, make certain that the frame fits the picture. (Here is where four corner clamps come in handy.) Follow this same procedure on the other three corners and allow the glue to dry thoroughly. Check for squareness by measuring diagonally across the frame each way. The two measurements should be equal. If not, a slight push on the long diagonal corner will square up your frame. Tack a strip of wood on the back diagonally from corner to corner to hold the frame square while the glue is drying. Carefully finish driving the brads with a small nail set so that the heads are about 1/16" below the surface. Fill the nail holes with a little wood filler and let dry. After the glued-up frame is completely dry, sand it lightly with fine sandpaper. You're now ready for staining or painting in whatever manner you choose (see Chapter 12). These designs also make excellent frames for mirrors.

Bookends

You can better organize and store your books if you use bookends. In order for a bookend to be heavy enough to hold a series of books, it must be either very heavy itself or it must be attached to some kind of base for the first few books to sit upon. This can be small

metal plates of various types and sizes, which can usually be purchased at a metal fabrication shop, sheet metal shop, or steel service center. Another method is to connect both bookends together with dowels. The ends then become a fixed distance apart, making the size of your display permanent. The actual size of your bookends will depend upon the size of your books. Because bookends are usually under pressure, make sure they are glued and nailed so they won't collapse. These can be even further strengthened by adding corner plates to the backside. It's also a good idea to add felt to the undersides of bookends to protect the surface on which they sit.

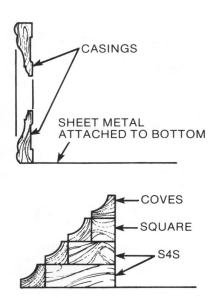

Bookend construction details.

Lamp Bases

Basically, lamps are all the same on the inside. They're just a socket and a switch attached to a wire that goes through a center tube and ends up with the wall plug. Usually there's also a wire harp attached to the socket which holds the lamp shade. Where lamps differ is on the outside. In most cases they're just a box. How the box is covered is what gives a lamp its uniqueness, charm, character, and beauty.

The lamp shown here (bottom left) is a narrow box made of S4S stock with squares of casing attached. Chair rail moulding, base, flat astragals, stops, battens, and shingle moulding can also be used. The top and bottom of the box is capped with a piece of S4S with a hole drilled for the center tube. Mitered stop moulding is attached to the bottom to form a wider base. A large square of lumber could also be used.

A simple box of plywood with a framework of casing is all there is to this lamp (bottom center). Besides the casing, base, batten, base caps, shingle moulding, coves, flat astragal, chair rails, and mullions can be used.

Cylindrical shaped lamps are also popular. The lamp shown here (bottom right) is just a top and bottom circle cut out of 3/4" lumber with half rounds attached. Be sure all the mouldings used here are perfectly straight, otherwise spaces will show through the lamp base. This design could also be done in a square, octagon, or hexagon shape. If those shapes are desired, use plywood under the moulding to eliminate the possibility of space gaps.

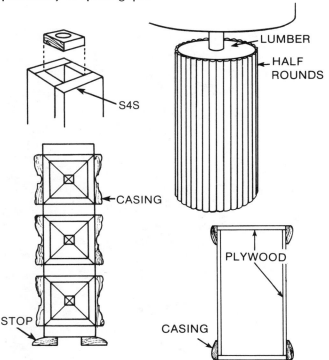

Lamp base construction details.

Wind Chime

Create your own wind chime with lattice, screen, rounds, half rounds, quarter rounds, dowels, squares, base caps, coves, and stops, all clustered together to form a melodious wind chime. The tones will vary according to the weight, length, and patterns of wood mouldings you choose. After you've made your selection, attach small eye hooks at the end and suspend them from a frame of squares with dowel cross pieces. The distance between them should be far enough apart to swing freely, but close enough to touch in a gentle breeze. Stain or oil as you desire, then hang it from your porch or a nearby tree.

Boxes (Cigarette, Jewelry, Utility, Etc.)

Handy little boxes can be used to store a variety of items, such as cigarettes, jewelry, stamps, or buttons. These boxes utilize a 1/4" plywood or hardboard for backing. Hardboard is fine for gluing but difficult to use for nailing. Your miter box is a must on these projects. The size of each box will depend on your needs. Remember, if you can't find the type of moulding shown here at your lumber yard, it is easy to substitute something you find available.

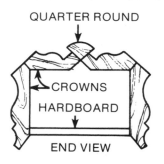

QUARTER ROUND

CROWNS

HARDBOARD

END VIEW

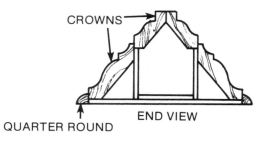

CROWNS

QUARTER ROUND

END VIEW

Other possible decorative box designs.

CHAPTER
—10—
PANELING

No wall covering material offers the natural warmth and quiet beauty that wood does. To man, the builder and the decorator, genuine wood has always been the stout heart of his home, offering man a way to create a mood, set a stage, warm a hearth, brighten a room, and reflect the good life. Paneling is available in many different species, patterns, and finishes, and there is something for every decor from colonial to contemporary. It can be applied as solid wood boards or as plywood or hardboard. Installation is simple; one needn't be a professional to add a professional touch of class to any decor (Fig. 10-1).

A

B

Fig. 10-1: (A) Plain walls become (B) distinctively beautiful with the addition of real wood paneling.

SOLID WOOD PANELING

Various types and patterns of woods are available for application on walls to obtain the desired decorative effects. For informal treatment, knotty pine, redwood, whitepocket Douglas fir, sound wormy chestnut, and pecky cypress may be used to cover one or more sides of a room. These may be finished natural or stained and varnished. In addition, there are such desirable hardwoods as red oak, pecan, elm, walnut, white oak, and cherry also available for wall paneling. Most types of paneling come in thicknesses from 3/8″ to 3/4″, widths from 4″ to 8″, and lengths from 3′ to 10′.

Paneling is also available in several textures and patterns. In addition to the popular straight tongue and groove boards, paneling is produced with moulded edges that create handsome shadow lines and decorative patterns. Most paneling is available either planed for smoother finishing or rough-sawn for a rustic, informal effect. Those with a rough-sawn texture are available in either the square-edged boards or the simple tongue and groove pattern.

When planning a wood paneled room, remember that if you wish to accent a wall, use boards of random widths; subdue it by the use of equal-width boards. Small rooms can be given the illusion of increased size by applying the paneling horizontally. Of course, paneling can be applied vertically, horizontally, diagonally, or in combined directions (Fig. 10-2).

Preparing to Panel

To estimate quantities of board paneling, measure wall height and width and multiply the areas to be paneled. Deduct for major openings such as doors, windows, and fireplaces. Then add 10 to 20% for waste in fitting, lap of boards, if any, and the difference of rough width from finished width.

Even though kiln-dried, solid wood is subject to shrinkage and swelling. After delivery, therefore, stack the lumber inside the house at a temperature as

A   B   C

Fig. 10-2: Three methods of installing solid wood paneling: (A) horizontally, (B) vertically, and (C) diagonally.

close to room temperature as possible. The paneling should never be stored where it will be exposed to weather or to excessive moisture. The building or room in which the wood planking is to be installed should be completely closed in and dry before installation begins. Masonry and other work involving moisture should be completed and dried. A moisture barrier such as polyethylene plastic sheeting (4 mils thick) should be provided behind paneling where any danger of moisture penetration exists. This is a requirement on outside walls and on all concrete or masonry walls. Also, if you intend to install paneling over a masonry wall that is often damp, it is a good idea to apply a wood preservative containing pentachlorophenol to the back of each panel. This will protect the paneling against moisture, mildew, fungus, and termites and other insects.

Before doing any installation, lay out the boards on the floor adjacent to the installation wall. Arrange the most attractive combination of widths, lengths, grain patterns, and shades of color. Then install the boards in the selected sequence. Use shorter pieces at the top and bottom of the wall area, where more than two pieces are required for wall height. Stagger the end joints to form a pleasing pattern on the wall, and avoid positioning two or more end joints near each other. Vary the widths to enhance the random effect. For best contrast, use narrow planks adjacent to wider ones. Figure 10-3 illustrates three patterns of panel arrangements. The channel rustic patterns provide strong vertical accents with bold shadow lines, while the bevel-edged tongue and groove and shiplap patterns offer the more subtle V-groove effect. Where no accent line at all is desired, square-edged adaptations are used to create tight, flush joints. Most patterns may be installed either vertically or horizontally; the choice is yours.

Fig. 10-3: Patterns of board arrangement: (top to bottom) channel rustic pattern, shiplap pattern, tongue-and-groove pattern.

How to Install Vertical Paneling

For most vertical applications over plaster or similar walls, 1 × 2 or 1 × 3 furring strips installed (nailed or glued) horizontally at 16″ or 24″ centers are recommended (Fig. 10-4). Where the wall is uneven or wavy, wooden wedges or shims should be used behind the furring strips to bring them into an even line (Fig. 10-5).

Starting at one corner, the first piece of paneling should be plumbed vertically with a plumb line (Fig. 10-6). This may necessitate trimming the corner grooved edge if the wall corner is not plumb. Succeeding panels are then applied by blind nailing through the tongue of the panel or are face nailed to the furring strips (Fig. 10-7).

Use 8d nails for 3/4″ boards when face nailing, 6d for blind nailing. Use proportionately smaller nails for thinner panelings. If face nailing is used, set the nails 1/32″ below the surface and fill the resulting holes with colored filler or stick putty.

As you install each board, check for plumbness, adjusting slightly on each panel as needed. The last panel may need to be beveled before it will fit. Apply surface treatment or finish following manufacturer's directions.

Fig. 10-6: The first piece of paneling should be plumbed vertically with a plumb line.

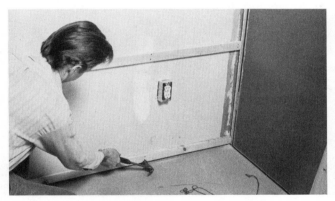

Fig. 10-4: Applying horizontal furring strips for vertical paneling.

Fig. 10-5: Shims placed under furring strips keep the nailing surface flush.

Fig. 10-7: Panels can be applied by either face nailing or blind nailing through the tongue.

How to Install Horizontal Paneling

While not as common as vertical paneling, horizontal applications have some definite advantages. This style allows longer and, therefore, fewer pieces to be used, it can be done quicker, and it makes a room seem longer or larger and a ceiling seem lower. Standard panels in uniform widths are best.

When applying horizontal paneling over uneven walls, nail furring strips vertically on 3′ centers. When solid wood paneling is to be applied horizontally on an existing wall that is reasonably sound and true, furring strips are not usually required. Once the trim has been removed and the studs located, the boards are nailed through the existing wall material into the studs. If the old wall surface is plaster or masonry, in poor condition, or not true, furring strips should be installed as for vertical solid paneling except that strips should run vertically rather than horizontally. Shim the strips to obtain a true nailing surface. Inside corners are formed by butting the panel boards flush with adjacent walls. If random widths are employed, boards should be well matched and accurately aligned. When nailing the boards, be sure to install them so that the tongue edge is up. This will permit you to blind nail through their tongues. Drive the nails in at an angle so they come out the back of each board behind the tongue. The nail heads, of course, will be hidden in the groove of the next board. At the top and bottom of the wall, be sure to leave an expansion space of about 1/4". These gaps will be hidden behind mouldings.

How to Install Diagonal Paneling

One of the popular diagonal patterns is herringbone. The herringbone style of application is perhaps the most exciting pattern in standard tongue and groove paneling, but it is also the most demanding in craftsmanship.

To install herringbone paneling, apply furring strips 18" on center. Apply stain to all paneling, moulding, and baseboard. Do this now to avoid any unstained areas, should the paneling shrink slightly after application. When these are dry, install the baseboard.

Next, use a long level to draw a plumb line at the center of three furring strips, A, B, and C (Fig. 10-8). The lines should be as close to 36" apart as possible in a 12' wall. This should divide the wall into four equal parts or units.

To apply the first panel, saw four 45° triangles as shown in Fig. 10-9. These triangles should be butted

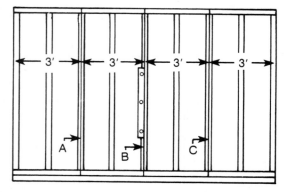

Fig. 10-8: Use a long level to draw plumb lines A, B, and C.

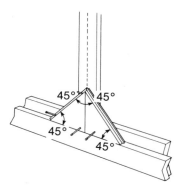

Fig. 10-9: Herringbone installation begins with pieces cut 45° on both ends.

together and nailed to strips A and C. Blind nail through the tongue and into the furring strips. An important craftsmanship point is to make the paneling butt flush with the baseboard. The vertical gap between boards will be covered with a moulding strip.

The succeeding planks are fitted by first making a 45° cut on one end, fitting the groove into the lower panel, and marking a plumb line as shown in Fig. 10-10. As you work up the wall, plumb lines must be drawn on both ends of the board before cutting to size. Install each piece clear across from center to center. Remember to blind nail wherever possible.

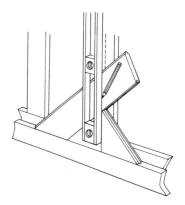

Fig. 10-10: Cut the second piece 45° on one end and cut along the plumb line on the other.

Miscellaneous Tips on Installing Paneling

Fit the solid paneling as closely as possible around the untrimmed door opening thickness. (The door, window, base, and ceiling mouldings should be removed before starting the job.) Fur out window and door frames to equal the thickness of the furring strips plus thickness of the paneling. To give the job a finished look, use moulding around windows and doors, along the floor and ceiling, and wherever else applicable.

In new work, wood paneling may be nailed to studs or furring in the same manner as plywood. A right-handed worker will prefer facing the tongues to the right and working from left to right, starting with a length nailed to a corner studding or furring. The boards that fill the space to the next stud are then laid out and cut to the proper length, the preceding one being used as a template to make sure that all are the same length. Each tongue should be fitted snugly into its groove. Be careful not to force the boards together too tightly. The boards between those anchored to studs can be secured to the top plate near the ceiling and to the base plate close to the floor. Warped lengths should be discarded. If possible, use only full-length pieces that extend from floor to ceiling, except where the wall is masked by bookshelves or built-ins. Corners must be solid, which will usually require ripping at least one board for its full length to take off the tongue (Fig. 10-11). The top of the paneling can be finished with a suitable cove or crown moulding.

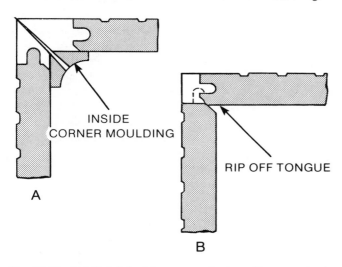

INSIDE
CORNER MOULDING

RIP OFF TONGUE

A

B

Fig. 10-11: (A) Finish inside corners by installing standard inside corner moulding or (B) by butting planks. Use outside corner moulding where required.

Adhesive for Solid Wood Paneling

Solid board paneling may be applied directly over sound, even walls using a ceramic tile type of adhesive or mastic. Ask your building supply dealer for advice concerning the type and brand available.

As in nailing, make sure the first panel is aligned vertically at the corner of the room. After fit is assured, use a putty knife to apply daubs of adhesive to the back of the panel. These should be about the size of a half dollar, at least 1/2" thick and spaced 18" apart near both edges of the panel. Place the panel in position and press it firmly to even out the adhesive and assure

a tight bond. Succeeding panels are treated the same: placed close to the previous panel, pressed into place, and then slid tightly against it.

PLYWOOD PANELING

The homeowner who is handy with tools can remodel a basement, living room, bedroom, kitchen, or attic with a minimum of money and labor by using plywood. Plywood panels come in woods ranging from richly figured oak, mahogany, birch, and walnut to fir and pine, allowing a choice of decorative material to meet every taste and budget. They can be applied effectively to either traditional or modern interiors.

One outstanding advantage of plywood for interiors is the elimination of periodic redecorating and patching of cracks. Plywood walls are kickproof, punctureproof, and crackproof. The only upkeep required is an occasional waxing. The large sheets, 4' wide, 8' long, and 1/4" thick, can be erected quickly and easily with ordinary hand tools.

Selection of a Panel Arrangement

The photographs in Fig. 10-12 suggest a few interesting ways to arrange panels in architecturally and decoratively correct designs. Many of these can be used on all the walls in a room, others are intended to create a point of interest or contrast in one part of the room only. In the latter cases, the rest of the room may be paneled with full length plywood in natural finish, or with less expensive or lower grade plywood, painted or papered. Plywood panels can also be used in combination with painted or papered plaster, with mirror, glass block, masonry, and other wall materials.

In choosing your panel arrangement, remember that it is best to start paneling at the openings, with vertical joints, and then divide the plain space in an orderly pattern, placing the panels in a reasonably balanced horizontal or vertical arrangement. Where the width of the wall is 10' or less, panels may be run horizontally in two or three pieces, with the openings cut out. Place vertical joints at each side of the top of doors and at the top and bottom of window openings. If the width of the door or window opening is more than 4', most designers do not hesitate to place panels horizontally. Remember, you can plan vertical arrangements to lend height and horizontal paneling to give breadth and sweep. Both can be combined in the same room with a pleasing effect. In certain woods, panels 9' or 10' long are available to solve special paneling problems.

Fig. 10-12: Designed plywood arrangements.

Estimating the Amount of Plywood Required

To estimate the number of panels required, measure the perimeter of the room. This is merely the total of the widths of each wall in the room. Use conversion Table 10-1 to figure the number of panels needed.

TABLE 10-1:   PANEL ESTIMATION

Perimeter (feet)	Number of 4' × 8' panels needed
36	9
40	10
44	11
48	12
52	13
56	14
60	15
64	16
68	17
72	18
92	23

For example, if your room walls measured 14' + 14' + 16' + 16', this would equal 60' or 15 panels required. To allow for areas such as windows, doors, fireplaces, etc., use the following deductions:

Door	1/2 panel
Window	1/4 panel
Fireplace	1/2 panel

If a room of this perimeter (60') had two windows, two doors, and a fireplace, the actual number of panels needed would be 13 (15 panels minus two total deductions). If the perimeter of the room falls in between the figures in Table 10-1, use the next highest number to determine panels required. These figures are for rooms with 8' ceiling heights or less. For walls over 8' high, select a paneling which has V grooves and that will "stack," allowing panel grooves to line up perfectly from floor to ceiling.

Installing Plywood Paneling

After purchasing the necessary paneling, store the panels in the room for a few days before you start the job. Spacers allow air to circulate around each panel. Whether new or old, the studs should be straight, dry, plumb, and true to assure a smooth, flat wall surface. If new framing is being installed, use only #1 Common, thoroughly dry, straight framing lumber of uniform width and thickness. Framing should be erected on 16" centers. If necessary, extra framing members should be installed to provide a nailing base for all edges of the panels. Where required, nail cats (horizontal framing members) at 4' heights for additional support of panels for every panel edge and for every 4' of panel. If you are in doubt about the dryness of the framing lumber, apply plywood strips (1/4" thick, 2-1/2" wide, and 4' long), with the grain running the short way over the face of the framing members. For studs spaced 16" on centers, use 1/4" plywood; for studs placed 24" or more on centers, apply 3/4" furring strips.

Plan the sequence of panels about the room so that the natural color variations form a pleasing pattern in complementary tones or in direct contrast. Hold each panel against the wall to see how it looks before you nail it.

There are several tricks for laying out panels to reduce cutting as well as to achieve a pleasing pattern of joints. To avoid intricate fitting around windows and doors, start full panels on each side of the openings. On plain walls, it is best to start at the center so that fractional panels will be the same at each end. You can keep all joints vertical, the simplest arrangement, or use the tops and bottoms of windows as guidelines for horizontal joints.

Be sure that the panels are square with the adjacent wall (at corners) and ceiling before nailing. If the panel is not square with the adjacent wall, scribe it to the corner (Fig. 10-13). Keep the bottom of each wall panel about 1/4" above the floor to allow space for the lever used to pry the panel tightly against the ceiling. As the panels go up, keep checking them for plumbness. Shim out the studs or fill hollows of the framing. Keep a level handy for truing up and down (vertical position). Moulding will take care of the irregular meeting with floor and ceiling. When nailing, start along one edge of the panel and work across the width so as to avoid bulges.

To locate an electrical outlet cutout on a panel, place the panel against the wall and, with a padded block over the approximate location of the outlet, tap it soundly with a hammer. The outlet box will indent the back side of the panel. Drill small pilot holes from the back (enlarge holes from finish side) and saw the outlet hole from the front side of the panel with a keyhole saw (Fig. 10-14). After the cutout has been made

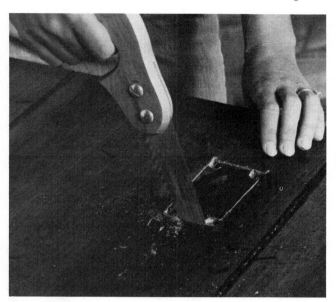

Fig. 10-14: Cut outlet box opening by drilling and sawing with a keyhole saw.

and the panel board installed, attach receptacle extensions to advance the receptacles flush with the panel surface. Building codes usually require the front of the receptacle to be placed within 1/8" of the panel face. You should check the building codes for your specific locality.

When cutting plywood with a handsaw, or on a table saw, plywood should be cut with the good face up. If you are using a portable electric handsaw, either circular or saber, cut the plywood with the good face down. With a handsaw, or on a table saw, permit only the teeth of the blade to protrude through the work. For smooth cuts, use blades that have teeth with no set and that are hollow ground. Special small-toothed blades are available for cutting plywood. Some additional tips for installing plywood paneling with nails are given in Fig. 10-15.

Installing with Adhesive

The application of plywood with panel adhesive is widely employed by homeowners. Its use largely eliminates the need for brads or nails and the resulting concealment of their heads. Generally, the adhesive comes ready to use in a tube with a plastic nozzle. This tube fits into almost any caulking gun, and the panel adhesive comes out of the nozzle as a heavy bead. If the wall is in good condition, smooth and true, the adhesive can be applied directly to the back of the panel all around the edges in intermittent beads about 3" long and spaced about 3" apart. Keep the adhesive at least 1/4" from the edges of the panel and be sure that it is continuous at the corners and around open-

Fig. 10-13: A panel edge can be cut to fit an out-of-square corner by tracing the corner with a scriber.

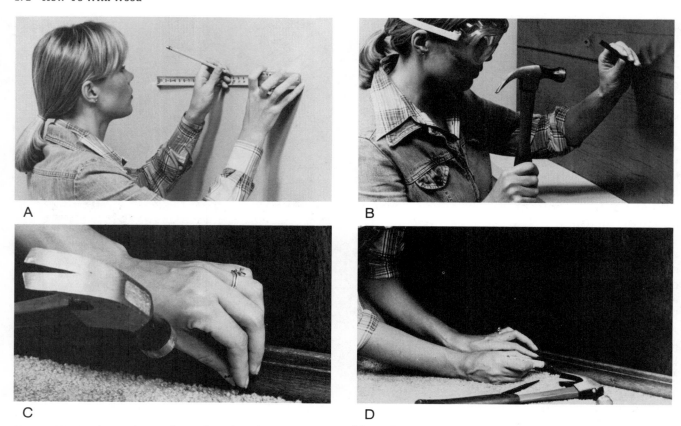

A   B

C   D

Fig. 10-15: Applying plywood panels with nails: (A) Measure 16" from the corner to locate the first stud. (B) To hide the nails, nail through the kerf and counterset the nails. (C) Face nail the mouldings. (D) After countersetting nails, fill with a stick putty of matching color.

ings for electrical outlets and switches. Additional adhesive should be applied to the back of the panel in horizontal lines of intermittent beads spaced approximately 16" apart. Once the adhesive is applied, the panel may be pressed against the wall. It may be moved as much as is required for satisfactory adjustment. To make this easier, drive three or four small finishing nails about half their length through the panel near the top edge. The panel can then be pulled away from the wall at the bottom with the nails acting as a hinge. After adjustment has been made, a padded block should be used to keep the panel pressed back on the wall, and then the nails are driven home. (These will be covered by a moulding.) A rubber mallet or a hammer and padded block should be used on the face of the panel to assure good adhesion between panel and wall.

This adhesive also may be used on furring strips and open studs. It is applied directly to each furring strip or stud in continuous or intermittent beads (Fig. 10-16). Panels are then applied by the same method as previously described. But never apply adhesives on plaster walls in poor condition, with flaking paint or wallpaper that is not tightly glued. If the plaster seems hard and firm and does not crumble when you drive a nail into it, it is probably safe for adhesives.

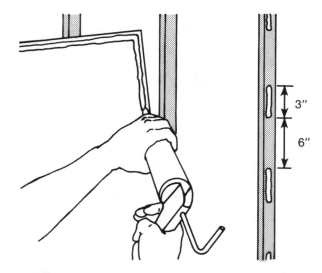

3"

6"

Fig. 10-16: Apply glue either continuously or intermittently to either the panel back or studs.

HARDBOARD PANELING

Hardboard specially manufactured for use as prefinished paneling is specifically treated for resistance to stains, scrubbing, and moisture. It is also highly resistant to dents, mars, and scuffs. In most cases, the material is prefinished in wood grains such as walnut, cherry, birch, oak, teak, and pecan, and in a variety of shades. It may be smooth-surfaced or random-grooved. In addition there are the decorative and work-saving plastic-surfaced hardboards which resist water, stains, and household chemicals exceptionally well. A typical surface consists of baked-on plastic. Most hardboard is sufficiently dense and moisture resistant for use in bathrooms, kitchens, and laundry rooms. The variety of finishes and sizes is extensive. Finishes include rich-looking wood grains, exceptional marble reproductions, plain colors, speckled colors, simulated tile, lace prints, wallpaper textures, and murals. Vinyl-clad panels are also available in decorative and wood grain finishes.

Use 3/16", 1/4", and 5/16" hardboards over open framing. All panel edges should be backed. Studs or framing members should be spaced no more than 16" on center. Use 1/4" or 5/16" board thicknesses for structural wall members. Hardboards 1/8" and 3/16" thick should be applied over solid backing. Quarter-inch-thick boards may be applied directly over studding or stripping not over 16" on center. Tips for installing a partial wall of hardboard paneling are given in Fig. 10-17.

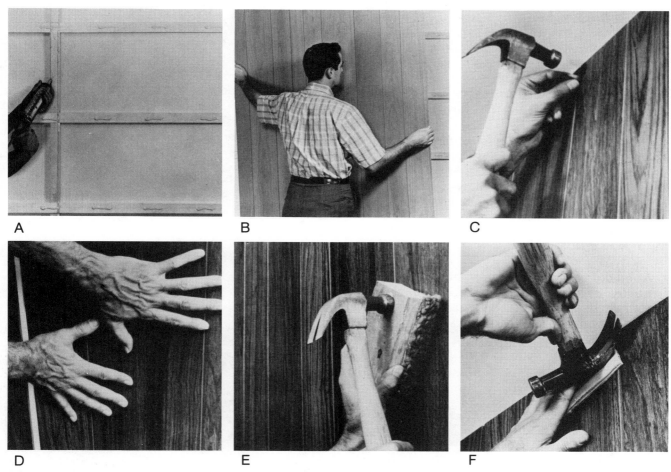

Fig. 10-17: (A) After making sure that all surfaces to which adhesive is to be applied are clean and dry, apply 1/8" thick continuous ribbon to furring or other surfaces to which panel edges are to be bonded. Apply intermittent ribbon (3" bead, 6" open space) to intermediate furring. Adhesive and room temperatures should be between 60° and 100° F during application. (B) Move panel into position over furring strips and immediately press into position. (C) Install two nails at top of the panel to maintain its position, leaving the heads exposed for subsequent easy removal. (D) With uniform hand pressure, press the panels firmly into contact with the adhesive bead. (E) After 15 to 20 minutes, reapply pressure to all areas to be bonded, using a padded block of wood and a hammer or mallet. A final set is thus provided. (F) Carefully remove the nails, protecting the panel surface with a scrap of carpeting. When installing base, follow the procedure shown in D. If prefinished plastic mouldings are not used, a wood moulding can be stained or painted to harmonize or contrast with the paneling.

CHAPTER

—11—

WOOD DOORS AND WINDOWS

In a previous chapter, we discussed the possibility of brightening any room in your house by an imaginative use of inexpensive mouldings. Without going into a major remodeling project, the outside of your house can also be given a new look by adding new windows and doors. Many different appearances are possible. Exchange double-hung windows for a slider or a casement window. Install a beautifully stained, carved panel door where a nondescript metal door now hangs (Fig. 11-1). There are many choices that are both beautiful and economical. Doors and windows and how they can beautify as well as weatherize your home are subjects discussed in this chapter.

WOOD DOORS

Wood doors have graced fine homes for decades. The entry to a home often creates a first impression. A beautifully designed wood door can create a favorable first impression. For aesthetic and practical reasons, more and more people are choosing wood doors to enhance the entrance to their home.

Wood Doors—a Beautiful Choice

Wood doors come in a wide variety of designs and prices, from early colonial panel doors to intricately detailed doors with the appearance of hand carvings (Fig. 11-2). Appealing grille and glass designs add a further dimension to the range of door styles that can be used. There's a door to fit any style home. Many of the popular carved designs are available in wood doors only. They all provide do-it-yourselfers with an inexpensive means of adding a distinctive difference to the front of the home.

Wood doors can be finished in a variety of colors and color combinations from antique to ultramodern. Unlike metal doors, wood doors readily take stain as well as paint finishes. When transparent stain is applied to a wood door, the grain becomes a decorative element, giving the door its own unique character. A wood door can be finished to complement any exterior decor.

Fig. 11-1: A panel door and a bow window are beautiful additions to any home.

Fig. 11-2: An intricately designed panel door.

Wood Doors—a Practical Choice

Wood has long been recognized as one of the finest natural insulating materials available. Its cellular structure provides a honeycomb of protection between the weather outside and the comfort inside. Wood is composed of many hollow cells of different sizes and shapes. These hollow cells give wood a considerable percentage of dead air volume. Because the insulating quality of air is very high compared with other materials, wood is an excellent insulator. For the purpose of comparison, wood as a material insulates four times as effectively as concrete block, six times as effectively as brick, 15 times as effectively as concrete, 400 times as effectively as steel, and 1,770 times as effectively as aluminum. Since heat travels through wood much more slowly than through metal, a wood door will feel warm while a metal door will feel chilly or cold.

Wood doors can be easily trimmed to meet the requirements of varying door frames—an important consideration in replacement and remodeling. Your first attempt at installing a door may not be perfect, but tight spots can be easily smoothed over with a jack plane to make even the most obstinate door open easily.

EXTERIOR DOORS

Exterior doors are usually 1-3/4" thick and not less than 6' 8" high. The main entrance door, as a rule, is 3' wide and the side or rear service door 2' 8" wide. The frames for these doors are made of 1-1/8" or thicker material, so that rabbeting of the side and head jambs provides stops for the main door. The wood sill is often oak for wear resistance, but when softer species are used, a metal nosing and wear strips are included. Many exterior doors are designed to be accompanied by a combination storm and screen door.

The frame is nailed to studs and headers of the rough opening through the outside casing. The sill must rest firmly on the header or stringer joist of the floor framing, which commonly must be trimmed with a saw and hand ax or other means. After finish flooring is in place, a hardwood or metal threshold with a plastic weather stop covers the joints between the floor and sill. The exterior trim around the main entrance door can vary from a simple casing to a molded or plain pilaster with a decorative head casing (Fig. 11-3). Decorative designs should always be in keeping with the architecture of the house. Many combinations of door and entry designs are used with contemporary houses, and manufacturers have millwork that is adaptable to this and similar styles. If there is an entry

hall, it is usually desirable to have glass included in the main door when no other light is provided in the hall.

Types of Exterior Doors

Exterior doors and outside combination and storm doors can be obtained in a number of designs to fit the style of almost any house.

Panel Doors. Doors in the traditional pattern are usually the panel type. They consist of stiles (solid vertical members), rails (solid cross members), and filler panels in a number of designs. Other doors have glazed (glass) upper panels with raised wood or plywood lower panels.

Exterior Flush Doors. Exterior flush doors should be of the solid-core type rather than hollow-core to minimize warping during the heating season. (Warping is caused by a difference in moisture content on the exposed and unexposed faces.)

Flush doors consist of thin plywood faces over a framework of wood with a wood-block or particleboard core. Many combinations of designs can be obtained, ranging from plain flush doors to others with a variety of panels and glazed openings. Bold designs can be achieved with wide moulding, painting in colors that contrast strongly with wide moulding and painting in colors that contrast strongly with the door face. Various accents can be achieved by choosing brighter shades, more subdued shades, or even the same color as the rest of the door, letting the 3-D effect come through subtly.

Combination Doors. Wood combination doors (storm and screen) are available in several styles. Panels that include screen and storm inserts are normally located in the upper portion of the door. Some types can be obtained with self-storing features, similar to those in window combination units. Heat loss through metal combination doors is greater than through wood doors of similar size and construction.

INTERIOR DOORS

The two general interior door types are the flush door and the panel door. Novelty doors, such as the folding door unit, can be flush or louvered. Most standard interior doors are 1-3/8" thick.

The flush interior door is usually made up with a hollow core of light framework of some type with thin plywood or hardboard (Fig. 11-4A). Plywood-faced flush doors may be obtained in gum, birch, oak, mahogany, and woods of other species, most of which are suitable for natural finish. Nonselected grades are usually painted, as are hardboard-faced doors.

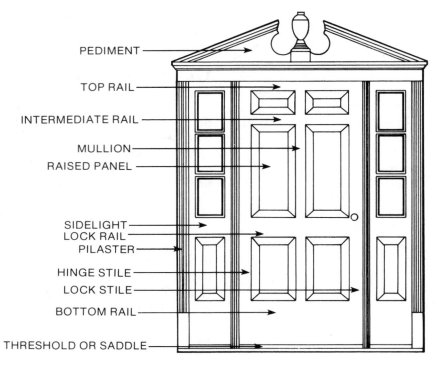

PEDIMENT
TOP RAIL
INTERMEDIATE RAIL
MULLION
RAISED PANEL
SIDELIGHT
LOCK RAIL
PILASTER
HINGE STILE
LOCK STILE
BOTTOM RAIL
THRESHOLD OR SADDLE

Fig. 11-3: Exterior door and trim parts.

The panel door consists of solid stiles (vertical side members), rails (cross pieces), and panel filters of various types. The five-cross panel and the colonial-type panel doors are perhaps the most common of this style (Figs. 11-4B and C). The louvered door (Fig. 11-4D) is also popular and is commonly used for closets because it provides ventilation. Large openings for

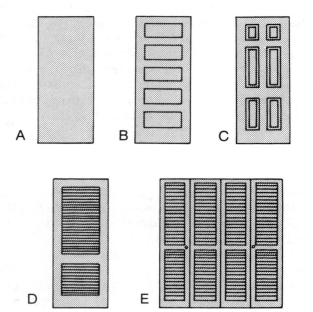

Fig. 11-4: Interior doors: (A) flush, (B) panel (five cross), (C) panel (colonial), (D) louvered, and (E) folding (louvered).

wardrobes are finished with sliding or folding doors that are either flush or louvered (Fig. 11-4E). Such doors are usually 1-1/8" thick.

Hinged doors should open or swing in the direction of natural entry, against a blank wall whenever possible, and should not be obstructed by other swinging doors. Doors should never be hinged to swing into a hallway.

DOORJAMBS AND TRIM

A door frame is the wood lining the door opening. It consists of two side jambs called the hinge jamb and the strike jamb, plus a connecting jamb called the header. These door linings are separated into two categories—interior openings and exterior openings. An exterior opening leads to the outside of a house. All other openings are considered interior openings.

Interior Jambs

Interior door frames are made up of two side jambs and a head jamb and include stop mouldings upon which the door closes. The most common of these jambs is the one-piece type (Fig. 11-5A). Jambs may be obtained in standard 5-1/4" widths for plaster walls and 4-5/8" widths for walls with 1/2" drywall finish. The two- and three-piece adjustable jambs are also

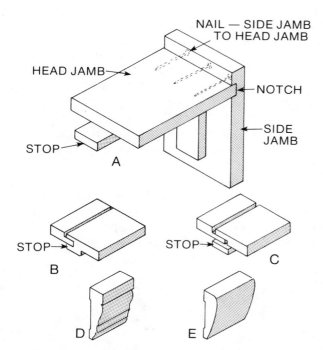

NAIL — SIDE JAMB TO HEAD JAMB

HEAD JAMB

NOTCH

SIDE JAMB

STOP

A

STOP

B

STOP

C

D

E

Fig. 11-5: Interior door parts: (A) doorjambs and stops, (B) two-piece jamb, (C) three-piece jamb, (D) colonial casing, and (E) ranch casing.

standard types (Figs. 11-5B and C). Their principal advantage is being adaptable to a variety of wall thicknesses. Some manufacturers produce interior door frames with the door fitted and prehung, ready for installation. Application of the casing (Figs. 11-5 D and E) completes the job. When used with two- or three-piece jambs, casings can even be installed at the factory.

Common minimum widths for single interior doors are: (a) bedrooms and other habitable rooms, 2′ 6″; (b) bathrooms, 2′ 4″; and (c) small closets and linen closets, 2′. These sizes vary a great deal. Sliding doors, folding door units, and similar types are often used for wardrobes and may be 6′ or more in width. In most cases, the jamb, stop, and casing parts are used in some manner to frame and finish the opening.

Standard interior and exterior door heights are 6′ 8″ for first floors, while 6′ 4″ doors may be used on the upper floors.

Exterior Jambs

Frames for exterior doors are thicker one-piece rabbeted jambs which are more weathertight and give added strength to support heavier exterior doors. The exterior frame may be equipped with a sill, weatherstrip, and an exterior casing. An exterior frame can also be purchased as an individual component part or as a prehung unit.

Installing Door Frames and Trim

For both new and old work, Fig. 11-6 shows the usual type of partition wall framing with the door opening made. Notice that a double header is installed at the top and that extra studs are set in at the sides. After preparing the opening, you are ready to install the door frame.

Installing Jambs. When the frame and doors are not assembled and prefitted, the side jambs should be fabricated by nailing through the notch into the head jamb with three 7d or 8d coated nails. The assembled frames are then fastened in the rough openings by shingle wedges used between the side jamb and the stud. One jamb is plumbed and leveled using four or five sets of shingle wedges for the height of the frame. Two 8d finishing nails are used at each wedged area, one driven so that the doorstop will cover it. The opposite side jamb is now fastened in place with shingle wedges and finishing nails, using the first jamb as a guide in keeping a uniform width.

Installing Casings. Casings are nailed to both the jamb and the framing studs or header, allowing about a 1/4″ edge distance from the face of the jamb. Finish or casing nails in 6d or 7d sizes, depending on the thickness of the casing, are used to nail into the stud. Fourpenny or 5d finishing nails or 1-1/2″ brads are used to fasten the thinner edge of the casing to the jamb. With hardwood, it is usually advisable to predrill to prevent splitting. Nails in the casing are located in pairs and spaced about 16″ along the full height of the opening and at the head jamb.

Casing used with any form of moulded shape must have a mitered joint at the corners. When casing is square-edged, a butt joint may be made at the junction of the side and head casing.

In fitting doors, the stops are usually temporarily nailed in place until the door has been hung. Stops for

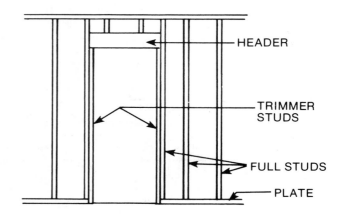

HEADER

TRIMMER STUDS

FULL STUDS

PLATE

Fig. 11-6: Rough framing for a door.

doors in single-piece jambs are generally 7/16" thick and may be 3/4" to 2-1/4" wide. They are installed with a mitered joint at the junction of the side and head jambs. A 45° bevel cut at the bottom of the stop, about 1" to 1-1/2" above the finish floor, will eliminate a dirt pocket and make cleaning or refinishing of the floor easier. Some manufacturers supply prefitted door jambs and doors with the hinge slots routed and ready for installation.

HANGING AN EXTERIOR DOOR

The first step in hanging a door is to cut and plane the door to fit the door frame. Measure the frame from the upper jamb to the sill and subtract 1/8" to determine the proper height of the door. Measure from side jamb to side jamb and subtract 1/16" to determine the width of the door. Cut the door to size and stand it in place to see if it fits. A flat bar can be used as a lever to raise and hold the door in position. If needed, mark areas to be further planed and take the steps necessary to make them fit.

Next, prop the door hinge-side up and plane a bevel of 1/16" on the inside edge the full length of the door. Then, separate the hinges by removing the pins. Measure from the top of the door down 7" and draw a straight line across the door's edge. Place the upper edge of the top hinge adjacent to and below the line. Position the hinge so that the hinge pin is at least 1/2" from the edge of the jamb to allow the hinge to swing 180°. The flat edge of the hinge should be no closer to the opposite side than 1/4" for doors up to 2-1/4" thick and no closer than 3/8" for doors over 2-1/4" thick. Draw an outline of the hinge in this position and as shown in Fig. 11-7, making sure that the pin side of the hinge is on the outside of the door. Follow the same procedure with the bottom hinge, measuring 11" up from the bottom of the door. The middle hinge should be centered between the other two hinges.

As you can see in Fig. 11-8, the installed hinge will be flush with the surface of the door. To accomplish this, a mortise must be cut into the edge of the door, either by hand or by using a router and template. Most do-it-yourselfers must resort to a hand chisel. The mortise must be as deep as the thickness of the hinge but no deeper. Usually this means chiseling out a mortise 1/8" deep using a 1-1/2" wood chisel to make the mortise. Begin by cutting with the chisel held upright with the flat side of the chisel parallel to the pencil lines, as in Fig. 11-9. After cutting out the perimeter of the mortise, chip the internal area of the mortise with successive cuts to the proper depth. Do this very carefully, removing a little of the wood at a time. After the mortise has been formed to the proper depth, install the hinges and secure each with one screw.

Fig. 11-8: The hinge should be recessed so that it is level with the surface of the door and jamb.

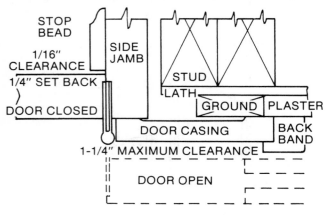

Fig. 11-7: Top view of 3-1/2" × 3-1/2" butt hinge mounted on door and jamb.

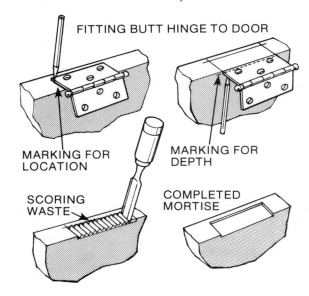

Fig. 11-9: Installing hinges.

Now that half of each hinge has been attached to the door, the placement of the hinges on the jamb must be determined. Measure from the top of the jamb down 7-1/8" and draw a line. This will allow 1/8" clearance between the top of the door and the top jamb. Position the half of hinge against and below the line. Outline the hinge and mark the depth of the mortise. Then chisel out the stock to make a mortise and install the hinge with one screw.

Once you have the top hinge secure, hang the door, hold the middle and bottom hinges against the jamb, and mark above and below each hinge. Remove the door, mark and mortise the jamb, and install the hinges, each with one screw. Then rehang the door and inspect to see that it fits properly. The clearance between the top and the jamb, as well as the back and the jamb should be 1/8". If the door binds when it is closed, adjust the hinges or plane the tight spots. When the door fits properly, install the remaining screws.

INSTALLING DOOR HARDWARE

Hardware for doors may be obtained in a number of finishes, with brass, bronze, and nickel perhaps the most common. Door sets are usually classed as: (a) entry lock for exterior doors; (b) bathroom set (inside lock control with safety slot for opening from the outside); (c) bedroom lock (keyed lock); and (d) passage set (without lock).

The use of three hinges for hanging 1-3/4" exterior doors and two hinges for the lighter interior doors is common practice. There is some tendency for the exterior side to warp during the winter because of the difference in exposure on the opposite sides. The three hinges reduce this tendency. Three hinges are also useful on doors that lead to unheated attics and for wider and heavier doors that may be used within the house.

Loose-pin butt hinges should be used and must be of the proper size for the door they support. For 1-3/4" thick doors, use 4" by 4" butts; for 1-3/8" doors, use 3-1/2" by 3-1/2" butts.

Types of door locks differ with regard to installation, first cost, and the amount of labor required to set them. Lock sets are supplied with instruction for installation. Some types require drilling of the edge and face of the door and routing of the edge to accommodate the lock set and faceplate (Fig. 11-10). A more common bored type (Fig. 11-11) is much easier to install as it requires only one hole drilled in the edge and one in the face of the door. Boring jigs and faceplate markers are available to provide accurate installation. The lock should be installed so that the doorknob is 36" to 38" above the floor line. Most sets come with

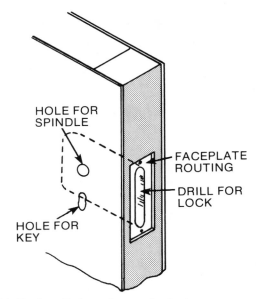

HOLE FOR SPINDLE
HOLE FOR KEY
FACEPLATE ROUTING
DRILL FOR LOCK

Fig. 11-10: Installation of a mortise lock.

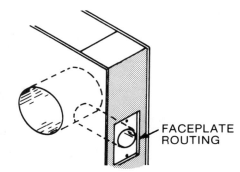

FACEPLATE ROUTING

Fig. 11-11: Installation of a bored lock set.

paper templates marking the location of the lock and size of the holes to be drilled.

The strike plate is routed into the doorjamb and holds the door in place by contact with the latch. To install the strike plate, mark the location of the latch on the doorjamb to determine the correct position of the strike plate. Rout the marked outline with a chisel and also rout for the latch. Door details are shown in Fig. 11-12. The strike plate should be flush with the edge of the jamb.

The stops, which have been set temporarily during the fitting of the door and the installation of the hardware, may now be nailed in place permanently. Finish nails or brads, 1-1/2" long, should be used. The stop at the lock side should be nailed first and should be set tight against the door face when the door is latched. Space the nails 16" apart in pairs.

The stop behind the hinge side is nailed next, and a 1/32" clearance from the door face should be allowed to prevent scraping as the door is opened. The head jamb stop is then nailed in place. Remember that when door and trim are painted, some of the clearance will be taken up.

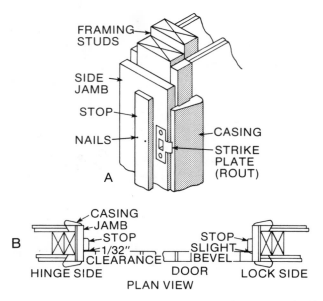

FRAMING STUDS

SIDE JAMB

STOP

NAILS

CASING

STRIKE PLATE (ROUT)

A

CASING
JAMB
STOP
1/32″
CLEARANCE
HINGE SIDE

B

STOP
SLIGHT
BEVEL
LOCK SIDE

DOOR

PLAN VIEW

Fig. 11-12: Door details (split jamb): (A) installation of strike plate and (B) location of stops.

Installing Exterior Door Locks

New locks and escutcheon plates can give new beauty to most entrance doors. The first step in replacing an old lock is to remove it completely from the door. Generally it is a good idea to fill all the holes created by the removal of the lock. An exception to this procedure occurs with some of the modern locks, which have large escutcheons that will cover the old holes. To fill the old mortise, make a plug of soft pine. When driving in the glued plug, make sure that the grain follows the grain of the stile. Fill all the screw holes with wood putty or plastic; let dry and then sand smooth.

When installing the new lock, use the cardboard template, or pattern, which comes with the lock, to locate all holes. To drill the large holes necessary with some locks, use an expansion bit, or start with a smaller hole and enlarge this with a keyhole saw. The cut for the face plate can be made with a chisel and hammer. Using the plate as a pattern, mark off the area that must be removed and carefully cut a shallow mortise just inside the mark.

After all the cuts are on the door, the new lock can be installed. Since each lock has its own special features, it is most important to follow the manufacturer's instructions to the letter. Figure 11-13 shows a typical installation of a front door lock set.

The last item to install is the striker plate against which the door latch hits as the door closes. Rub some chalk on the tip of the latch and close the door. Repeat this for the deadbolt. Cut a couple of notches in the frame where these marks indicate depressions are needed. (The plate also requires a shallow mortise so it will fit flush with the frame.) Hold the striker plate in position, mark off the two mortises, and then cut them out inside the marks. To complete the job, attach the striker plate with the screws provided.

WOOD WINDOWS

For any number of reasons, you may be faced with the task of installing windows. This is not necessarily a job for a professional; you, yourself, can install new windows in your home. You can beautify your home by changing window styles (for example, installing a picture window in place of double-hung windows). Modern air tight windows with double glazed panes will make your home more energy efficient. In the long run, you will be paying yourself to renovate your home.

WINDOWS AND ENERGY CONSERVATION

Most homeowners today are concerned about energy conservation. Many are trying to cope with rising energy costs by adding insulation or supplementing a heating system with a wood stove. Another alternative is to install beautiful, snug-fitting, wood windows.

Wood is a natural insulator—its cellular structure contains thousands of air pockets that trap warm air and slow down the convection loss of heat. Metal windows do not have this natural insulating property and are inferior to wood windows from the standpoint of energy conservation. Wood windows are also treated with preservatives to ward off insect attack, decay, and stains. Many are sheathed in vinyl or aluminum, reducing the need for maintenance and painting (Fig. 11-14). The result is an energy efficient, long lasting, maintenance-free window.

Heat Loss Through Windows

Windows lose heat in two ways: infiltration and conduction (Fig. 11-15). In the first, cold air infiltrates from the outside, passing around the frame and through small openings between the frame and sash. The problem of infiltration of the cold air from the outside is significantly reduced by efficient design of the windows. Quality windows come equipped with frames that are sealed and screwed for maximum weather tightness, with vinyl jamb liners for smooth, tight operation, and "cushion" aluminum weather strips in the top and bottom sash.

A   B

C   D

Fig. 11-13: When installing a lock set, (A) follow the manufacturer's instructions and use the template provided for drilling and cutting holes. (B) Drill from one side of the door until the point of the bit protrudes from the opposite side, then reverse the procedure and (C) complete drilling the hole from the other side. (D) Use a sharp wood chisel to cut away wood. Leave at least 1" of solid wood in the stile behind the lock set to maintain strength of the door. Be sure to install the striker plate accurately.

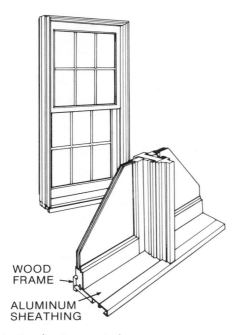

WOOD
FRAME

ALUMINUM
SHEATHING

Fig. 11-14: An aluminum window.

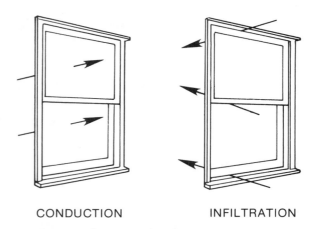

CONDUCTION   INFILTRATION

Fig. 11-15: Conduction and infiltration.

Conduction is accomplished as heat passes through the glass and sash. Heat loss by conduction can be reduced by adding a pane or two (Fig. 11-16). Some windows are double glazed; they have two panes instead of one. A window with three panes is called triple glazed. The third pane is usually removable and

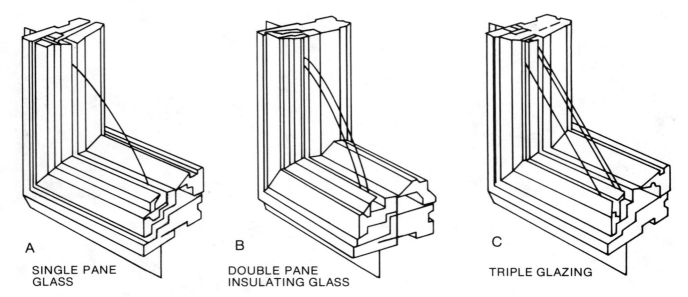

A	B	C
SINGLE PANE GLASS	DOUBLE PANE INSULATING GLASS	TRIPLE GLAZING

Fig. 11-16: Glazing reduces the amount of heat loss due to convection.

functions as a storm window. The additional panes create air spaces in much the same way as insulation does in your walls and ceiling.

The difference between single and multi-glazed windows is evident when sitting near a window. Heat is soaked out of the air near the single pane window, making the room feel cooler near the window than in other areas of the room. To compare the insulating value of double and triple glazed windows, tests were conducted in a controlled environment where the outside temperature was 0°F, the wind velocity was 15 mph, and the inside room temperature was 70°F. The inside surface temperature of the single pane glass was 14°F. The use of double pane insulating glass raised the inside glass surface temperature from 14°F to 42°F. With triple glazing the inside glass surface temperature rose to 52°F. These temperature differences translate into lower heating cost and greater comfort.

Passive Heating and Cooling

The size and style of window can also affect your heating and cooling cost. Windows act as passive solar heat collectors, permitting the sun into a room and trapping its heat. On houses in cold climates, southern exposures should have larger windows to take advantage of the winter sun, while the east and west and especially the north sides of a house should have smaller windows (Fig. 11-17). Replacing drafty single pane windows with larger glazed windows is a double boost in energy savings (Fig. 11-18).

Windows keep cold air out and warm air in during the winter months, but when hot weather arrives, the windows work in reverse, conserving the air-conditioned air and shutting out the hot summer air. In warm climates, summer solar heat gain can be reduced by facing the largest windows north and facing smaller windows to the east, west, and south. Double pane insulating glass reduces the summer conducted heat gain through the window, and for additional shielding, reflective insulating glass that absorbs and reflects heat is also available.

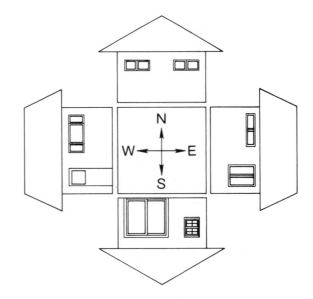

Fig. 11-17: Orienting large windows where they will receive the greatest amount of sunlight reduces heating costs on sunny winter days.

Fig. 11-18: *Replacing small single pane windows with larger glazed ones decreases energy loss, brightens the interior, and beautifies the exterior of your home.*

The style of window can also affect your summer cooling costs. Some windows open wider than others and admit more of the cooling summer breezes. Casement windows can open to 100% of their sash opening area, double-hung and sliding windows to nearly 50%, and awning windows to about 25% (Fig. 11-19). Those with greater sash opening area should be placed where they can be opened to the prevailing winds and take advantage of natural cross ventilation.

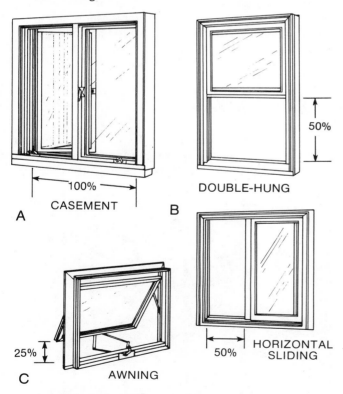

Fig. 11-19: *Some windows can be opened to a greater percentage of their sash opening than others: (A) casement—100%, (B) double-hung and horizontal sliding—50%, and (C) awning—about 25%.*

PARTS OF A WINDOW

The parts of a double-hung window are shown in Fig. 11-20. The three basic parts of any window frame are the head jamb, side jambs, and sill. The number of window parts depends, of course, on the style of window. Window parts are defined in the following:

• *Apron.* The inside trim of a window placed against the wall directly below the stool.
• *Casing.* The finish trim around door and window openings.
• *Drip Cap.* An exterior moulding used over doors and windows to direct water away from the frame.
• *Jamb.* The inner surface lining the sides and top of door and window frames.
• *Light.* A window pane. The sheet of glass in a section of a window or door.
• *Mullion.* A vertical divider between two adjacent windows.
• *Muntin.* The moulding separating the glass panes or lights of a window.
• *Rail.* The horizontal crosspiece of a window; it is also the top piece of a balustrade.
• *Sash.* Either the framework which holds the glass in a window or the movable part (or parts) of the window itself.
• *Sill.* The lowest horizontal member in a window.
• *Stile.* The vertical frame member of a window.

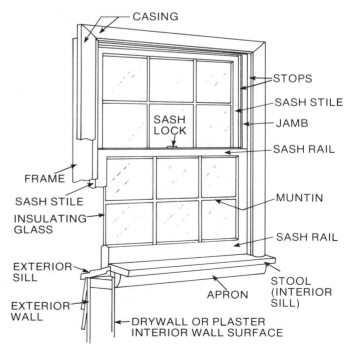

Fig. 11-20: *Components of a window—including the framing parts, casement, and exterior wall cross section.*

• *Stops.* Narrow wood strips which keep double-hung windows in place.
• *Stool.* A flat moulding fitted over the window sill between the jambs.

TYPES OF WINDOWS

Windows are available in many types, each having advantages. The principal types are double-hung, casement, stationary, awning, and horizontal sliding. Tables showing glass size, sash size, and rough opening size are available at lumber dealers, so that the size of windows and wall openings can be matched.

Double-Hung Windows

The double-hung window (Fig. 11-21) is perhaps the most familiar window type. It consists of an upper and lower sash that slide vertically in separate grooves in the side jambs or in full-width weather stripping. This type of window provides a maximum face opening for ventilation of one-half the total window area. Each sash is provided with springs, balances, or compression weather stripping to hold it in place in any location. Compression weather stripping, for example, prevents air infiltration, provides tension, and acts as a counterbalance; several types allow the sash to be removed for easy painting or repair. The jambs (sides and top of the frames) are made of nominal 1" lumber; the width provides for use with drywall or plastered interior finish. Sills are made from 2" lumber and sloped for good drainage. Sashes are normally 1-3/8" thick, and wood combination storm and screen windows are usually 1-1/8" thick.

Sashes may be divided into a number of lights by small wood members called muntins. A ranch-type house may look best with windows whose top and bottom sashes are divided into two horizontal lights. A colonial or Cape Cod house usually has each sash divided into six or eight lights. Some manufacturers provide preassembled dividers or grilles that snap in place over a single light, dividing it into six or eight lights. This simplifies painting and other maintenance.

Assembled frames are placed in the rough opening over strips of building paper put around the perimeter to minimize air infiltration. The frame is plumbed and nailed to the side studs and header through the casings or the blind stops at the sides. Where nails are exposed, such as on the casing, use the corrosion resistant type.

Hardware for double-hung windows includes the sash lifts that are fastened to the bottom rail (although they are sometimes replaced by a finger groove inserted in the rail) and sash locks or fasteners located at the meeting rail. They not only lock the window, but draw the sash together to provide a "windtight" fit.

Double-hung windows can be arranged in a number of ways, as a single unit, doubled (or mullion) type, or in groups of three or more. One or two double-hung windows on each side of a large stationary insulated window are often used to effect a window wall. Such large openings must be framed with headers large enough to carry roof loads.

Casement Windows

This type of window (Fig. 11-22) is characterized by a side-hinged sash, usually designed to swing outward because it can be made more weathertight than the

Fig. 11-21: A double-hung window.

Fig. 11-22: A casement window.

in-swinging style. Screens are located inside these out-swinging windows, and winter protection is obtained with a storm sash or by using insulated glass in the sash. One advantage of the casement window over the double-hung type is that the entire window area can be opened for ventilation. Weather stripping is also provided for this type of window, and units are usually received from the factory entirely assembled with hardware in place. Closing hardware consists of a rotary operator and sash lock. As in the double-hung units, casement sash can be used in a number of ways, as a pair or in combinations of two or more pairs. Style variations are achieved by divided lights. Snap-in muntins provide a small, multiple-pane appearance for traditional styling.

Stationary Windows

Stationary or picture windows (Fig. 11-23) used alone or in combination with double-hung or casement windows usually consist of a wood sash with a large single light of insulated glass. They are designed to provide light, as well as for attractive appearance, and are fastened permanently into the frame. Because of their size (sometimes 6′ to 8′ wide), 1-3/4″ thick sash is used to provide strength. The thickness is usually required because of the thickness of the insulating glass.

Other types of stationary windows may be used without a sash. The glass is set directly into rabbeted frame members and held in place with stops. As with all window-sash units, back puttying and face puttying of the glass (with or without a stop) will assure moisture resistance.

Awning Windows

An awning window unit (Fig. 11-24) consists of a frame in which one or more operative sashes are installed. It is often made up for a large window wall and consists of three or more units in width and height.

Sashes of the awning type are made to swing outward at the bottom. A similar unit, called the hopper type, is one in which the top of the sash swings inward. Both types provide protection from rain when open. Jambs are usually 1-1/16″ or more thick because they are rabbeted, while the sill is at least 1-5/16″ thick when two or more sashes are used in a complete frame. Each sash may also be provided with an individual frame, so that any combination of width and height can be used. Awning or hopper window units may consist of a combination of one or more fixed sashes and one or more of the operable type. Operable sashes are provided with hinges, pivots, and sash-supporting arms.

Weather stripping and storm sash and screens are usually provided. The storm sash is eliminated when the windows are glazed with insulated glass.

Fig. 11-24: An awning window.

Horizontal-Sliding Window Units

This type of window looks like a casement sash. However, the sashes (in pairs) slide horizontally in separate tracks or guides located on the sill and head jamb. Multiple window openings consist of two or more single units and may be used when a window wall effect is desired. As in most modern window units of all types, weather stripping, water-repellent preservative treatments, and sometimes hardware are included in these fully factory-assembled units.

Fig. 11-23: A stationary window.

INSTALLING A WOOD PATIO DOOR

A large sliding window that functions as a door is the patio door. The first consideration when installing a wood patio door is the size of the opening. Whether you must cut an opening in an existing wall or you are installing the door in an existing opening, make sure the opening is the correct size to accommodate the patio door (Table 11-1). If an oak sill is to be used under the patio, add this thickness to the opening dimension for height.

TABLE 11-1: DIMENSIONS FOR PATIO DOOR OPENINGS

Door Size	Rough Opening	Masonry Opening
6' patio	6' 4-5/8" × 6' 10-1/2"	6' 6-1/2" × 6' 11-1/4"
8' patio	8' 4-5/8" × 6' 10-1/2"	8' 6-1/2" × 6' 11-1/4"
9' patio	9' 6" × 6' 10-1/2"	9' 8" × 6' 11-1/4"
12' patio	12' 6" × 6' 10-1/2"	12' 8" × 6' 11-1/4"

Assembling the Frame

Lay out all the frame sections on a clean flat area or on saw horses as shown in Fig. 11-25. Caulk all the joints between the members (Fig. 11-26); for example, caulk where the sill and head are screwed to the jambs and at the outside casing miters. Screw the sill and the jambs together using two #8 × 1-1/2" slotted flat-head screws in each corner. Keep the inside of the sill flush with the inside edge of the jambs. Keep the ends of the sill flush with the outside surface of the jambs. Screw the head to the jambs using two #8 × 1-1/2" slotted flathead screws in each corner.

Installing the Frame

When you have the frame assembled and caulked, run caulking compound across the opening to provide a tight seal between the door frame and the sill.

Fig. 11-25: Assembling the frame.

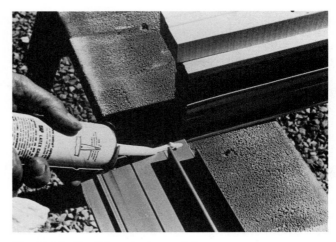

Fig. 11-26: Caulking the frame joints.

Position the frame into the opening from the outside. Use a long carpenter's level to check the levelness of the sill (Fig. 11-27). If it is not level, use shims to make it so. Secure the sill to the frame with #8 × 1-1/2" screws. Also, check to see if the jambs are plumb and straight (Fig. 11-28). Shim solidly (five shims per jamb) between side jambs and the jack studs. Secure the side jambs using three #8 × 2" screws in each jamb (Fig. 11-29). Always use predrilled starter holes. Secure the head jamb using four #8 × 2" pan-head sheet metal screws (two in each track). Again, check to see that the installed frame is level and plumb. Fasten the brick moulding with 10d casing nails (Fig. 11-30) and install flashing above the head casing.

Installing the Fixed Panel

After determining which way the door is to slide, fasten three retainer clips to the "fixed" jamb. Posi-

Fig. 11-27: Check to see if the sill is level.

tion the retainer clips approximately 3" from the top, 3" from the bottom, and in the center of the jamb (Fig. 11-31). Then, screw the gold aluminum extrusion onto the bottom of the fixed panel using three #8 × 1" roundhead screws (Fig. 11-32). Position the fixed panel from the outside onto the outer track (Fig. 11-33). Slip the top edge in place first and swing in the bottom. Be sure that the bottom of the panel sets into the grooves of the sill. Use a 2 × 4 as a lever to force the panel into the run of the side jamb, making sure that it is level and square and that the bottom extrusion is seated in the sill grooves (Fig. 11-34). Secure this panel in place by screwing #6 × 3/4" panhead screws through the hole of the retainer brackets and into the panel rail. Caulk the outside where the fixed panel meets the jamb.

Fig. 11-28: The jambs must be plumb and straight.

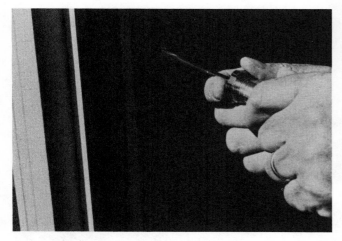

Fig. 11-29: Attach the jambs with screws.

Fig. 11-30: Attach brick moulding with 10d casing nails.

Fig. 11-31: Fasten retainer clip to the jamb.

Fig. 11-32: Attach aluminum extrusion to bottom of the fixed panel.

Fig. 11-33: Placing the fixed panel in position.

Fig. 11-34: Bottom extrusion fits into sill grooves.

Installing the Sliding Panel

To install the sliding panel, attach the sliding panel plastic interlock to the outer edge of the meeting rail, keeping it flush with the bottom of the panel and flush with the bevel (Figs. 11-35A and B). Next, fasten two panel guides to the top of the sliding panel approximately 2" in from each side (Fig. 11-36). Working from the inside, slip the top edge of the sliding panel up and into the inside track of the head channel. Swing the

bottom of the panel in and down so that the rollers will rest on the track in the sill (Fig. 11-37). To level the sliding panel, turn the screw at the base of both sides of the panel (Fig. 11-38). Turn the screws clockwise to raise and counterclockwise to lower. To prevent damage to the adjustment screw, take the weight off the rollers while adjusting. With this done, remove the vinyl plug in the sill located on the inside of the fixed panel.

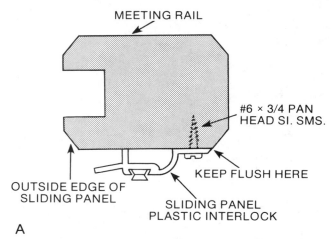

A

B

Fig. 11-35: Fastening sliding panel plastic interlock.

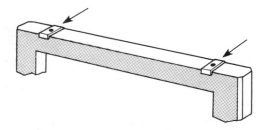

Fig. 11-36: Attaching panel guides.

Fig. 11-37: Positioning the sliding panel in place.

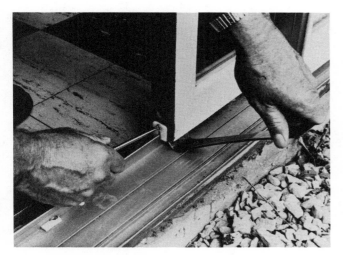

Fig. 11-38: Level the sliding panel by adjusting screws.

INSTALLING A PICTURE WINDOW

One of the easy ways to update your home, both inside and out, is to add a picture window. As stated earlier, most such windows are manufactured as a complete unit, ready to be installed into the wall. A number of types are sold by various makers. The technique of installation varies but little for the different kinds.

The job can be done from inside or outside the house, depending on the type of exterior wall and how quickly the window will be installed. If there is

extensive remodeling being done on the interior at the same time and dust in the room is not a problem, it is easier to remove the gypsum wallboard or plaster and frame the new opening from the inside. If it is desirable not to make dirt inside the house and the job can be done in a day or a weekend, remove the siding or shingles along with the sheathing to expose the framing. Do not try to cut into the wall with a power saw; you might hit wiring, and insulation will fly around. Remove the insulation and any wiring that might be in the area to be enlarged for the new window. Relocate the wiring.

Since the opening for a picture window is more than three studs wide, it is necessary to shore up the ceiling just inside the opening so that the second floor or attic joists will not sag. The shoring can be simply a length of 2 × 4 held flat against the ceiling by two or three vertical 2 × 4s wedged tightly against the main floor. Once the shoring is in place, the studs can be removed to create the new opening.

As shown in Fig. 11-39, frame the new opening to the required rough opening size specified for the window selected. Note that the trimmer studs on each side of the opening support the header, which is needed to bridge the opening and support the structural load above it. The header is made by doubling two 2 × 6s or 2 × 8s, depending on the width of the opening. Double 2 × 4s are the sufficient header size for openings up to 3'; 2 × 6s should be used for openings up to 6'; and 2 × 8s for headers over openings from 6' to 12'. Install short cripple studs beneath the sill framing and between the lintel and the top plate of the wall framing, spacing them 16" on centers, the same as the framing studs. Staple the insulation back into position around the new opening.

Once the opening is framed on the side of the wall that was removed, an accurate opening to match can be cut in the untouched wall simply by sawing along the edge of the header, the trimmer studs, and the rough sill.

If the outside of the wall was removed, cut the sheathing to fit around the opening and nail it in place. Then set the window in place and level it, using shims if necessary to hold it in position. Fasten the window by driving nails through the outside casing into the trimmer studs on each side. For additional support, drive nails or screws up through the window head into the overhead beam (the header or lintel). Knee brackets, available from the window manufacturer, are recommended under a unit that is cantilevered out beyond the wall. Knee brackets are not needed beneath a full-height unit set on an extension of the flooring. The drip cap, usually made of vinyl or aluminum and supplied by the manufacturer, is nailed along the top edge of the window frame.

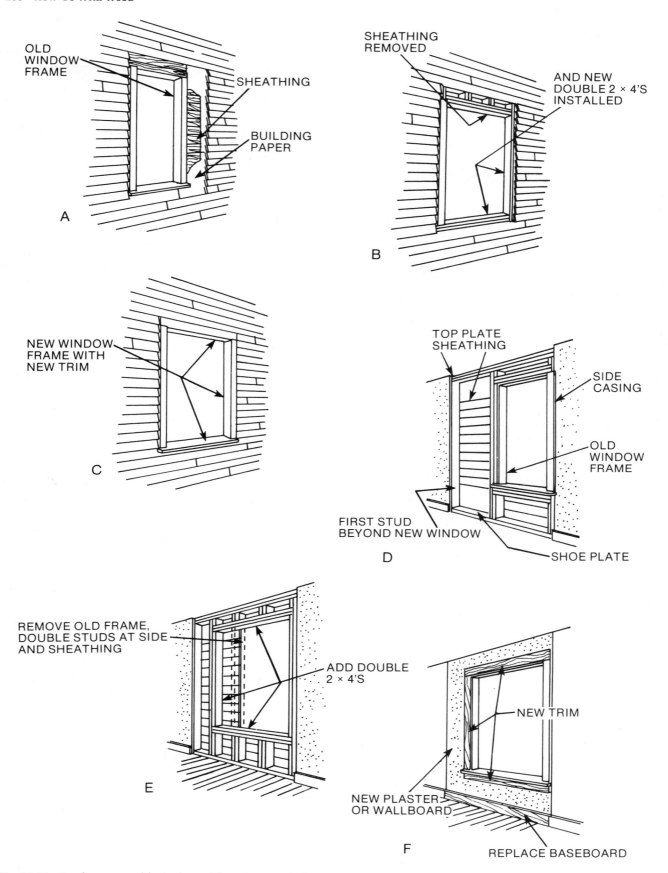

Fig. 11-39: Replacing an old window with a picture window.

Bow and bay windows installed beneath a wide second floor or roof overhang require nothing more than caulking to seal joints against the weather, but a decorative roof is required above the window when it is installed in a flat wall. This roof, often supplied knocked down by the manufacturer, is installed against the wall sheathing and sealed by nailing flashing over the joints, later to be covered with roofing and further protected by fitting the siding or shingles around it.

Complete the job by reinstalling the shingles or siding around the new window and caulk the meeting joints on all sides of the window for a tight seal. Install the stool, apron, and casing around the interior of the window and paint or stain these members as desired.

When any other type of new window is installed, the same basic procedure is followed as for a picture window. That is, cut a hole in the wall for the new window, removing the studs, sheathing, and siding from the new opening. Install a new 2 × 6 header and two 2 × 4s from the header to the horizontal 2 × 4 that rests on the floor. Make a new sill of double 2 × 4s. Install the new window as directed by the manufacturer, and complete the repair of the finish surfaces, inside and out, as described for picture windows.

REPLACING A WINDOW

If you just wish to replace an old window with a new one, remove the old unit as previously described. Then replace the window with a new one of the same size. It may be necessary to shim the new window at the top and sides to make it level.

To enlarge an existing window opening, it is first necessary to remove the old sash. To do this, remove the inside trim and outside casing. With a crowbar gently force the window away from the studs, removing the nails until the window is free. Then mark the size of the new window and cut out the necessary opening. Add the necessary new framing, double 2 × 6 headers at the top and twin 2 × 4s at each side. A double 2 × 4 sill completes the framing. The new window can be secured in position and the wall refinished around it.

Odd-shaped openings such as those originally fitted with tall, narrow windows can be reduced in height by blocking the opening to the required size. Usually, these tall windows were set low in the wall, with the head at door height and the sill close to the floor, so just nailing new sill framing across the opening at a height appropriate for the new window often will bring the rough opening to size. If the opening is still a bit wide, nailing trimmer studs at one or both sides will reduce the width.

Replacement windows set in framed walls and some brick veneer and masonry walls do not always require jamb extenders; recessing the window so that the in-side of the jamb is flush with the interior wall may be sufficient. Jamb extenders of various widths are available to adapt windows readily to a wide range of standard wall thicknesses. Where wall thicknesses are not standard, jambs can be fitted by ripping off enough material from the edges of an oversize set of jamb extenders to bring them flush with the existing interior wall surface. Alignment of these jamb extenders is easy and fast; the tongued edge of the extender fits snugly into a groove in the jamb and is secured by nailing.

Unless the existing exterior wall covering is to be replaced with new material, any gaps around the new window and the existing siding or shingles should be filled in with matching material and the joints caulked where the siding material meets the exterior casing. A plywood panel or any low-maintenance material, trimmed with moulding for a decorative effect, can be nailed beneath the new window if necessary to fill the space formerly occupied by a tall window, or a veneer of used brick can be laid up to the sill to retain the continuity of a masonry wall.

The interior wall should be refinished. The installation of a stool and apron at the sill and interior casing around the jamb completes the replacement window on the inside.

INSTALLING WINDOW TRIM

The casing around the window frames on the interior of the house should have the same pattern as that used around the interior door frames. Windows may be trimmed in two ways: conventional framing (Fig. 11-40) or picture framing (Fig. 11-41). In conventional

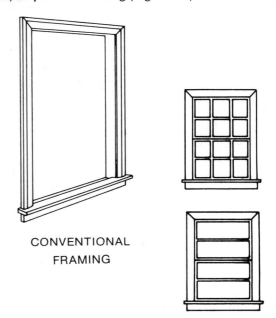

CONVENTIONAL
FRAMING

Fig. 11-40: Conventional window framing.

framing, the trim that is used for a double-hung window frame includes the sash stops, stool, and apron (Fig. 11-42). In picture framing, the stool is replaced with a stop, and casing is substituted for the apron.

The stool is the horizontal trim member that laps the windowsill and extends beyond the casing at the sides, with each end notched against the wall. The apron serves as a finish member below the stool. The window stool is the first piece of window trim to be installed and is notched and fitted against the edge of

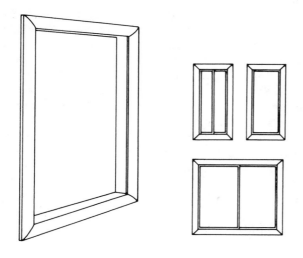

PICTURE FRAMING

Fig. 11-41: Picture window framing.

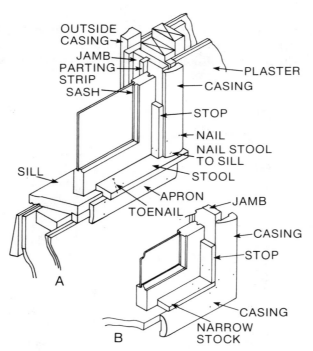

Fig. 11-42: Installation of window trim: (A) with stool and apron, and (B) enclosed with casing.

the jamb and the plaster line, with the outside edge being flush against the bottom rail of the window sash. Using 4d or 5d finishing nails, the stool is blind-nailed at the ends so that the casing and the stop will cover the nail heads. Predrilling is usually necessary to prevent splitting. The stool should also be nailed at midpoint to the sill and to the apron with finishing nails. Face-nailing to the sill is sometimes substituted or supplemented with toenailing of the outer edge to the sill.

The casing is applied and nailed so that the inner edge is flush with the inner face of the jambs and so that the stop will cover the joint between the jamb and casing. The window stops are then nailed to the jambs so the window sash slides smoothly. Channel-type weather stripping often includes full-width metal subjambs into which the upper and lower sash slide, replacing the parting strip. Stops are located against these instead of the sash to provide a small amount of pressure. The apron is cut to a length equal to the outer width of the casing line. It is nailed to the windowsill and to the 2 × 4 framing sill below.

When casing is used to finish the bottom of the window frame as well as the sides and top, the narrow stool butts against the side window jamb. Casing is then mitered at the bottom corners and nailed as previously described.

QUALITY CONTROLS ON WINDOW CONSTRUCTION

The National Woodwork Manufacturers Association (NWMA) has established standards for the window-making industry. Its quality procedures specify the species, grade, and moisture content of the wood used; the type of preservatives, weather stripping, and glass to be used; and the performance requirements of strength and infiltration. Don't buy a window that hasn't met at least the minimum requirements established by the NWMA. The Association has initiated a testing, inspection, and labeling program so that you may be assured that the window unit you purchase has been tested and meets the requirements of the standard. The NWMA supplies labels such as the one in Fig. 11-43 for windows that pass the test. Look for the label when you are purchasing any window.

Fig. 11-43: Typical quality mark of the National Woodwork Manufacturers Association.

CHAPTER
—12—

FINISHING WOOD

After working carefully on the construction steps of a project, the final stage is finishing, a process as critical as any of the preceding ones. To get a first rate finish, you'll have to take the care *and* as much time as is necessary to do a good job. You cannot hurry through the finishing steps. This chapter concentrates on clear and stain furniture finishes for your fine woodworking projects. Paint finishes are less complicated and, if you follow the manufacturer's recommendations for priming and finishing coats, are quick and easy to apply.

The purpose of the finish is twofold. First, the finish helps protect the wood from dirt, abrasion, indentations, stains, and color changes due to light or atmospheric pollutants. And more importantly, it protects the wood against moisture damage. Secondly, the finish serves an aesthetic purpose by enhancing the wood's natural grain and color, enriching the color or even changing the color entirely.

The final finish is a combination of two elements—the surface condition of the wood and the finishing treatment you apply to it. When planning the final finish, these two elements must be planned to complement each other and both must be done properly.

SURFACE PREPARATION

The first thing you must do is evaluate the surface condition of your wood based on four points—trueness, evenness, smoothness, and quality. *Trueness* refers to how close a surface comes to being perfectly round or flat or whatever the intended geometry of the surface is. *Evenness* can be ruined by raised grain, mismatched joints, or careless handling or sanding. *Smoothness* is the absence of such irregularities as knife checks, marks from careless scraping, tear-outs, and knife marks from machine planing. *Quality* of the surface of wood can be affected by seasoning checks, compression failures, hammer indentations, cell structure bruises, and so on.

Before you even attempt to develop a good surface, be certain that you are working with seasoned wood. Seasoning brings the lumber close to the moisture content to which it normally stabilizes. Check with your dealer to be certain that the wood product you purchase is of the appropriate moisture content for your particular project. For instance, lumber graded by the Western Wood Products Association is available with a moisture content not exceeding 15% (MC-15), a moisture content not exceeding 19% (S-DRY), or a moisture content of over 19% (S-GRN). Purchasing seasoned wood of appropriate moisture content will help you avoid warping, twisting, cracking, and nail-popping.

Planing and Sanding

The first step in surface preparation is to remove high spots with a well-sharpened, fine-set plane. The plane can also be used to take off sharp corners and edges. Be especially careful not to plane against (perpendicular to) the grain because the splinters are difficult to repair.

The next step is to develop surface smoothness by sanding. Abrasive paper comes in a variety of fineness grades, grit types, paper backing weights, and general types. It is also available with open or closed coats. All of these characteristics are designated on the back of the paper. The best sanding method involves using a progression of grit sizes, from coarse to fine (Fig. 12-1). The scratch pattern of each replaces the coarser pattern of the previous one, resulting in an increasingly fine surface. Three of the more commonly used abrasive papers are given in Table 12-1. Each has a different method of designating grit sizes. Regardless of the type or grade of sandpaper you use, be sure to always sand parallel to, rather than across, the grain.

To obtain the smoothest possible surface, use a technique called *grain raising*. After the surface has

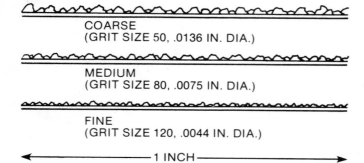

COARSE
(GRIT SIZE 50, .0136 IN. DIA.)

MEDIUM
(GRIT SIZE 80, .0075 IN. DIA.)

FINE
(GRIT SIZE 120, .0044 IN. DIA.)

◄──────── 1 INCH ────────►

Fig. 12-1: Sandpaper is available in grades ranging from coarse to fine. As this drawing shows, a grit size of 120 is much finer than a grit size of 50.

TABLE 12-1: COMMON ABRASIVE PAPER

Grit Size	Aluminum Oxide or Silicon Oxide	Garnet	Flint
Super fine	12/0—600	10/0—400	
	11/0—500	9/0—320	
	10/0—400	8/0—280	
Extra fine	9/0—320		
	8/0—280		
	7/0—240	7/0—240	
Very fine	6/0—220	6/0—220	4/0
	5/0—180	5/0—180	3/0
			2/0
Fine	4/0—150	4/0—150	
	3/0—120	3/0—120	
			0
	2/0—100	2/0—100	
			1/2
Medium	1/0—80	1/0—80	
			1
	1/2—60	1/2—60	
Coarse	1—50	1—50	1-1/2
			2
	1-1/2—40	1-1/2—40	
			2-1/2
Very coarse	2—36	2—36	
	2-1/2—30	2-1/2—30	3
	3—24	3—24	

been sanded down, wipe it with a slightly damp cloth. The wood fibers at the top of the surface will absorb the moisture and expand. These fibers will project above the surface after the wood dries, stabilizing the wood surface. The projecting fibers can then be removed by a very light sanding with extremely fine paper. Be careful only to remove the fibers sticking up, without further abrading the surface.

If you plan to use a water-base stain, you *must* use this grain raising process with a dripping wet cloth. Otherwise, the water base in the stain will cause the grain to rise after the surface is finished.

Filling Holes and Blemishes

Countersunk nails and screws, damaged areas, and natural blemishes in the wood surface leave holes that should be filled as a part of surface preparation. A number of common compounds are available for this purpose, some of which are mixed commercially, others which you mix yourself (Fig. 12-2). Some common fillers include plastic wood, plastic water putty, wood compound paste, and oil putty. You can also make your own putty by mixing fine sawdust from the wood you're working with and white glue, hot animal glue, or vinyl resin.

Regardless of the type of filler you select, it is all used in much the same manner. Simply work the putty into the holes with a knife or chisel (Fig. 12-3), leaving a slight excess above the surface to allow for shrinkage. Allow the filler to dry for at least an hour, then sand the area flush with the wood surface. If the excess is not *completely* removed, it will clog the pores of the wood, preventing the absorption and/or adhesion of the finish. If the affected area is deep, fill the void part way. Allow the first fill to set, then finish filling the area and sand when dry.

Fig. 12-2: Various materials that can be used for filling and sealing.

Fig. 12-3: Applying wood putty to cracks and holes.

Composite boards, such as particleboard and Waferwood, are somewhat more porous than most finished lumber. Surface characteristics vary from one board to another. Some provide a surface which can be painted without using a filler. Others require a filler to reduce the porosity of the surface. It is a good idea to test scraps to determine the best method for obtaining the desired surface finish.

If a very smooth finish is desired, the particleboard surface should be filled with a paste wood filler or a sanding sealer prior to applying finishes. If the surface is unusually porous, both a filler and sanding sealer should be used. Factory-filled boards, with a surface ready for painting, are available. Some manufacturers apply a resin impregnated fibrous sheet to the faces of their particleboards to provide an excellent base for painting.

Repairing Dents and Hammer Marks

Dents and hammer marks can sometimes be removed without filler. Since this type of void is caused by compression of the wood fibers, the area can often be restored by returning the fibers to their normal shape. This can be done by wetting the affected area with a few drops of water, allowing the water to soak into the wood and be absorbed by the wood cells. The cells will then expand and take their original shape.

To speed the process, use a needle to make holes in the affected area approximately as deep as the depression. Then soak the area with hot water.

When the depression has expanded sufficiently, allow the area to dry, and then sand it flush with the wood surface.

FINISHING TREATMENTS

You should choose a finishing treatment based on three primary factors—the wood involved, the protection required, and the final effect you wish to achieve. All of these factors must be taken into consideration. For instance, if you disregard the type of wood you're working with when selecting stain color, the stain color could dry to a completely different shade than you expect.

Regardless of the finishing treatment you select, the primary objective of any treatment is to prevent moisture exchange. No finish is totally effective, but the finish will decrease the rate of moisture exchange enough to limit the effects of extremes in humidity.

In any instance, multiple coats of finish are better than a single coat. Be certain that all areas of the surface are treated and finished in exactly the same way,

with equal coatings, equal numbers of coats, equal drying times for each layer, and so on. An even moisture barrier is crucial, since an uneven barrier would permit unequal moisture exchange.

The basic steps for finishing are:

1. Surface preparation.
2. Staining (unless you plan to paint or preserve the wood's natural color).
3. Filling.
4. Sealing or priming.
5. Finishing with a top coat, paint, or enamel.
6. Rubbing and/or buffing the top coat.

Since we've already discussed surface preparation, we'll go on to steps 2 through 6. These suggestions apply generally to all finishes, but always read and follow the product manufacturer's instructions as you work with specific finish treatments.

Staining

Stains are used to darken wood's natural color. Most stains are designed to bring out, rather than obscure the wood's texture and grain. Some woods, such as walnut and cherry, are most attractive if treated with clear finishes and no stain. But in most cases, you'll probably find it necessary to stain the wood to bring out the richness and beauty of its figure.

Stains are generally applied with a brush or soft cloth, uniformly and in the direction of the grain. In most cases, the stain is allowed to soak in or set, and the excess is wiped off. However, there are a number of different types of stains, and a few are discussed here briefly. Check with your supplier and the manufacturer's suggestions for further information on individual products. It's always a good idea to test stain on scraps of the wood you're using to be sure you'll get the effect you desire (Fig. 12-4).

Fig. 12-4: To see the effect of stain and finish on the final color of wood, make a sample board. Apply different stains; when they are dry, add the finishing coat.

Pigmented Wiping Stains. Pigmented wiping stains are generally more opaque than most stains; therefore, they're used in instances when you wish to obscure the grain pattern, darken the wood considerably, or give two different, adjacent pieces of wood a uniform color. Some of the color is dissolved in the oil base, and other pigments are solids which must be frequently stirred into suspension before and during use.

Pigmented wiping stains can be purchased ready made, or you can mix them to the shade you desire. Some of the more popular recipes are provided for you in Table 12-2. But don't let yourself be limited; one of the main benefits of mixing your own stain is the opportunity to experiment and develop the exact shade you desire.

Penetrating Oil Stains. Penetrating oil stains are similar to pigmented wiping stains, except that there are no suspended pigment particles and no sealer action. These stains can be used on all types of wood, but they will not produce the same color on different woods. They will produce the proper color only on the woods for which they are intended. Table 12-3 summarizes common shades and the colors they normally produce.

After working with oil stains, immediately soak used cloths in water or destroy them. If oily cloths accumulate, they may possibly begin to burn by spontaneous combustion.

Water Stains. Water stain is purchased in the form of a powder or liquid concentrate and is mixed according to the instructions on the label. This allows you to select or mix any shade you might desire (Table 12-4). These stains penetrate quickly and deeply, producing a clear, transparent finish. Keep in mind, however, that water stains seem relatively dull and flat when dry. It is only after the top coat has been applied that the true color appears. Water stain will not penetrate previously finished wood, even if every trace of the old finish has been removed.

Alcohol Stains. This type of nongrain-raising stain uses alcohol as a base, but otherwise has characteristics similar to those of water stains. As with other stains

TABLE 12-2:   PIGMENTED WIPING STAINS

Cherry Stain
8 ounces Burnt Sienna
1 pint turpentine
6 ounces boiled linseed oil
1/2 ounce drier

Cherry Stain Light
4 ounces Raw Sienna
4 ounces Burnt Sienna
1 pint turpentine
6 ounces boiled linseed oil
1/2 ounce drier

Pumpkin Brown Maple
8 ounces Burnt Sienna
A trace Ultramarine Blue
1 pint turpentine
6 ounces boiled linseed oil
1/2 ounce drier

Honey Brown Maple
6 ounces Burnt Sienna
2 ounces Ultramarine Blue
1 pint turpentine
6 ounces boiled linseed oil
1/2 ounce drier

Yellowish Maple
6 ounces yellow (French) Ochre
1 ounce Burnt Sienna
1 ounce Ultramarine Blue
1 pint turpentine
6 ounces boiled linseed oil
1/2 ounce drier

Light Oak
6 ounces Raw Sienna
2 ounces Raw Umber
1 pint turpentine
6 ounces boiled linseed oil
1/2 ounce drier

Dark Oak
4 ounces Raw Sienna
2 ounces Burnt Umber
2 ounces Burnt Sienna
1 pint turpentine
6 ounces boiled linseed oil
1/2 ounce drier

Red Mahogany
6 ounces Burnt Sienna
2 ounces Rose Pink
1 pint turpentine
6 ounces boiled linseed oil
1/2 ounce drier

Brown Mahogany
6 ounces Vandyke Brown
2 ounces Rose Pink
1 pint turpentine
6 ounces boiled linseed oil
1/2 ounce drier

Walnut
4 ounces Vandyke Brown
4 ounces Burnt Umber
1 pint turpentine
6 ounces boiled linseed oil
1/2 ounce drier

Dark Walnut
8 ounces Vandyke Brown
1 pint turpentine
6 ounces boiled linseed oil
1/2 ounce drier

Silver Gray
4 ounces Lamp Black
4 ounces White Lead
1 pint turpentine
6 ounces boiled linseed oil
1/2 ounce drier

Fruitwood
6 ounces Vandyke Brown
2 ounces Burnt Umber
1 pint turpentine
6 ounces boiled linseed oil
1/2 ounce drier

TABLE 12-3: PENETRATING OIL STAINS

Shade	Approximate color on wood of same name
Fumed Oak	dark brown
Golden Oak	light golden brown
Light Oak	yellowish
English Brown	dark chocolate brown
Brown Mahogany	reddish brown
Red Mahogany	deep reddish brown
Golden Maple	yellowish
Reddish Maple	pumpkin red
Light Maple	creamish white
American Walnut	brown (dark)
French Walnut	brown (light)
Ebony	black onyx (any wood)

TABLE 12-4: WATER STAINS

Black—Jet	Oak—Fumed
Blue	Oak—Reddish
Bismark Brown—Reddish	Oak—Golden Dark
Bismark Brown—Yellowish	Oak—Flemish
Brown—Seal	Orange
Brown—Adam	Red—Scarlet
Brown—Sheraton	Red—Medium
Green—Olive	Red—Blood
Green—Light	Red—Rose
Mahogany—Light	Red—Eosine Yellowish
Mahogany—Brown	Rosewood
Mahogany—Pinkish	Silver Gray
Mahogany—Red	Violet—Purple
Mahogany—Yellowish	Walnut—Circassian
Maple—Antique Light	Walnut—Medium
Maple—Yellowish	Walnut—Dark
Maple—Reddish	Yellow—Lemon
Oak—Weathered	Yellow—Canary
Oak—Early English	

purchased in powder or liquid concentrate form, be sure to check the package label to see what type of base the dye is intended for before you purchase and mix the stain. The variety of alcohol stain shades is limited (Table 12-5), but it's possible to combine powders to produce nearly any shade imaginable.

Because of the alcohol base, this type of stain is very fast drying and will evaporate almost immediately

TABLE 12-5: ALCOHOL STAINS

Black—Nigrosene	Mahogany—Yellowish
Blue—Violet	Mahogany—Adam Brown
Bismarck Brown—Reddish	Maple—Reddish
Bismarck Brown—Yellowish	Oak—Fumed
Brown—Seal	Oak—Reddish
Brown—Adam	Oak—Golden Yellow
Green—Sage	Oak—Dark
Green—Yellowish	Orange
Silver Gray	Walnut—Circassian
Mahogany—Medium	Yellow—Lemon

when applied to raw wood. This can be an advantage when you're in a hurry, but makes it almost impossible to stain a large area without lap or streak marks.

Varnish Stains. Varnish stain is a mixture of varnish and penetrating oil stain. This type of stain can be purchased ready-to-use in a number of shades, or you can mix your own by combining a penetrating oil stain and clear varnish. Varnish stains give color and a protective coat in one operation, making them ideal for applications where the appearance is not essential. For instance, the interiors of cabinets or closets require only coloring to make the surface inconspicuous.

However, varnish stains do not produce a professional looking finish. This type of stain does not penetrate the surface, and the varnish diminishes the transparency and clarity of the stain. Regardless of the care taken in application, varnish stains dry muddy, streaky, and with a rough, semigloss finish.

Do not use multiple coats of varnish stain. Doing so will only obscure the wood as the finish becomes increasingly opaque. Should you wish to add further top-coating, switch to regular varnish.

Wax Stains. This type of stain usually consists of penetrating oil stain mixed with wax and a drying agent. Wax stains are manufactured in common colors and finishes, but work best with the type of wood for which they are intended. They should be tested on sample wood before being used on your project to be sure that the effect is what you want. Wax stains do not fill the pores of the wood. They produce a smooth, open grain effect.

Chemical Stains. Chemical stains are available in crystal, powder, or liquid forms. Those which are not in liquid form must be dissolved in water according to the manufacturer's directions. These stains combine chemically with the wood and cause a reaction to take place that permanently colors the wood. A few of the chemicals used to stain wood are shown in Table 12-6.

TABLE 12-6: CHEMICAL STAINS

Chemical	Color Produced
Permanganate of potash	medium brown
Household lye	light brown
Sal soda	yellowish brown to medium brown
Vinegar and iron filings	gray
Ammonia (26%)	various shades of brown

Chemical stains are caustic and can be quite dangerous. They should be handled with great care. It's wise to wear rubber gloves, old clothes, and eye protection when using such chemicals. Also, be sure to store the chemical solutions in glass containers, never metal containers.

Filling

Wood fillers are used to fill the pores of the wood to make the surface even. There are two types of wood fillers—paste wood filler, used for filling the pores of open grain wood; and liquid filler, used for filling the pores of close grain wood. Fillers are optional with close grain woods, but are a must for a smooth, non-textured finish on open, coarse-grained woods. The types of filler required for various woods are given in Table 12-7.

Fillers are composed of tiny particles of silica mixed with linseed oil and turpentine or other paint solvent. Oil color is added to filler to match the filler to stained surfaces. A number of colors are available, but in cases where you can find no prepared filler in the shade you desire, oil color can simply be added to alter the shade. As you select a shade, remember that the filler should be slightly darker than the color of the stained wood, since the filler will dry a little lighter than its original color.

Application of Filler. To apply a paste filler, proceed as follows:

1. Clean the dust from the surface with steel wool (Fig. 12-5).

2. Apply the filler quickly and generously to a limited area at a time. Use an old, stiff, short-bristle brush and rub it in a little with the grain of the wood (Fig. 12-6). Then brush it smooth with the grain. Stir the mixture thoroughly before each application.

3. Clean off the surplus filler by wiping across the pores with waste wool or burlap. The main idea is to pad the excess filler into the pores of the wood (Fig. 12-7).

4. In 5 to 20 minutes, the filler will start to lose its wet appearance. As soon as the filled pores begin to ap-

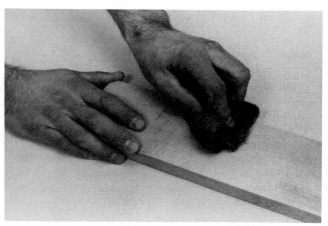

Fig. 12-5: Cleaning the surface before applying a filler with steel wool.

Fig. 12-6: Brush the filler with the grain of the wood.

TABLE 12-7:   FILLER FOR VARIOUS WOODS

No filler needed	Thin filler*	Medium filler	Heavy filler
Aspen	Alder	Amaranth	Ash
Basswood	Beech	Avodire	Bubinga
Cedar	Birch	Butternut	Chestnut
Cypress	Cherry	Korina	Elm
Ebony	Gum	Mahogany	Hickory
Fir	Maple	Orientalwood	Kelobra
Gaboon	Sycamore	Primavera	Lacewood
Hemlock	Tupelo	Rosewood	Lauan (Phillipine
Holly		Sapeli	mahogany)
Magnolia		Tigerwood	Locust
Pine		Walnut	Oak
Poplar		Zebrawood	Padouk
Redwood			Teakwood
Spruce			

*Liquid filler may also be used.

Fig. 12-7: Pad in the excess filler with a coarse cloth across the grain.

Fig. 12-9: Clean corners and grooves with a picking stick made from a pointed dowel.

pear flat, wipe with a clean cloth across the grain (Fig. 12-8). Difficult places can be wiped with a cloth over a soft, pointed, wooden stick (Fig. 12-9). In working large projects, watch the place where you started applying the filler; this may appear flat and require wiping before the whole job is coated with filler. If the filler sets up too hard for easy wiping, moisten the wiping cloth with mineral spirits. Inspect the work. If the pores are not filled level, apply a second coat of slightly thinner filler immediately, wiping off in the same way.

5. Finish wiping with clean cloths, stroking with the grain (Fig. 12-10). Paste filler should dry at least 12 hours unless it is a fast-drying type, which is ready for coating in 3 to 4 hours. However, the slow-dry type is generally the best, and 24 to 48 hours is not too much

time to allow for drying. In any case, it is of the greatest importance that the filler be bone dry before any other coating is applied. The dry filler should be sanded lightly with 150 to 240 grit abrasive paper and wiped off with a cloth moistened with mineral spirits.

Shellac makes a good liquid filler in many instances. White shellac is best for natural and light-colored finishes, and orange shellac is best for dark colors. For medium-dark finishes, mix white and orange shellac. As a filler, mix the shellac with shellac solvent or denatured alcohol. Shellac is usually a 4-pound cut (4 pounds of shellac dissolved in 1 gallon of alcohol). For use as a filler, shellac should be a 2-pound cut (2 pounds of shellac dissolved in 1 gallon of alcohol). By adding 1 gallon of alcohol to a gallon of 4-pound-cut shellac, a shellac suitable for filling can be obtained. Apply one or two coats and allow each coat to set hard

Fig. 12-8: Wipe off with a clean cloth.

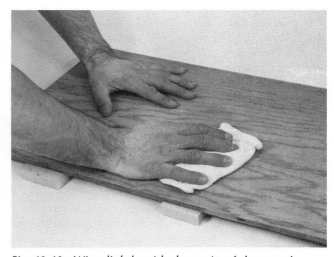

Fig. 12-10: Wipe lightly with the grain of the wood.

before applying the next coat. Sandpaper each coat when dry, and clean dust from the surface before applying the next coat of filler. But, remember that some of the synthetic varnishes do not adhere well to shellac.

Sealing

Shellac was long recognized as "the" sealer for under varnish, paint, and lacquer. But, with the introduction of synthetic varnishes, some of these formulations do not adhere well to shellac and, thus, it is most important to check the instructions on the can to determine whether or not the varnish material can be used over shellac. If it can be used over shellac and for undercoat for paint and enamel, the shellac is applied in the manner described in the section on sealing the filler. Use a 2-pound cut. When the shellac is dry, it should be sanded with 220 to 240 grit abrasive paper.

A thin or wash coat of shellac before filling offers the following advantages: It may be used over oil stain as a seal; it promotes better wiping of the filler; and it stiffens wood whiskers for sanding after the application of water stain. The wash coat must never be so heavy that it partly blocks the pores—properly applied, a wash coat over stain is invisible.

Two coats of pure white shellac, thinned to a 2-pound cut, may be applied to wood as a base for most lacquers. Both coats should be sanded with very fine abrasive paper. This reduces the amount of lacquer required and is economical in time and cost.

Another popular sealer for varnish and lacquer is a special product known as sanding sealer. It is made of a lacquer-shellac base, and it dries ready to recoat in about an hour. It brushes easily, has a good hard surface, and contains a sanding agent that permits clean, powdery sanding without gumming.

Sealing Fir and Other Softwoods. Fir and some other softwoods need a good sealer because of the special character of the grain figure, which is made up of alternate hard summer growth and softer spring growth. If you do not use a sealer, the first coat of paint or stain penetrates unevenly and results in a "wild overconspicuous grain."

To tame or quiet this grain, several special types of resin sealers have been developed. They may be purchased from lumber, paint, or hardware dealers. If the resin sealer is used properly, it allows the stain to soften the darker markings and deepen the lighter surface. The finish will be soft and lustrous, with the wild grain figures pleasantly subdued. For application details, follow the manufacturer's directions.

Finishing with a Top Coat

There are a number of materials which can be used for the final finish on your project. Consider these four main factors before selecting a final finish:

1. The ease of application.
2. Drying speed.
3. Durability.
4. The effect on the color and texture of the wood.

Shellac. Shellac is one of the oldest types of finishing materials and is still popular today because it's quick drying, durable, and strong. It is also easy to apply, requiring only three to six coats applied at intervals of 3 hours to produce an excellent build on the surface. When the dry surface is rubbed with steel wool or pumice stone and oil, a beautiful finish is produced.

There are limitations to the types of applications that shellac is suited for. Shellac is not waterproof and will turn white if subjected to moisture. Therefore, it is not the recommended finish for coffee tables, kitchen tables, outdoor furniture, siding, or structures. It is not heatproof. If subjected to heat, the surface will soften or even blister and crack, resulting in an irreparable mark. Since shellac is made with alcohol, it will absorb and be damaged by any trace of alcohol. It should not be used on bars or tables which may have alcohol spilled on them, since liquor will act as a solvent and remove the finish to the bare wood.

Shellac may be purchased in a number of "cuts," which indicate the amount of lac flake dissolved in the alcohol base. The standard cut is a 5-pound cut (5 pounds of lac flake in 1 gallon of alcohol). To reduce shellac to thinner consistencies (a 2- to 3-pound cut is recommended for final finishing), consult Table 12-8.

Particleboard usually contains a small amount of paraffin wax which is added during manufacturing to retard the rate of water absorption. If the paint or finish contains materials which are good solvents for wax, some of the wax will be absorbed in the wet paint film and form areas with a slower drying rate. The wax can be effectively isolated from interior finishes by applying a thin barrier coat such as shellac, which is not a solvent for wax. Shellac applied to exterior surfaces may result in poor weather resistance.

Applying Shellac. Shellac may be applied by brushing or spraying. Before you use shellac, shake or stir it thoroughly. The first two coats should be thinned to a 1- or 2-pound-cut consistency, while a 3- or 4-pound cut is best for the final coat. A 1/2-pound cut is ideal for a wash coat before staining, and a 1/2- or 1-pound cut makes a good sanding sealer.

TABLE 12-8: THINNING SHELLAC

To convert	Add denatured alcohol
1 quart 5-pound cut to 3-pound cut	1 pint to quart
1 quart 5-pound cut to 2-pound cut	1 quart to quart
1 quart 4-pound cut to 3-pound cut	1/2 pint to quart
1 quart 4-pound cut to 2-pound cut	3/4 pint to quart

To apply shellac, use a soft varnish brush (Fig. 12-11). Brush the shellac on with the grain in long running strokes—one stroke to apply, one stroke to tip off. Work quickly, and do not brush back and forth over the surface. If you brush excessively, the shellac will pile up in ridges and show laps. Sags, runs, and brush marks can be smoothed out by lightly stroking the wet surface with the tips of the bristles. If you miss a spot, let it go until the next coat, as it is very difficult to do any touching up without damaging the finish.

Allow 2 to 4 hours for drying between first and second coats and 6 to 8 hours between subsequent coats. To remove specks and dirt between coats, go over the

Fig. 12-11: Shellac is easy to apply with a brush.

surface with extra fine paper or 3/0 grade steel wool after the shellac has dried. Sandpaper with the grain of the wood. After each sanding, brush the surface, and rub with a cloth dampened with benzine to remove the dust before applying another coat. When sanding, use either cheap flint paper or one of the open-coated papers, because shellac will gum it up rapidly. Of course, the open-coated paper can be washed and brushed out with alcohol, dried, and reused.

In general, take the same precautions when applying shellac as outlined for varnish. Shellac is very thirsty; therefore, avoid muggy, warm days for your shellac work. Never apply shellac over a damp surface, for the moisture will cause the shellac to cloud. Two thin coats are always better than one thick one; it not only gives a better finish but makes brushing much easier.

When you are applying the shellac with a spray gun, avoid excessive air pressure—30 to 40 pounds pressure is about right. Too much pressure may produce "orange peel"—an undesirable rippled finish.

Varnish. Varnish produces a very hard finish, resistant to alcohol, heat, and water, and it levels to a smooth, uniform coat when properly applied. Only two or three coats are necessary to build a sufficient finish, flexible enough to resist cracking, mars, and dents.

However, varnish is slow drying and therefore requires at least 24 hours of drying time under ideal conditions to obtain good results. Varnish must be allowed to dry in a draft-free, dust-free room at 70° to 80°F under normal humidity.

However, faster-drying varnishes are now available. They possess the same qualities as the traditional type varnishes but will dry in a few hours because of their synthetic resins and chemical composition.

Many types of varnishes are available for specific applications. These include cabinet varnish, rubbing varnish, flat varnish, interior spar varnish, exterior spar varnish, and polyurethane UVA. Consult your dealer for more information on the types of varnishes if you are interested in any of these specific types.

Applying Varnish. For average work, use a full-chisel varnish brush about 2" wide. You will also want to have on hand two or three brushes of various kinds and sizes in order to handle every job to best advantage. There are many instances where a small brush comes in handy. Brushes must be kept clean and properly stored after use.

Varnish should never be used directly from the can. That is, pour a small amount into a separate container (Fig. 12-12). The handle of the container should be shortened and rolled over to form a comfortable loop for the thumb. Stretch a wire (called a strike wire) across the can, opposite the thumb loop, and use it to wipe your brush on. Do not wipe the brush on the edge of the container, as the granules of dried varnish on the rim will fall down into the varnish. Incidentally, varnish cups with a strike wire already attached are available at most paint stores and home centers. Stir the synthetic varnish (Fig. 12-13) before and during use; never shake.

When applying synthetic varnish, dip the brush into the material and brush it back and forth on clean, heavy wrapping paper to work the varnish evenly through the bristles. Never use newspaper or other paper that gives off lint. Too much varnish on the brush will cause it to drip or run onto the handle. For this reason, never dip the brush into the varnish by more than one-third its length, and always remove any excess from the brush on the strike wire before applying it to the surface.

Fig. 12-13: Stir synthetic varnish well before use.

When brushing varnish, hold the brush much as you do a pencil, using an easy wrist motion. Hold the brush at an angle of about 45°, so that the "chisel" of the brush meets the surface and puts the maximum amount of bristle in contact with the wood (Fig. 12-14). Be careful to use light, even strokes. Too much pressure on the brush can cause bubbles to form. Actually, brushing consists of three operations:

1. To *cut in,* start from the corners and work toward the center (Fig. 12-15A). Make every effort to flow the varnish on, rather than "scrubbing" it on.

Fig. 12-12: A varnish cup with a "strike wire" can be made from a tin can. The wire is a piece of coat hanger stuck through two nail-punched holes in the can and bent over.

Fig. 12-14: The proper brush angle for varnishing is approximately 45°.

2. Next, *cross brush* the panel in such a manner that the bristle tips are dragged along the entire length of the panel in a single stroke. Where this is impractical, the tips of the bristles should be touched to the panel at one end and then dragged about halfway across before curving gently up away from the surface. The next stroke is then started at the opposite end and brought back far enough to overlap the end of the stroke just completed (Fig. 12-15B); that is, lift the brush quickly as the strokes overlap. Never finish off by touching the bristle tips to the surface in the middle of a panel or strip since this will leave a line that must be smoothed later.

3. Finally, wipe off the brush on the strike wire to remove all excess finish material. Now, brush lightly with the grain with only the tips of the bristles touching the surface (Fig. 12-15C). This operation is called *tipping off*. Always brush from the edge to the center, overlapping in the middle. Clean the brush on the strike wire after each stroke.

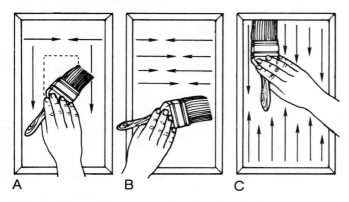

Fig. 12-15: (A) The area to be varnished is first cut in or lined, using a suitable brush. (B) Cross brushing is done across the grain, applying a full-bodied coat. (C) Tipping off is done with a nearly dry brush, which should just barely touch the varnish coat.

Tabletops and similar large flat surfaces should be worked in much the same way, except that cross brushing may be eliminated. Instead, apply the flow coat with the grain, beginning on the side away from you, and work from the center, brushing to the right and left (Fig. 12-16). Now tip the surface, using a running stroke from one end of the work to the other, with the bristles of the brush barely touching the work. If you do not catch runs, sags, curtains, dry spots, or other potential surface blemishes while tipping off in a given area, forget about them until the surface is hardened. At that time, sand them level, and build up with the next coat. Any rebrushing of a partially set area can cause other problems.

Finish the edges with a small brush, working from the center toward each corner. Do not let the brush run over onto the wet varnish coat on the surface.

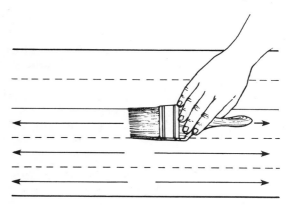

Fig. 12-16: On large surfaces, brush the varnish with the grain and from center to ends, never from end to end.

On vertical surfaces, the procedure should be changed slightly to prevent curtains or sags on the finished work. Employ short, quick strokes, working an area of about 6" square, back and forth across the surface, starting from a corner at the top. Then, tip off the surface by brushing down halfway and up halfway, so that the brush is lifted from the surface in the central portion. When varnishing objects that may be easily lifted, turn the item upside down, place it on a work bench (boards on saw horses are good), complete the entire understructure first, and then do the upper part. In other words, always apply the varnish to hard-to-reach areas first. Leave the easier-to-reach portions for last. Start on the farthest part of a surface and work toward yourself, rather than working away from yourself.

Lacquer. Lacquer is used for most commercial finishing since it can be sprayed on, recoated in a matter of hours, and requires only a day or two to build up a sufficient finish. Lacquer withstands moisture and heat, and will retain a clear, transparent finish indefinitely. Some special lacquers are also alcohol-proof.

However, since lacquer dries so quickly, it must be sprayed on to achieve a high quality finish. Spraying requires special equipment. A few lacquers are designed specifically for brushing and work well on small objects for interior use, but simply do not achieve the top-notch finish possible with other finishing materials on larger projects.

Lacquer and lacquer sealers are now available in aerosol spray cans. These lacquers are very handy for use on small areas and patch-up work.

Applying Brushing Lacquers. A good brushing lacquer is very thin—almost like water—and thus, brushes very easily. When applying, keep the following points in mind:

1. When filling the brush from the container, do not rub off the excess lacquer on the top of the container

as you do with paint; if you do, the quick-drying lacquer will become sticky and foul the brush on successive trips to the container. For this reason, it is best to squeeze off any excess against the inner side of the container.

2. Place the articles to be lacquered in a well-lighted area so that the light will be reflected from the freshly finished surfaces and will show up any improperly covered areas. The surfaces to which lacquer is being applied should be in a horizontal position.

3. Finish any removable parts separately with the surfaces held horizontally to prevent sags and runs that may occur when a wet coat is applied to a vertical or oblique surface.

4. Avoid brush marks by using a rather large brush (2" to 3") of medium soft grade. The larger brush holds more lacquer than a small one which means much more rapid flowing of the lacquer and less danger of laps or uncovered streaks.

5. When applying lacquer to uneven surfaces, such as carvings and beadings, make sure that the lacquer does not accumulate in the hollows. Pick up or pull out the excess with the tip of the brush.

6. "Flow" the lacquer by using a rather full wet brush—do not work back and forth as in varnishing. Spread each brushful with the grain of the wood; then, turn the brush around and draw it over the surface in the opposite direction. This is enough brushing. Next, dip the brush in lacquer deeply enough to fill it well, and then touch the tip of the bristles to a drip wire over the container to prevent the lacquer from dripping off the brush. If this is done quickly, the next brushful of lacquer may be applied to the edge of the previous brushful without roughness. It is best to coat an entire surface quickly and fully by brushing with the grain whenever possible.

7. Add a small amount of thinner if the lacquer does not spread well. Lacquer causes more "pull" on the brush than the varnish does. Use a thinner prepared for the lacquer that is being used.

8. Use bold, rapid strokes when applying lacquer with a brush (Fig. 12-17). Carry each stroke as far as

possible without running the lacquer into separate thin lines. Overlap prior strokes only slightly. If the surface is large, it is best to work from opposite ends, blending the strokes in the center (Fig. 12-18).

9. Any runs or streaks found on surfaces should be removed with lacquer thinner before you apply lacquer.

10. Sanding between coats of lacquer is not necessary unless there is roughness.

11. Undercoats must be fully dry before applying brushing lacquer; otherwise, they will be softened or raised and will cause roughness.

12. Avoid application of lacquer in damp or rainy weather, because *blushing,* a white deposit in the film, may be the result.

Fig. 12-18: When finishing a long, flat area, start away from the last stroke and end overlapping it.

Penetrating Finishes. Penetrating oil finishes give wood its most natural look. The color of the wood is intensified and grain pattern is accentuated, but the wood texture is unaltered.

Penetrating finishes accentuate every imperfection in the wood surface. Therefore, an absolutely topnotch surface condition must be achieved before the finish is applied. Grain-raising and final sanding are a *must.*

Applying Penetrating Resin-Oil Finishes. When applying the penetrating resin-oil finish, use a cloth pad, brush, or 2/0 steel wool; or on horizontal surfaces, pour it on (Fig. 12-19). Whenever possible, turn the work so that the surface that is being worked on is flat. This permits the material to stand on the wood and penetrate as deeply as it can. When using a brush, lay the finish on as thick as possible without runoff. When using a wad of cloth or steel wool, swab the finishing material around on the surface, using only light pressure (Fig. 12-20). This helps to work the finish into the wood.

Keep the surface wet for at least half an hour, often longer, depending on the specific manufacturer's recommendations. If a dull spot appears on the surface,

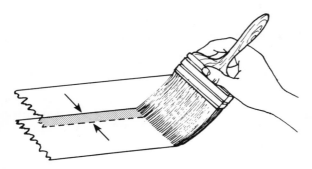

Fig. 12-17: Apply brushing lacquer with rapid strokes, lapping the sides of each stroke.

Fig. 12-19: A good way to apply penetrating resin-oil finish on a horizontal surface is to pour it on.

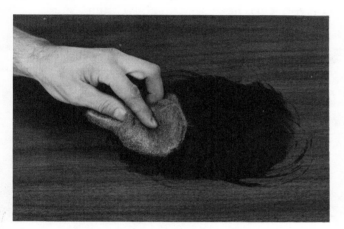

Fig. 12-20: Swab the penetrating resin-oil around on the surface with a wad of fine steel wool using light pressure.

Fig. 12-21: Wipe all the finish off the surface.

The time between coats may vary from 4 to 24 hours, depending on the manufacturer's recommendation. The second and third coats are applied and wiped off in the same manner as the first. No sanding is required between coats; many expert finishers rub the surface with 4/0 steel wool between coats. This smooths down any places where the grain may be slightly raised and ensures a more satiny finish for the final coat.

It must always be remembered that oiled cloths are easily combustible. To prevent fire, they should be burned or washed soon after being used. Should there be any delay, spread them out flat or hang them on a line. If left too long, they will harden. Store the cloth that was used for applying the mixture in the container with any unused portion of the mixture.

No Finish

You may be surprised to know that no treatment at all is considered to be a viable alternative in wood finishing. Some wood applications need no finish, and for their intended end-use, may be most attractive and/or useful without a finishing treatment of any kind. Carvings, sculptures, trays, cutting blocks, bowls, and utensils are a few of the items which may be most appealing and functional with a natural finish. Such items can be lightly sanded with fine-grade paper to remove accumulated dirt and dust as often as they would normally be oiled or polished.

Wood exposed to exterior conditions will weather through a combination of physical, mechanical, and chemical influences: Windborne particles abrade the surface; wetting and drying cause expansion, compression, shrinkage, and surface checking; ultraviolet radiation contributes to surface deterioration; and freezing of absorbed water causes structural break-

indicating that all the material has soaked in, apply more to keep the surface wet.

After the wood has soaked up all the liquid it will take, use clean cloths (preferably old and lint-free) to wipe all the surface resin off (Fig. 12-21). Check the surface for small areas of liquid which are often forced to the surface by air bubbles or heat and wipe the surface completely dry. If any trace of the finish remains on the surface, it will dry to a rather unpleasant sheen. Should this occur, it can usually be corrected by brushing on more resin finish and then wiping it clean in a few minutes. If the finish resists normal cloth wipe-up, moisten a pad of 3/0 steel wool in the liquid resin and gently rub.

It is usually wise to plan two or three applications of penetrating resin finishes, since the material continues to soak in and permeate the pores and spaces in the wood after it is wiped. Remember that the more resin that is absorbed—with no surface coating—the tougher the finish and the harder the surface will be.

down. Yet, weathering will wear away only about 1/4" of exposed wood surface per century.

You may find the weathered look of unfinished exterior siding quite appealing. Some species of wood, such as redwood, weather to an especially attractive natural finish. Over a period of years, dark wood generally tends to lighten and light wood darkens. Should you wish to speed up the weathering process, simply spray the wood surface with water occasionally.

Exterior Wood Finishing

Exterior wood applications require special consideration, since they will be subjected to the weather forces of wind, water, and sunlight. As mentioned earlier, some applications may be left unfinished, but remember that they will be completely vulnerable to weathering and its degenerative effects.

To preserve the natural appearance of the wood, a water-repellent preservative may be used to reduce swelling and shrinkage and to protect against mildew and decay. This type of treatment only darkens the wood very slightly. However, this is a temporary measure and will have to be repeated approximately every six months. (If you decide to stain after using a water-repellent preservative, wait at least 90 days after its last application.)

Natural-tone stains are often used for longer lasting, natural looking protection. Semitransparent stain (light-bodied penetrating stain) will change the wood's color but not its texture or grain. Solid color or opaque (heavy-bodied) stain may be used to completely obscure the wood's natural grain. Paint is also a popular choice.

To obtain an immediate, uniformly weathered appearance, commercial bleaching oils or weathering stains, which act chemically on the wood, may be used. These products help avoid uneven color changes on different exposures of the wood surface.

As you decide on a finish for exterior applications, consider the effect you want, the amount of protection you feel is necessary, and how often you're willing to refinish the surface. Remember that in general, paints and heavier finishes provide greater protection and require less frequent refinishing than light stains. Regardless of the type of finish you choose, *always* purchase a finishing product designed for exterior applications, and follow the manufacturer's directions.

Index